Song
of the
Vikings

Song

of the

Vikings

SNORRI AND THE MAKING
OF NORSE MYTHS

NANCY MARIE BROWN

palgrave
macmillan

For

S. Leonard Rubinstein,
Samuel P. Bayard, and Ernst Ebbinghaus

SONG OF THE VIKINGS
Copyright © Nancy Marie Brown, 2012.
All rights reserved.

First published in 2012 by PALGRAVE MACMILLAN® in the U.S.—a division of St. Martin's Press LLC, 175 Fifth Avenue, New York, NY 10010.

Where this book is distributed in the UK, Europe, and the rest of the world, this is by Palgrave Macmillan, a division of Macmillan Publishers Limited, registered in England, company number 785998, of Houndmills, Basingstoke, Hampshire RG21 6XS.

Palgrave Macmillan is the global academic imprint of the above companies and has companies and representatives throughout the world.

Palgrave® and Macmillan® are registered trademarks in the United States, the United Kingdom, Europe, and other countries.

ISBN: 978-0-230-33884-5

Library of Congress Cataloging-in-Publication Data

Brown, Nancy Marie.
   Song of the Vikings : Snorri and the making of Norse myths / Nancy Marie Brown.
      pages   cm
   Includes bibliographical references and index.
   ISBN 978-0-230-33884-5 (hardback)
   1. Snorri Sturluson, 1179?–1241—Criticism and interpretation. 2. Old Norse literature—Influence. 3. Literature and society—Scandinavia—History. I. Title.
PT7335.Z5B76   2012
839'.63—dc23

2012012031

A catalogue record of the book is available from the British Library.

Design by Letra Libre

First edition: October 2012

10 9 8 7 6 5 4 3 2 1

Printed in the United States of America.

Contents

Iceland in Snorri's time.
Copyright © Jeffery Mathison.

VATNSFJORD

HOLAR
ORLYGSSTAD
THINGEYRI

HVAMM
SAUDAFELL

HELGAFELL
STAD
DEILDAR-TUNGA
REYKHOLT
SURT'S CAVE
STAFHOLT
BORG
BAER
GARD
HAUKADALE
THINGVELLIR
SKALHOLT
BESSASTAD
EYR
KELDUR
ODDI
WESTMAN
ISLANDS

GRIMSEY

GRUND

ICELAND

N

MOUNT
HEKLA

7 DAYS' SAIL TO NORWAY

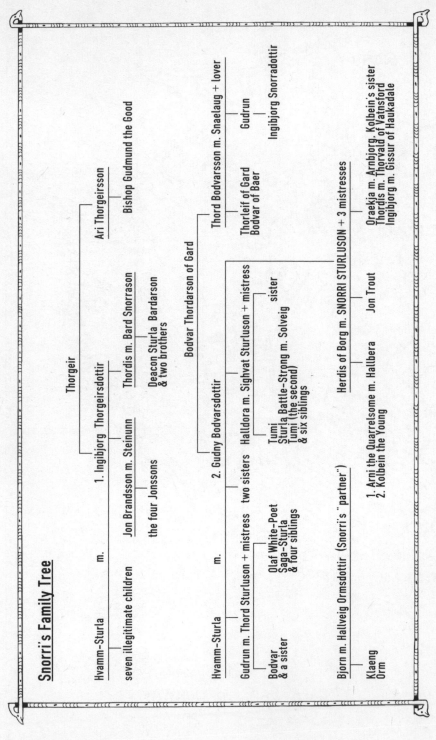

Snorri's Family Tree

Hvamm–Sturla   m.

seven illegitimate children

Thorgeir

1. Ingibjorg Thorgeirsdottir

Jon Brandsson m. Steinunn

the four Jonssons

Thordis m. Bard Snorrason

Deacon Sturla Bardarson
& two brothers

Ari Thorgeirsson

Bishop Gudmund the Good

Hvamm–Sturla   m.

Gudrun m. Thord Sturluson + mistress

Bodvar
& a sister

Olaf White–Poet
Saga–Sturla
& four siblings

two sisters

2. Gudny Bodvarsdottir

Halldora m. Sighvat Sturluson + mistress

Tumi
Sturla Battle–Strong m. Solveig
Tumi (the second)
& six siblings

Bodvar Thordarson of Gard

sister

Thord Bodvarsson m. Snaelaug + lover

Thorleif of Gard
Bodvar of Baer

Gudrun

Ingibjorg Snorradottir

Bjorn m. Hallveig Ormsdottir (Snorri's "partner")

Klaeng
Orm

1. Arni the Quarrelsome m. Hallbera
2. Kolbein the Young

Herdis of Borg m. SNORRI STURLUSON + 3 mistresses

Jon Trout

Oraekja m. Arnbjorg, Kolbein's sister
Thordis m. Thorvald of Vatnsford
Ingibjorg m. Gissur of Haukadale

Design by Jeffery Mathison and Newgen KnowledgeWorks.

Preface

GANDALF

What troubles the gods? What troubles the elves? . . . Would you know
more, or not?

—Snorri, *Edda*

*I*n the late 1920s J. R. R. Tolkien provoked an argument. Oppos-
ing him, among others, was C. S. Lewis. Tolkien had not yet written The
Hobbit or The Lord of the Rings. Lewis had not yet written The Chronicles
of Narnia. They were debating the appropriate curriculum for English majors at
Oxford University, where they both taught.

Tolkien believed too much time was spent on dull and unimportant writers
like Shakespeare, whom Lewis revered. Instead, Tolkien thought, students should
read Snorri Sturluson.

Who?

And not only Snorri but the other fine authors of the Icelandic sagas and the
the Eddic poems. And the students should read them in Old Norse.

Lewis had read the mythological tales from Snorri's Edda in English as a boy.
He found the Norse myths more compelling—as stories, he said—than even the
Bible. Like Tolkien, he was drawn to their Northernness: to their depictions of
dragons and dwarfs, fair elves and werewolves, wandering wizards, and trolls that
turned into stone. To their portrayal of men with a bitter courage who stood fast
on the side of right and good, even when there was no hope at all.

It's even better in the original, Tolkien said. He had been reading Old Norse
since his teens. He loved the cold, crisp, unsentimental language of the sagas, their
bare, straightforward tone like wind keening over ice. Reading Snorri and his peers

was more important than reading Shakespeare, Tolkien argued, because their books were more central to our language and our modern world. Egg, ugly, ill, smile, knife, fluke, fellow, husband, birth, death, take, mistake, lost, skulk, ran-sack, brag, *and* law, *among many other common English words, all derived from Old Norse. As for Snorri's effect on modernity, it was soon to mushroom.*

Tolkien convinced his colleagues to substitute Snorri for Shakespeare by start-ing a club called the Kolbítar. A coalbiter in the sagas is a lad who lounges by the fire instead of working; roused, he transforms into a hero, an outlaw, or both. These academic coalbiters lounged by the fire translating medieval Icelandic poetry and prose aloud. They began with the myths in Snorri's Edda. *A few years later, having finished the major Icelandic sagas and the mythological verse in the* Poetic Edda, *the club morphed into the Inklings, where they read their own works.*

One of those works was The Hobbit.

I first heard The Hobbit *read aloud when I was four. I discovered* The Lord of the Rings *when I was thirteen. Through college, Tolkien was my favorite au-thor, his books my favorite works of literature—despite the scorn such a confession brought down on an English major at an American university in the late 1970s, where fantasy was derided as escapist and unworthy of study.*

Then I took a course in comparative mythology. To learn about the gods of Scandinavia, I was assigned The Prose Edda, *a collection of mythological tales drawn from the work of the thirteenth-century Icelandic writer Snorri Sturluson. Page forty-one in the paperback edition of Jean Young's 1954 translation was the turning point of my literary life.*

I read: "The gods seated themselves on their thrones and held counsel, and remembered how dwarfs had quickened in the earth. . . . By the decree of the gods they acquired human understanding and the appearance of men, although they lived in the earth and in rocks. Modsognir was the most famous, and next to him Durin."

Durin?

I knew that name. In the list of dwarfs that filled the rest of page forty-one and spilled onto forty-two, I recognized several more: "Bifur, Bafur, Bombor, Nori, Ori, . . . Oin . . . Gandalf—"

Gandalf? I sucked in my breath. What was Tolkien's wizard doing in medieval Iceland?

I read Tolkien's biography and learned about the coalbiters. I met a professor with a bookcase full of Icelandic sagas that he lent me, one after the next. When I ran out of translations, I found another professor to teach me Old Norse. As I con-templated earning a PhD, I went to Iceland and, like William Morris and many other writers before and since, traveled by horseback through the wind-riven wil-derness to the last homely house. I wondered why Iceland's rugged, rain-drenched landscape seemed so insistently familiar—until I learned that Tolkien had read Morris's Journals of Travel in Iceland, 1871–1873 *and created from them the character of the home-loving hobbit Bilbo Baggins and his soggy ride to Rivendell.*

The name of the wizard, Tolkien acknowledged, he had plucked from Snorri's list of dwarfs, though Gandalf had nothing dwarfish about him. (In the first draft of The Hobbit, *the wizard's name was Bladorthin.) Gandalf's physical descrip-tion and his character, Tolkien wrote, were Odinic. They derived from Snorri's tales of the Norse god Odin, the one-eyed wizard-king, the wanderer, the shaman and shape-shifter, the poet with his beard and his staff and his wide-brimmed floppy hat, his vast store of riddles and runes and ancient lore, his entertaining after-supper tales, his superswift horse, his magical arts, his ability to converse with birds.*

But who was Snorri Sturluson? Thirty years after meeting his Gandalf on the page, I finally thought to answer that question.

Introduction

THE WIZARD OF
THE NORTH

Odin was the cleverest of all. . . . He talked so glibly and shrewdly that all
who heard him must need take his tale to be wholly true.

—Snorri, *Heimskringla*

In the year 1220 Snorri Sturluson sailed home from Norway. He was one of the richest men in Iceland, holder of seven chieftaincies, owner of five profitable estates and a harbor, husband of an heiress, lover of several mistresses, a fat man soon to go gouty, a hard drinker, a seeker of ease prone to soaking long hours in his hot tub while sipping stout ale, not a Viking warrior by any stretch of the imagination, but clever. Crafty, cunning, and ambitious. A good businessman. So well versed in the law that few other Icelanders could outargue him. A respectable poet and a lover of books. At age forty-two he was at the height of his power.

Snorri, son of Sturla, was a contemporary of Saladin, who battled Richard the Lionheart and his crusaders in Jerusalem. During Snorri's lifetime, Genghis Khan and his Mongol horde broke through the Great Wall of China and plundered Beijing, then turned west to conquer Russia, Hungary, and Poland. Francis of Assisi, charmed by birds and wild beasts, founded the mendicant order of Franciscan monks at this time. Just before Snorri's birth, Thomas Beckett, archbishop of Canterbury, was killed by four knights hoping to win the favor of King Henry II of England. Three years before Snorri's visit to Norway, Henry's son, King John, signed the Magna Carta, acknowledging that his power as king was limited by English law. In 1217 John's ten-year-old successor, Henry

III, struck up a friendship with the fourteen-year-old king of Norway, Hakon, who many years later would order Snorri put to death. The two boy-kings sent each other presents: From Norway came thirteen Icelandic falcons (three white and ten gray), walrus ivory and elks' antlers, a live elk, and, some years later, a live polar bear. From England came the earliest romances of King Arthur and his Knights of the Round Table (written in Anglo-Norman French), as well as an architect who built Hakon a great stone hall modeled on Henry's palace at Westminster.

Snorri had spent the years 1218 to 1220 traveling abroad. On the quay at Bergen, departing for home, he tossed off a praise poem about Earl Skuli, said to be the handsomest man in Norway for his long red-blond locks. In response the earl gave Snorri the ship he was to sail in and many other fine gifts. Young king Hakon honored Snorri with the title of landed man, or baron, one of only fifteen so named. The king also charged Snorri with a mission: He was to bring Iceland—then an independent republic of some fifty thousand souls—under Norwegian rule.

Or so says one version of the story. The other says nothing about a threat to Iceland's independence. Snorri was not asked to sell out his country, simply to sort out a misunderstanding between some Icelandic farmers and a party of Norwegian traders. A small thing. A few killings to even out. A matter of law.

Iceland was a seven-day sail west of Norway. Tipped on the southern edge of the Arctic Circle, the island earns its name: It holds the largest glacier in Europe. The first sight sailors see, as they approach Iceland, is the silvery gleaming arc of the sun reflecting off the ice cap. Closer in, the eye is struck by the blackness of the shore, the lava sand, the cliffs reaching into the sea in crumpled stacks and arches, the rocks and crags all shaped by fire. For Iceland is a volcanic land. Even when an eruption is not in progress, steam from its hot springs rises high in the air. Fire and ice have shaped this island. Its central highlands— half its total area—are desert: ash, ice, moonscapes of rock. Grass grows well along Iceland's coasts, but little else thrives. There are no tall trees—and so no shipbuilding: a dangerous lack for island dwellers. Other natural resources are equally scarce. Iceland has no gold, no silver, no copper, no tin. The iron is impure bog iron, difficult to smelt. The first settlers, Vikings emigrating from Norway and the British Isles between 870 and 930, chose Iceland because they had nowhere else to go. Nowhere they could live free of a king. At least, that's how the story goes.

Iceland has many such stories.

The arctic winter nights are long. To while away the dark hours Icelanders since the time of the settlement told stories, recited poems, and—once the Christian missionaries taught them the necessary ink-quill-and-parchment technology in the early eleventh century—wrote and read books aloud to each other.

Three of those books, including the most influential, are linked to Snorri Sturluson. Writers of prose in his day did not sign their works, so we can't be absolutely certain of his authorship. He was named as author of the *Edda* in the early 1300s, of *Heimskringla* by the 1600s (supposedly based on a now-lost medieval manuscript), and of *Egil's Saga* not until the 1800s. The arguments in each case are, to me, convincing. The three works chime. Together they create a world.

No one knows what *Edda*, the title of Snorri's first book, means. It could mean "the book of Oddi," the name of the farm where Snorri grew up. It could mean "great-grandmother"; Snorri himself uses the word that way in a list of poetic synonyms for women. *Edda* could derive from an Icelandic word meaning "wits, poetry, or song" or from a Latin word meaning "the art of poetry." In the hands of a punster, it could mean "the art of great-grandmother's old-fashioned songs," a title that aptly describes Snorri's *Edda*, which he wrote to teach the boy-king of Norway how to appreciate Viking poetry.

Viking poems often allude to legends and myths, so Snorri included many such tales in his *Edda*. All the stories we know of the Vikings' pagan religion, the Norse myths of Valhalla and the Valkyries, of elves and dwarfs and dragons, of one-eyed Odin and the well of wisdom, of red-bearded Thor and his hammer of might, of two-faced Loki and the death of beautiful Baldur, of lovesick Freyr and lovely Freyja, the rainbow bridge, the great ash tree Yggdrasil, the world-wrapping Midgard Serpent, Heimdall's horn, the eight-legged horse Sleipnir, Ragnarok or the Twilight of the Gods; all the stories we know of the gods whom we still honor with the names Tuesday, Wednesday, Thursday, and Friday—for all these stories Snorri is our main, and sometimes our only, source. Introducing the 1954 translation of Snorri's *Edda*, an Icelandic scholar remarked that no one now read it "as a textbook on mythology." He was wrong. *All* textbooks on Norse mythology rely on Snorri's creation. There is little else to go on. We have poems containing cryptic hints. We have rune stones whose blunt images and few words tantalize. Only Snorri gives us stories, with beginnings and endings

and explanations. Our modern understanding of the ancient Scandinavian be-
lief system, and especially what a 1909 translator called its "peculiar grim humor," is a product of Snorri's imagination.

Snorri is the Homer of the North—and also its Herodotus. The title of
his second book, *Heimskringla,* means "The Round World" or "The Orb of
the Earth" (from its first two words). In it Snorri traces the history of Norway
from its founding in the shadows of time by Odin the wizard-king (who later
was revered as a god, Snorri explains) to 1177 A.D., the year before Snorri's
birth. *Heimskringla* is a long and complex book, structured as sixteen individual sagas; it fills eight hundred pages in a modern paperback edition. Each
of the sixteen sagas tells the story of a king of Norway and his kinsmen. The
famous phrase, "The history of the world is but the biography of great men,"
was inspired by this book: Snorri is indeed a deft biographer. Through his vivid

Detail of a runestone from Gotland, Sweden. Because of Snorri's tales of the eight-legged horse,
Sleipnir, the rider is thought to be Odin. But when art historians interpreted a prehistoric
painting of an eight-legged horse at Chauvet Cave in France, they explained the extra legs as
an attempt to show great speed. Now in the Statens Historiska Museum, Stockholm. Photo by
akg-images.

portraits of kings and sea kings, raiders and traders, Snorri created the Viking image so prevalent today, from the heroes of sports teams to the bloodthirsty berserks of movies and video games to the chilling neo-Nazi.

In his third book, *Egil's Saga*, Snorri expanded that image, creating the two competing Viking types who would give Norse culture its lasting appeal. *Egil's Saga* may be the first true Icelandic saga, establishing the genre and granting the word *saga* the meaning we still use today: a long and detailed novel about several generations of a family. *Egil's Saga* begins with a Viking named Evening-Wolf (reputed to be a werewolf) and his two sons; one son also had two sons, one of whom is Egil. In each generation one son is tall, blond, and blue eyed, a stellar athlete, a courageous fighter, an independent and honorable man who laughs in the face of danger, dying with a poem or quip on his lips. The other son is dark and ugly, a werewolf, a wizard, a poet, a berserk who works himself into a howling frenzy in battle (and is unbeatable), a crafty schemer who knows every promise is contingent. Both sons, bright and dark, are Vikings.

Snorri not only gave us the Norse gods and kings and Vikings: The modern perception of Icelanders as a fiercely independent people is also due, in good part, to him. Tiny Iceland, current population 320,000 (the size of Pittsburgh or Des Moines), ranks number 175 on the United Nations' list of the most populous countries, a little ahead of Barbados and Vanuatu. Yet Iceland has a permanent representative at the UN, and a few years back it applied for a seat on the Security Council. Iceland faced down Britain about fishing rights in the 1970s, became a member of the "coalition of the willing" fighting in Iraq in 2003, and refused to knuckle under to the demands of the European Union in 2008 when the Icelandic banks collapsed. In 2011 Iceland stood up to the United States over WikiLeaks.

The country's unshakable sense of its own worth is grounded in a speech Snorri wrote about freedom. Ironically Snorri's greed and ambition cost Iceland its independence—no matter what, exactly, he promised the boy-king of Norway on the quay at Bergen in 1220. In 1262, twenty-one years after his death, Iceland became a colony of Norway (both Iceland and Norway later were subsumed by Denmark). The golden age was over. Iceland descended into its own dark ages of colonial repression. For hundreds of years the island was known to the rest of the world only for its rich offshore fishing grounds, its barbaric people (said to wash in urine and dine on candle wax), and its volcanoes, one of which was known as the Mouth of Hell.

Then in the early 1600s Snorri was resurrected. Translations from Old Norse appeared throughout Europe. The craze led in one direction to the gothic novel and ultimately to modern heroic fantasy. Snorri influenced writers as various as Thomas Gray, William Blake, Sir Walter Scott, the Brothers Grimm, Thomas Carlyle, Henry Wadsworth Longfellow, Alfred Lord Tennyson, Robert Browning, Richard Wagner, Matthew Arnold, Henrik Ibsen, William Morris, Thomas Hardy, J. R. R. Tolkien, Hugh MacDiarmid, Jorge Luis Borges, W. H. Auden, Poul Anderson, Günther Grass, Gabriel García Márquez, Ursula K. LeGuin, A. S. Byatt, Seamus Heaney, Jane Smiley, Neil Gaiman, and Michael Chabon.

In another direction the rediscovery of Snorri's works led to Hitler's master race.

Snorri may be the most influential writer of the Middle Ages: His *Edda*, according to the 1909 translator, is "the deep and ancient wellspring of Western culture."

The fat poet setting sail from Norway in the fall of 1220 had no idea of his future importance. He had not yet written any books. Snorri's ambition was to rule Iceland. Whether as the leader of a group of more or less equal chieftains or as the king's earl made no difference to him, so long as he was rich, respected, and indulged.

The voyage did not go well. It was late in the year to sail, and the weather in the North Atlantic was fierce. His new ship lost its mast within sight of Iceland; it wrecked on the Westman Islands off the southern coast. Snorri had himself and his bodyguard of a dozen men ferried over to the mainland with their Norwegian treasures. They borrowed horses and rode—bedecked in bright-colored cloth like courtiers, wearing gold and jewels and carrying shiny new weapons and sturdy shields—to the nearby estate of the bishop of Skalholt. There Baron Snorri's new title was ridiculed. Some Icelanders even accused him of treason, of having sold out to the Norwegian king.

From then until his death in 1241, Snorri would fight one battle after another (in the courts or by proxy), double-crossing family and friends to see who would be earl of Iceland, deputy to Norway's king. Snorri would die in his nightshirt, cringing in his cellar, begging for his life before his enemies' thugs. He did not live up to his Viking ideals, to the heroes portrayed in his books. He did not die with a laugh—or a poem—on his lips. His last words were "Don't strike!" As the poet Jorge Luis Borges sums him up in a beautiful poem, the writer who "bequeathed a mythology / Of ice and fire" and "violent glory" to us was a coward: "On / Your head, your sickly face, falls the sword, / As it fell so often in your book."

Yet his work remains. Because of Snorri's wizardry with words, the gods and heroes of the Vikings live on, and our modern culture is enriched by northern fantasy. In the twenty turbulent years between his Norwegian triumph and his ignominious death, while scheming and plotting, blustering and fleeing, Snorri did write his books. He covered hundreds of parchment pages with world-shaping words, encouraging his friends and kinsmen to cover hundreds of pages more.

It's difficult to reconcile this unscrupulous chieftain with the witty story-teller of the *Edda, Heimskringla,* and *Egil's Saga.* But Snorri never wrote about himself. We have no letters, only poems and tales. He appears in two sagas by his nephew, Sturla Thordarson, one written on a king's commission, the other presumably for posterity. In neither book does Snorri come off well; no one knows what grudge the nephew held to portray his uncle so poorly. Unhelpfully, Sturla's two sagas also contradict each other. Saga-Sturla, as I will call him to distinguish him from a cousin of the same name, grew up with Snorri on his kingly estate of Reykholt in the west of Iceland. Saga-Sturla learned to read there, in his uncle's fine library. He met writers and poets who came to copy Snorri's books and discuss them, to declaim their own poetry and old poems they had memorized, and to avail themselves of Snorri's liberal food and ale and lounge in his luxurious hot tub. True, Snorri may have stolen his nephew's inheritance from his grandmother. And Snorri did leave Saga-Sturla in the lurch on at least one battlefield. The rest we will never know.

Snorri's books, however, may reveal how he saw himself. He is captivated by complex, contradictory characters: the shape-shifter, the man in disguise, the split or two-faced hero, both good and evil, beautiful and troll-like. He begins the *Edda* with an ancient Swedish king going to interview the gods: "He set out to Asgard and traveled in secret and assumed the form of an old man and so disguised himself." But the gods saw him coming and created for him a vast illusion.

In *Egil's Saga* the hero Egil is ugly and troll-like, "never at a loss for words," but "a hard one to handle," while his beloved (and doomed) brother, Thorolf, is handsome, popular, and "skilled in everything talented men of the time chose to do." Together they make one complete man. When Thorolf is killed, Egil is forever scarred and damaged.

Then there is Odin, the one-eyed wizard-king, of whom Snorri writes in *Heimskringla*, "When he sat with his friends he was so fair and noble in looks that all were joyful," while to his enemies Odin appeared terrifying. Odin was a human king: Only after death was he deified, Snorri says here, though he'll give a different account of Odin's origins in his *Edda*. But Odin was a king with the skills of a wizard. "He could change himself and appear in any form he would," Snorri writes, including bird, beast, fish, or dragon. Odin raised the dead and questioned them. He owned two talking ravens who flew far and wide, gathering news. He worked magic with runes and spoke only in verse or song. With a word he "slaked fire, stilled the sea, or turned winds in what way he would." He knew "such songs that the earth and hills and rocks and howes opened themselves for him," and he entered and stole their treasures. "His foes feared him, but his friends took pride in him and trusted in his craft."

Long after King Odin's death, when he had become a god, Snorri says, the missionary king Olaf Tryggvason, who forced Norway to become Christian around the year 1000, held a feast to celebrate Easter. An unknown guest arrived, "an old man of wise words, who had a broad-brimmed hat and was one-eyed." The old man told tales of many lands, and the king "found much fun in his talk." Only the bishop recognized this dangerous guest. The bishop convinced the king that it was time to retire, but Odin followed them into the royal chamber and sat on the king's bed, continuing his wondrous stories. The bishop tried again. "It is time for sleep, your majesty." The king dutifully closed his eyes. But a little later King Olaf awoke. He asked that the storyteller be called to him, but the one-eyed old man was nowhere to be found.

Nowhere but in Snorri's books. And perhaps in his soul. For without Snorri Sturluson, sitting at our bedsides and chattering glibly along seven hundred years after his death, we would have no tales of Odin the wanderer, king of the Viking gods, wizard of the North, who gave up an eye for a single sip from the well of wisdom.

To understand Snorri Sturluson, we must begin with Odin.

One

ODIN'S EYE

Wisdom is memory.

—Snorri, *Edda*

*I*n the beginning, Snorri writes, there was nothing. No sand, no sea, no cooling wave. No earth, no heaven above. Nothing but the yawning empty gap, Ginnungagap.

All was cold and grim.

Then came Surt with a crashing noise, bright and burning. He bore a flaming sword. Rivers of fire flowed till they turned hard as slag from an iron maker's forge, then froze to ice.

The ice sheet grew, layer upon layer, till it bridged the mighty, magical gap.

Where the ice met sparks of flame and still-flowing lava from Surt's home in the South, it thawed, dripping like an icicle to form the first frost giant, Ymir, and his cow.

Ymir drank the cow's abundant milk. The cow licked the ice, which was salty. It licked free a handsome god and his wife. They had three sons, one of whom was Odin, the ruler of heaven and earth, the greatest and most glorious of the gods: the All-Father.

Odin and his brothers killed Ymir. From his body they fashioned the world: His flesh was the soil, his blood the sea. His bones and teeth became stones and scree. His hair became trees, his skull was the sky, his brain, the clouds.

From his eyebrows they made Middle Earth, which they peopled with humans, crafting the first man and woman from driftwood they found on the seashore.

So Snorri explains the creation of the world in the beginning of his *Edda*. Partly he is quoting an older poem, "Song of the Sibyl," whose author he does not name. Partly he is making it up—especially the bit about the world forming in a kind of volcanic eruption and then freezing to ice. If this myth were truly ancient, there would be no volcano. Norway, Sweden, and Denmark, the Scandinavian homelands, are not volcanic. Only Iceland—discovered in 870, when Norse paganism was already on the wane—is geologically active. In medieval times Iceland's volcanoes erupted ten or a dozen times a century, often burning through thick glaciers. Nothing is as characteristic of Iceland's landscape as the clash between fire and ice.

Ymir's cow may be Snorri's invention, too. No other source mentions this monstrous cow, nor what the giant Ymir lived on, but like all wealthy Icelanders, Snorri was a dairyman. He was also a Christian. It suits his wry sense of humor for the first pagan god to be born from a salt lick.

Snorri goes on: Odin established the godly city of Asgard. There he built his feast hall, Valhalla, with its roof of golden shields and 540 doors. In a silver-roofed palace nearby sat his throne, from which he watched over all the nine worlds, from the highest bright heaven to the damp, dark underworld called Hel. He could see the lands of the Aesir gods (like him) and the Vanir gods (enemies at first, then in-laws and allies), the lands of the frost giants like Ymir and fire giants like Surt, the lands of the light elves and dark elves, of the dwarfs in their halls of stone, and Middle Earth, the land where humans lived.

Odin could see what everyone was doing everywhere. In case he missed something, his ravens, Thought and Memory, flew over all the nine worlds each day collecting news. Sometimes Odin wandered the nine worlds himself. One of his first quests was to search out the well of wisdom: He traded an eye for a single sip of enlightenment.

Odin One-Eye was Snorri's favorite of all the Norse gods and goddesses. Following tradition, he placed Odin, god of Wednesday (from the Old English spelling, Woden's Day), at the head of the Viking pantheon of twelve gods and twelve goddesses. Then Snorri increased Odin's power. Rather like the Christian God the Father, Snorri's Odin All-Father governed all things great and small.

Icelanders had in fact long favored Thor, the god of Thursday. They named their children after the mighty thunder god: In a twelfth-century record of Iceland's first settlers, a thousand people bear names beginning with *Thor*. None is named for Odin. Nor did the first Christian missionaries to Iceland find cults of Odin. Odin is rarely mentioned in the sagas. For a good sailing wind Icelanders called on Thor. But Snorri wasn't fond of Thor—except as comic relief. Thor was the god of farmers.

Odin was a god for aristocrats—not just the king of gods but the god of kings. He had the best horse, eight-legged Sleipnir; Snorri told two memorable tales about Odin's horse. Odin had a gold helmet and a fine coat of mail, a spear, and a gold ring that magically dripped eight matching rings every ninth night. No problem for him to be a generous lord, a gold giver. Finally Odin gave men the gift of poetry. At least in Snorri's mythology he did. Snorri's tale of the divine mead that turns all drinkers into poets is dismissed by modern critics as "one of his more imaginative efforts."

The story begins with the feud between the Aesir gods and the Vanir. They declared a truce, and gods from each side spat into a crock to mark the peace. Odin took the spittle and made it into a man. Truce Man traveled far and wide, teaching humans wisdom, until he was killed by the dwarfs. (They told Odin that Truce Man had choked on his own learning.) The dwarfs poured Truce Man's blood into a kettle and two crocks, mixed it with honey, and made the mead of poetry. To end a feud, the dwarfs gave the mead to the giant Suttung, who hid it in the depths of a mountain with his daughter as its guard. Odin set out to fetch the mead. He tricked Suttung's brother into helping him, and they bored a hole through the mountain. Odin changed into a snake and slithered in, returning to his glorious god form to seduce Suttung's lonely daughter. He lay with her for three nights; for each night she paid him a sip of mead. On the first sip he drank the kettle dry. With the next two sips he emptied the crocks. Then he transformed himself into an eagle and took off. Suttung spied the fleeing bird. Suspicious, he changed into his giant eagle form and made chase. It was a near thing. To clear the wall of Asgard, Odin had to squirt some of the mead out backward—the men who licked it up can write only doggerel. The rest of the mead he spat into vessels the gods had set out when they saw him coming. He shared this mead with certain exceptional men; they are called poets.

Though Odin is sneaky, two faced, arrogant, and avaricious in Snorri's tales, he is no dim-witted muscleman like Thor, no flirtatious mare like the trickster god, Loki. In all his writings Snorri never once made Odin look ridiculous. Perhaps that's because Snorri's own father, Sturla of Hvamm, was once likened to the one-eyed god.

The tale of Hvamm-Sturla and Odin One-Eye is the first to mention Snorri himself, though his role is only a small one when he was three years old.

It begins beside the river Hvita in the West of Iceland, where lay the rich farm of Deildar-Tunga. It was not a large farm, but rich in its ability to make hay, for it owned extensive water meadows along the river banks. Even better, these were *warm* water meadows. The Hvita is an ice-cold glacial river. Its name, White River, denotes not white-water rapids but milky glacial till. Yet not far from the river, beneath a bluff painted pink with mineral deposits, bubbled a hot spring: the highest-volume hot spring in all of Iceland, an island riddled with more than 250 hot springs. The hot spring at Tunga provided warm water for cooking and bathing and washing clothes, but these were minor benefits compared to its effect on the hay fields. The hot water that spilled into the river and spread over the floodplain made the grass sprout sooner after winter and stay green longer in the fall. Grass was the foundation of Iceland's economy: Hay was the only crop that grew well in the island's harsh climate. Thanks to his hot spring, the farmer at Tunga could make more hay than his neighbors and so keep more cows, sheep, and horses. Cows were highly valued because the Viking diet was based on milk and cheese. Sheep were milked as well (sheep's milk is richer in vitamin C; vital in a land where no vegetables grow), but sheep were prized mostly for their wool: Cloth was Iceland's major export. Horses were necessary for transportation, since Iceland has few navigable rivers.

The wealth of the farmer at Tunga—reckoned, the usual way, in cows or "cow equivalents" (six ewes equaled one cow)—was eight hundred head of cattle. Eighty head was considered a large farm. No wonder the two biggest men in the district took notice when, in 1180, between the Winter of Sickness and the Summer of No Grass, Tunga fell vacant. The farmer and his wife had gone on a pilgrimage to Rome to pray for children. Neither returned, and word came they had died en route. But who succumbed first? Ownership of the farm hung on that question.

Based on reports from travelers, the chieftain Pall Solvason, who lived up the river at Reykholt, announced that the farmer had died first, whereupon all his wealth went by law to his wife. She was Pall's daughter. When she died childless, rich Tunga came to him. Pall took over the property.

Just wait one moment, said the chieftain Bodvar Thordarson, whose estate was a few miles down the river. If the wife died first, her husband, *by law,* would inherit. When he died, the property went to his sister, who was Bodvar's client.

It would be fair, said Bodvar, to give the sister a share. He asked for the value of forty cows. Pall rather ungraciously said no.

Bodvar rode to Tunga with a troop of sixty armed men. This time he asked for the value of sixty cows. Pall still said no—but hurriedly vacated the farm. Bodvar and his sixty men built a high wall around the farmhouse and settled in. Soon the value of the estate dropped from eight hundred cows to four hundred: Bodvar kept holding feasts for his warriors, slaughtering Tunga's fat cattle.

Pall took him to court.

Iceland was an anomaly in the Middle Ages. It bowed to no king. The first settlers, coming to this cold and windy island outpost in the late 800s, had disliked the very idea of a king. Many had fled Norway, having lost their lands in the bloody civil war by which Harald Fair-Hair unified the country, becoming the first king of all Norway in about 885. King Harald claimed every farm and forest for himself and reapportioned the land to those who would pay him taxes. He gave the Norwegians three choices: swear oaths of loyalty, leave, or face the consequences, which included torture, maiming, and death. Some who left went first to the British Isles, only to be pestered by kings, oaths, and taxes there, too. They sailed on to Iceland to be free of such nonsense.

But after fifty years of anarchy the Icelanders deemed some form of government to be necessary, and in 930 a cabal of wealthy men worked out a way to share power. They divided the island into four quarters: North, South, East, and West. Three spring assemblies were to be held in each quarter (four in the larger North Quarter) to discuss local matters and to resolve disputes. Each spring assembly would be governed by three chieftains, for a total of thirty-nine. To these posts they appointed themselves.

In theory the thirty-nine chieftains of Iceland were equals, but some grew more powerful than others, for this new system of government was organized not geographically but by alliances. Uninhabited when it was discovered in 870, Iceland was home to at least ten thousand people by 930. (By Snorri's day the population would be fifty thousand.) There were no towns on the island, and there would not be until the eighteenth century. Instead Icelanders lived on farms scattered around the periphery of the island, which has at its center a vast uninhabitable wasteland of volcanoes and glaciers. Some farms were immense, supporting as many as one hundred people; others were small, farmed by one nuclear family. Every farmer who owned at least one cow or boat or fishing net for each of his dependents had to ally himself with a chieftain, pay him taxes, and, if requested, accompany him to assemblies or fight in his battles. The farmer could choose which of the thirty-nine chieftains he wanted to support, and he could change his allegiance once a year. But generally only the richer farmers dared annoy the local chieftain by choosing a more distant one.

Usually it paid to support a chieftain who lived close by. He was nearer to hand if the farmer was robbed, or his hay stores ran out during a harsh winter, and travel wasn't so onerous when the farmer was invited to a Yule feast or summoned for a raid (as Bodvar had summoned his sixty armed men to Tunga). Yet two chieftains often lived within a day's ride of each other. In that case it paid to choose the one who was less easily bullied, for the support of a chieftain was a family's only protection from a rival clan. Only a chieftain could bring a lawsuit to one of the assemblies, and only a chieftain could answer it.

In addition to the spring assemblies held in each quarter of the country, once a year, on the tenth Thor's Day of summer, in the great rift valley of Thingvellir beside its deep blue lake, Iceland's thirty-nine chieftains and their wives and children and followers gathered for the Althing, the general assembly of all Iceland. The Althing was a grand party. Thousands of people stayed for two weeks in tents and turf-walled booths on the banks of the Axe River, drinking ale, telling tales, taking part in horse fights and wrestling matches, races and dice games, making wedding plans or finalizing divorces, witnessing court cases, and wrangling about the law. Though carrying weapons was not allowed, the assembly was not always peaceful. The summer of 1178, the year of Snorri's birth, was known as the Stone-Throwing Summer for a fight that broke out at the Althing and left one dead and several wounded. But battles of bandied words were more common, for the Althing was Iceland's answer to a king.

Disputes between Icelanders of any rank could be settled at the Althing by appeal to Iceland's laws. There were five law courts: one for each quarter plus an appeals court, each with thirty-six judges. The chieftains chose the judges, each chieftain nominating and vetoing a certain number. Presiding was Iceland's only elected official, the lawspeaker. The first lawspeaker brought the laws of western Norway to Iceland in 930. For nearly two hundred years, until 1118, the lawspeaker recited one-third of the law code at each Althing. The place where he stood, called the Law Rock, was a height of land that formed a natural amphitheater. The chieftains gathered around the Law Rock and after the recitation debated, adjusted, and agreed upon the laws, for, as the sagas say, "With laws shall our land be built up, but with lawlessness laid waste."

Almanna Gorge, the western edge of the rift valley of Thingvellir, Iceland, where the yearly assembly of all chieftains was held. The white flagpole marks the Law Rock. Photo by the author.

Iceland had laws concerning stolen horses, rented cows, dogs that bit, or bulls that ran amok in the neighbor's haystacks. There were laws about betrothals and divorces, buying sheep, or claiming debts. There were laws concerning the welfare of orphans, widows, the sick, the disabled, and the poor.

There were laws about renting land or investing in a trading ship. Numerous laws defined homicide, setting the compensation a killer should pay a victim's family to avoid being exiled from the island. And Iceland had inheritance laws that clearly laid out the order in which property descended after its owner's death.

By the time Pall Solvason summoned Bodvar to court at the Althing to determine who owned the rich farm of Deildar-Tunga and its voluminous hot spring, Iceland's law code had been in writing for more than sixty years. Still, there were frequent lawsuits—and many feuds—over the inheritance of real estate. No law book could determine, for example, if the travelers Pall Solvason had quoted had told the truth concerning the time of his daughter's death relative to her husband's. Knowing the law was not enough to win a case at the Althing. As elsewhere in the medieval world, might made right.

Pall Solvason was an aristocrat. In addition to being a chieftain, he was an ordained priest; just a few years before, he had been a candidate for bishop of Skalholt, one of two bishoprics in Iceland. Pall was well educated and ran a school and a book-making scriptorium at Reykholt; he was known as "an old and honored teacher" and had many influential friends. To back up his claim to Tunga, Pall recruited the bishop of Holar and four chieftains, including the most popular chieftain at the time, Jon Loftsson of Oddi, who in later days was dubbed the uncrowned king of Iceland. These men would stand beside Pall in court, lending him their authority and, if necessary, their fighting men.

Bodvar recruited only one man: his son-in-law, Snorri's father, Sturla, the chieftain of Hvamm.

"Oh, the devil is standing by Sturla," said one of Pall's men, who fancied himself a poet:

> He's stalling the work of justice.
> Sly in his words, he's hiding
> Under the chieftain's cloak.

Sturla of Hvamm was an upstart from a middling family. The first famous name in his family tree is five generations back and on the distaff side: The grandfather of his father's grandmother was Snorri of Helgafell, a crafty chieftain who died in 1030. Sturla inherited wily Snorri's chieftainship. He also inherited his ancestor's wits and sarcastic sense of humor. But not the family estate, Hvamm, in the rich area known as the Dales. That Sturla bought at a bargain price, by bullying its previous occupant.

Sturla's career as a chieftain began, according to the anonymous *Saga of Hvamm-Sturla,* with the case of the stolen cloth. It seems a trivial task—but in Iceland, more often than not, a chieftain's daily job was to adjudicate just such petty disputes, to see that they didn't escalate (like this one did) into a blood feud. The problem began when Skeggi, one of Sturla's men, saw he was missing three yards of linen. A homeless woman, who slept in the sheep sheds and made her living gathering edible seaweed, was accused of the theft. She was not very bright, but she had a lover, so Skeggi accosted the man, who took offense and sought the advice of another chieftain. At an autumn feast, right under Sturla's nose, the offended lover sank an axe into Skeggi's head. The killer then fled.

Sturla gathered rumors and sent out spies. He found the man hiding far to the east and put pressure on those protecting him. At the Althing the killer was outlawed and exiled from Iceland, his helpers were fined, and the one who owned Hvamm was convinced he no longer wanted to live there.

Sturla was brash. He was ruthless and stubborn and a good fighter, taking risks other chieftains could not stomach. Once, he was outnumbered nine to one and did not back down. When someone grazed sheep on his stepson's land, Sturla had the sheep slaughtered and piled in a heap. When another man's sheep were stolen, Sturla rushed off alone after the gang of thieves. His wife called up their men and sent them after him, two to a horse. They fought a pitched battle in which at least three men were killed, one lost a hand, another's arm was broken in two places, and the leader of the thieves—Sturla's rival, the neighboring chieftain Einar of Stadarhol—took a sword thrust in the side and lost a lot of blood. He begged for quarter. Sturla graciously granted it. Such was the life of an Icelandic chieftain.

Sturla was eloquent. Like many chieftains, he was well trained in the law. But not all chieftains were such effective lawyers. When he was prosecuting a lawsuit, Sturla held the court spellbound—so he often triumphed over his rival Einar, who lisped. But Einar was richer and better connected than Sturla, with a bigger extended family: It was Einar who gathered 450 men to threaten Sturla's sixty, then looted and burned down Sturla's house.

Sturla took him to court. He agreed to let Einar's good friend, the bishop of Skalholt, arbitrate if he would first swear the leveling oath, asserting that the two chieftains were equals and that the bishop would have reached the same verdict if their positions had been reversed. Sturla valued his reputation more than his purse. The bishop swore the oath, then told Einar to return the stolen goods and give Sturla the value of ten cows for his house. Ten cows was not a lot.

"I revere the bishop's oath as I revere the Easter mass," Sturla said sarcastically. "I cannot estimate it in coin but this is an honor for us, even though many men will not consider the fine large or the verdict lucrative." Many men in fact thought the bishop had cheated, and Sturla's popularity soared.

So when the case of Deildar-Tunga and its hot spring came before the court at the Althing in 1180, and Bodvar and Sturla faced off against Pall, the bishop of Holar, and four other chieftains, no one was surprised to see them not back down. Bodvar and Sturla simply refused to settle.

They agreed only to come to Reykholt, Pall's estate, in the autumn to talk things over again. Many notable men, the saga says, came to that meeting, gathering outside on the grass in the sunny lee of the house. Bodvar now insisted that his client Vigdis get not forty cows as her inheritance from her brother, not sixty cows, but a full third of the value of Tunga: 266 cows. Pall did not like that at all, and the talks dragged on and on.

Pall's wife, Thorbjorg, now enters the story. Thorbjorg of Reykholt had a temper, we are told, and that day she lost it. She ran into the circle of men with a kitchen knife in her hand and thrust it at Sturla's eye, saying, "Why should I not make you look like Odin, whom you so wish to resemble?"

Someone grabbed her from behind, and the blade missed Sturla's eye, slashing across his cheek.

His men sprang to their weapons.

"Don't attack anyone," Sturla said, "before I say *who* is to be attacked." His hand was pressed against his cheek as he spoke, and blood poured down between his fingers. "There's no need to lose our tempers just because women have odd ways of showing their devotion. Thorbjorg and I have been friends for a long time," he added suggestively. Bodvar and Pall, he said, should conclude their negotiations about Tunga, and then he and Pall would discuss this little scratch.

Wounding a chieftain unprovoked was a serious matter. Pall agreed to all Bodvar's demands, giving Bodvar's client one-third of the value of Tunga. Pall then, after a little more arm-twisting by the notables present, offered Sturla self-judgment for his wife's attack.

To be offered self-judgment was an honor. It meant Sturla could assess whatever fine he wished, and Pall would pay it. Sturla could exile Pall, take his chieftaincy or his estate, or even have him or his wife put to death. But he wasn't expected to. When a man was given the great honor of self-judgment, he was expected to be magnanimous. He was expected to ask for a token payment and to earn his enemy's undying friendship.

"Take care," Sturla said ominously, "that if I am to estimate my own worth you won't find it excessive."

Pall insisted. They shook hands on it.

Sturla then assessed an outrageous sum, the highest fine for a slight wound in the history of Icelandic law: the equivalent of two hundred cows, to be paid promptly in gold, silver, land, livestock, or other goods. Kill a man, and the fine might be half that.

Pall flinched. It would take some time to get it together, he said.

He sent his son scurrying south to Jon Loftsson, the uncrowned king of Iceland. Jon said it wasn't right for Sturla to bully such a notable teacher as Pall. At the Althing the next summer Jon informed Sturla's father-in-law Bodvar that he would not allow the judgment to stand.

"Some of Pall's friends will lose their heads if Sturla suffers any disgrace," Bodvar warned.

"If Sturla has one of Pall's men killed," Jon countered, "I will have three of Sturla's men killed."

Sturla climbed to the Law Rock and waited till a crowd formed. "Pall gave me self-judgment," he said, tracing the scar on his cheek, "but now the most notable men in Iceland are called on for help so that this case can be settled by arbitration." Among those notable men, he said, "I name Jon Loftsson first of all, the most prominent man in this country and one to whom everyone appeals his lawsuits. And I don't know what else is more likely to help my prestige than to try what honor he will offer me." He withdrew his self-judgment and put the whole case in Jon's hands.

Jon thought Sturla spoke well. He reduced Pall's fine to thirty cows but offered to foster Sturla's youngest son, three-year-old Snorri.

Fosterage was common in medieval Iceland. One way a chieftain amassed power was by acquiring more kinsmen, who were honor bound to support him in court or on the battlefield. Families were enlarged by birth (a chieftain could never have too many sons, legitimate or illegitimate), by marrying off grown

children, or by fosterage. Children were fostered out to end a feud by binding
the two families together with kinship ties. A wealthy but childless man might
foster his chieftain's son to have help working the farm—and a guarantee that
no one would seize the property before the old man was ready to give it up.
Friends would foster each other's children to raise their friendship to the level
of kinship. A chieftain unsure of a neighbor's allegiance might thrust a child on
him to claim his loyalty. Or, as in this case, a child might be fostered as a form
of legal compensation, a fine paid to the father, with the assurance that the two,
father and foster father, would never again find themselves on opposite sides
in court.

Jon's offer, however, was unusual. The foster father was considered socially
inferior to the true father, and offering to foster another man's child was to
publicly acknowledge that fact. While in this case everyone knew it wasn't true,
the fiction was enough to enhance Sturla's prestige.

Jon invited Sturla to bring the little boy south to his estate at Oddi in time
for his church's annual dedication festival, and when Sturla turned for home he
carried additional gifts from Jon. He would never see his son again. Sturla died
two years later, in his bed at age sixty-eight, leaving behind a young widow and
fourteen children.

But his reputation was set. After the Viking Age, as Icelanders reckon time,
comes the Saga Age. After the Saga Age comes the Age of the Sturlungs: The
turbulent early thirteenth century in Iceland is named for Sturla of Hvamm
and his sons.

Little Snorri Sturluson, just five years old when his father died, profited
even more by Jon Loftsson's offer: At Oddi he received the best education to be
found in Iceland at the time.

The benefit to us—to all of Western culture—is immeasurable, for it was at
Oddi that Snorri became a writer.

Oddi, which means "Point," lay in the South of Iceland, in a triangle of
land between two branches of the River Ranga. To its north loomed Hekla, the
cloud-hooded volcano known to Europeans in the Middle Ages as the Mouth
of Hell. Hekla erupted twice during Snorri's lifetime, perhaps also once when
he was five, for the annals record "darkness across the south" that year. As a
cleric would report a few years later, "There are . . . mountains in this land,
which emit awful fire with the most violent hurling of stones, so that the crack

Hekla, the Icelandic volcano known in the Middle Ages as the Mouth of Hell, dominates the skyline north of Oddi, where Snorri grew up. Photo by the author.

and crash are heard throughout the country. . . . Such great darkness can follow downwind from this terror that, on midsummer at midday, one cannot make out one's [own] hand."

To the east of Oddi the ice caps rose, tier upon tier of vast blank whiteness, their glimmering domes mingling with the clouds so that on some days the horizon disappeared. Snorri's contemporaries were aware that active volcanoes lurked beneath the ice. A thirteenth-century poet told how "glaciers blaze," "fire unleashes storms," and "a marvelous mud begins to flow."

To Oddi's south stretched the sea. It couldn't be seen from Jon Loftsson's farmstead, but the jagged black teeth of the Westman Islands, where the nearest safe harbor lay, dominated the southern horizon. Lava also spouted from the sea in Snorri's lifetime, forming rugged black islands that rose above the waves only long enough for a few intrepid souls to row out and give them a name, the Fire Islands.

To the west of Oddi, Iceland's volcanic core revealed itself in hot springs, mud pits, screaming steam vents, and the great geysers that shot water more than two hundred feet into the air. Wastelands of black sand, ropy lava, or angular clinker taxed the most sure-footed riding horse. Even Thingvellir, the valley where the Althing met each summer, a day's ride northwest of Oddi, was marked by fire. The Law Rock itself was a lava hill, as was pointed out by Snorri's ancestor, wily Snorri of Helgafell. The occasion was the Althing of the year 1000, when Iceland's chieftains debated whether the land should become Christian, as the king of Norway urged. A rider broke into the proceedings to shout, "Earth fire! In Olfus!" A volcano had erupted on a chieftain's farm.

"It is no wonder. The gods are angry at such talk," people muttered.

"And what were the gods angry about," said Snorri of Helgafell, "when they burned the place we're standing on now?"

No one had an answer for that, and Iceland became Christian by parliamentary decree. Earth fire—lava—was just something Icelanders lived with, like the glacial rivers that burst in raging floods, the sea ice that clogged the island's shores, the constant whining wind, and the winter's darkness.

Though surrounded by fire and ice, the farm of Oddi itself lay sheltered behind a clump of hillocks in a wide green oasis of marsh and meadow crisscrossed by silver streams filled with fish. In some sheltered spots barley could be coaxed to grow. Thickets of birch and willow covered the slopes and gills of the nearby mountains. Twisted and stunted by the wind, the trees were useless as lumber but good for making charcoal and fashioning into small tools.

Jon Loftsson's estate encompassed several farms—seven, according to a document from 1270—where cattle, sheep, and horses were raised. With the estate came rights to collect bog iron or driftwood, to catch fish or birds, and to graze animals on other lands. Oddi included more than one church and collected the tithe for each: Certain farms in the valley paid the estate eighty-four sheep a year, while from every farm in a nearly fifty-mile radius Oddi received one cheese. Other farms tithed in beef, cloth, grain, fish, or salt.

Jon Loftsson's income from the tithe was sufficient to outfit each church with beeswax candles and embroidered altar cloths, incense and chrism, communion wine and wheat for the sacred hosts, bejeweled chalices, brightly painted icons, and even stained glass windows in at least one case. Everything but the cloth had to be imported. Jon could feed and clothe the deacons and priests, their wives and families (Icelandic churchmen routinely married in those days, though they were not supposed to), and the students, like little Snorri, at the church school.

Still, Jon had the means to hold a festival each year on December 9 to celebrate the Mass of Saint Nicholas, for whom the church at Oddi was named. The lovely Stave Church Homily might be read that morning from the great illuminated book of sermons resting on the lectern, since the priest "knew that the congregation would take his words more seriously if they could see that he was reading from a book." The four pillars of the church, this homily taught, were wisdom, righteousness, temperance, and fortitude, while its floor was paved with obedience, humility, and patience. It's clear Jon aspired to be a pillar, not a paving stone. He had a beautiful singing voice, and as a deacon he had mastered the mysteries of Gregorian chant. After church his men amused themselves with chess or dice, wrestling or ball games that resembled rugby, trials of strength like stone lifting, and horse races or horse fights in which two stallions were provoked to attack each other. Then came the feast at which both men and women could eat to bursting and get drunk on ale, beer, mead, or wine poured from a silver pitcher into a golden bowl. Stories were told, poems crafted and recited, songs sung to the thrumming of a harp, dances danced, and gifts liberally distributed—for the uncrowned king of Iceland lived like a king.

It came naturally: Jon Loftsson had royal blood. As Snorri would record years later in his collection of kings' sagas, *Heimskringla,* Jon's mother was an illegitimate daughter of the warrior-king Magnus Bare-Legs, so-called for his fondness for Scottish kilts. A son of King Sigurd Jerusalem-Farer, who fought in the Holy Land, King Magnus Bare-Legs ruled Norway from 1093 to 1103.

Jon Loftsson was born in Norway in 1124 and was raised for his first eleven years by the priest of Cross Church in Konungahella. The town, now in Sweden, was then a major Norwegian market town, and the church sported several souvenirs of King Sigurd's crusade, including a large silver processional cross containing a splinter of the True Cross. Jon's Icelandic father retrieved him from Konungahella in the nick of time. A week later pirates from Wendland (now parts of Germany and Poland) attacked the town. Jon's foster mother showed her spunk by slipping away to an outlying farm and sending around the war arrow to call up help, but it was too late. The town was burned and many of the townsfolk enslaved. Jon's foster father, the priest, was equally heroic. Trapped in the church, he ceremoniously presented the leaders of the pirates with a silver-gilt scepter and a gold ring; in return he asked to carry the holy cross as he was led into slavery. When he stepped onto the Wendish ship, Snorri wrote, "there came a great terror over the heathens," for the deck of the ship "became so hot that all thought they were going to be burnt up." The Wends set priest and cross in the ship's boat and, with a boat hook, pushed them back to shore.

Jon Loftsson did not return to Norway until 1164, when he was forty years old. On that occasion he came to see his uncle be consecrated bishop of Skalholt by the archbishop of Trondheim, who oversaw the Icelandic church.

Jon Loftsson and his uncle attended the festive crowning of another king Magnus, this one an eight-year-old boy. The king's mother was a daughter of King Sigurd Jerusalem-Farer. Magnus's father, a comparative nobody, convinced the archbishop to perform the ceremony, saying, "Though Magnus was not chosen king according to what has been the old custom of the country, yet can you with your power give him consecration as king, as God's law prescribes." Though Norway, unlike Iceland, had been a kingdom since the late 800s, this king Magnus was the first to be crowned by the church, not elected by the chieftains. Times were changing, and the repercussions of this breach in tradition would soon affect Iceland.

Norway had no jurisdiction over Iceland—yet. But Icelanders had long found it wise to make friends with the king. Norway was their main trading partner. It was also their source of ships. Iceland had no trees tall enough to build an ocean-going ship. Without access to the king's forests, the Icelanders were trapped on their windswept island. Knowing this, they struck a balance between fealty and freedom. Individuals swore oaths to the king and received ships, grain, gold, and other rewards. The island as a whole—with its Althing and body of laws—remained aloof. Yet by 1164 the archbishop of Trondheim already had jurisdiction over the Icelandic clergy, and the Norwegian church was well on its way to becoming a major political power in the North. When king and church joined forces at the crowning of young king Magnus, Iceland's independence was doomed.

None of this was apparent to Jon Loftsson and his uncle. For them the highlight of the day was the magnificent feast at which the young king and his father distributed presents. The best gift, to Jon Loftsson, was public recognition of his kinship with the king. Though Icelanders had no king—and professed to want no king—they were delighted to put on all the airs that royalty could claim. They believed, as did all Christians, that with royal blood came the divine right to rule.

Jon Loftsson, the uncrowned king of Iceland, was a proud man, wrote a cleric who quarreled with him: He was ambitious, obstinate, and pushy. "He would not give way for anyone or leave off what he began." Snorri picked up all these traits in the sixteen years he lived with his foster father at Oddi, from 1181 until Jon's death in 1197 at the age of seventy-three. Snorri also learned to share Jon's fascination with kingship. Though Snorri had no royal blood himself, to be the uncrowned king of Iceland was his deepest desire.

About Snorri's formal education at Oddi, we know little. No stories about his childhood are related in the sagas, but from other sources we can piece together an idea of what his schooldays were like.

The school at Oddi was set up in about 1100 by Jon Loftsson's paternal grandfather, the priest Saemund the Wise. A fantastic set of legends centers on Saemund, but little real information remains. In his youth Saemund studied in "Frakkland," perhaps in Paris at the university that would become the Sorbonne—though the legends say Saemund studied at the Black School run by Satan himself, where the students lived in the dark and studied books written in letters of flame. Satan claimed the last student out the door each year as his payment, but Saemund outfoxed him. He wore a great cloak; when Satan grabbed him, Saemund shrugged off his cloak and slipped away safe. Or, says another tale, when Satan cried, "Halt, you are the last!" as Saemund was about to step into the sunshine, Saemund pointed to his shadow on the wall and replied, "No, there's one behind me." He had no shadow for the rest of his days.

Saemund tricked the devil into ferrying him dryshod from Norway to Iceland. He tricked the devil into building a bridge over the river Ranga and into fetching Saemund's hay into his barn ahead of a rainstorm. He tricked the devil into changing into a gnat and crawling into a bunghole, which Saemund promptly plugged. To get out the devil had to promise to come when Saemund whistled.

These magical tales were first written down in the 1800s, but one survives from Snorri's days in the *Saga of Bishop Jon,* written by the Icelandic monk Gunnlaug Leifsson, who died in 1219. (Gunnlaug rather liked magicians; he also translated into Icelandic the fabulous "Prophecies of Merlin" from Geoffrey of Monmouth's *History of the Kings of Britain.*) Saemund had studied abroad so long, Gunnlaug wrote, that he forgot everything from his youth—even his name. But his friend Jon Ogmundarson finally found him. He described Iceland, then Oddi, to Saemund before finally sparking a glimmer of memory. Said Saemund, "Now I seem to remember that there was a hillock in the home field of Oddi where I always played." His friend convinced him to come home, but Saemund knew his schoolmaster would never give him leave. So they made a plan and on a cloudy night slipped away. The schoolmaster searched but could not find them until the next night, when the skies cleared and he could read the stars.

Saemund read the stars, too. He saw his schoolmaster coming. "Quick," he said, "fill my shoe with water and put it on my head."

"Bad news!" said the schoolmaster. "The Icelander has drowned my student." He turned back. The next night he looked again. He located Saemund and rode after him.

"Quick," said Saemund, "fill my shoe with blood and put it on my head."

"Bad news!" said the schoolmaster. "The Icelander has murdered my student."

The third night he searched the skies once more. "Aha!" he cried. "You are still alive, which is good, but I have taught you more than enough, for now you get the better of me. So fare you well and much may you accomplish."

This story was written down in Latin in the 1120s by the English cleric William of Malmesbury—but his hero was not the Icelander Saemund the Wise. It was the scientist pope, Sylvester II, born Gerbert of Aurillac and known in his lifetime as the leading astronomer of his age. After his death in 1003 he acquired a reputation as a wizard. Chances are that Saemund heard the tale of Gerbert the Wizard in Paris and brought it home, where it became attached to Saemund himself.

As for his own nickname, "the Wise," we can only wonder how Saemund earned it. He wrote a brief *Kings' Book,* chronicling the ten kings of Norway from 850 to 1047, but it no longer exists. He was consulted by Ari the Learned, who wrote the first history of Iceland in about 1120. Hundreds of years later, in 1643, because of an Icelandic antiquarian's wild guess, Saemund's name was attached to the manuscript of mythological poems now called *Saemund's Edda,* or the *Poetic Edda,* and thought to be one of Snorri's sources for his own *Edda,* which is often called the *Prose Edda.* Even if Saemund had nothing to do with the *Poetic Edda,* we can imagine that he liked to tell magical tales like the one about the scientist pope; that he might have told tales of the Viking gods; and that later generations, equating the old gods with devils, as churchmen commonly did, turned him into a benevolent wizard who could outwit Satan himself. We can also speculate that the subjects taught at his school at Oddi included the ancient stories and poems that inspired Snorri's *Edda.*

While our picture of Snorri's school at Oddi is drawn from legend and conjecture, we know a bit more about another Icelandic school from the 1100s. This school was established by Saemund's friend Jon Ogmundarson who, after rescuing Saemund from his star-reading schoolmaster in Paris, returned home to become the bishop of Holar in the North of Iceland. According to the monk Gunnlaug, Bishop Jon's schoolhouse stood to the west of the church; archaeologists have recently located its foundations there. The schoolmaster at Holar was a young Swedish cleric named Gisli Finnsson, known for his book learning. He was an excellent interpreter of the Bible and a good teacher of Latin— so good that the architect who was rebuilding the church next door, after it had burned down, listened in on Gisli's lessons and mastered Latin that way.

Another of the teachers at Holar was a French cantor named Rikini, who knew by heart all the chants sung for every church service of the year. Rikini taught singing and versifying. A third teacher was a nun named Ingunn. She taught Latin "to whoever would learn" and corrected the Latin in books that were read aloud to her while she was busy with her embroidery or weaving.

Bishop Jon Ogmundarson didn't always keep a close eye on his students. "It was the custom of the older men to teach the younger," Gunnlaug wrote, "and the younger men devoted their spare time to the writing of books." Elsewhere he adds other occupations for that spare time: "Some read holy books, some wrote, some sang, some studied, and some taught." And some sneaked off and raided the library. One, a boy sent to Holar at age twelve, was found engrossed in a copy of Ovid's *Art of Love*. Bishop Jon took the book away, noting that it was hard enough for a young man to control his sexual urges without reading erotic poems.

Why did a church-run school own a copy of Ovid's *Art of Love?* Perhaps it was bundled, as manuscripts often were, with Ovid's *Metamorphoses*, a popular textbook for Latin classes in the Middle Ages. We have no catalog of Holar's library (or of the library of any Icelandic school from the time), though we do know that one Icelandic monastery owned 120 books in 1184. Books commonly used to teach Latin elsewhere in Europe were Donatus's *The Minor Arts* and its sequel, *The Major Arts*; Priscian's *Introduction to Grammar*; Cicero's *On the Art of Speaking*; Horace's *Odes* and *Satires*; and Virgil's *Aeneid*. Icelanders in the twelfth century were also familiar with Plato's *Timaeus*, Sallust's *Histories*, Isidore of Seville's *Encyclopedia*, Honorius's *Elucidarius*, Gregory the Great's *Dialogues*, the anonymous *Physiologus*, Alcuin's *On Virtues and Vices*, Geoffrey of Monmouth's *History of the Kings of Britain*, and the works of the Venerable Bede, such as *On the Metrical Arts* and the *Ecclesiastical History of the English Peoples*.

Snorri shows little sign of having read these books. If he took Latin, it did not stick. He never quotes Latin books (not even the Bible) or uses Latin words. He never parades his classical learning, as his peers did. He has only the roughest grasp of the great classical stories like the fall of Troy: When he refers to Troy in the *Edda* and *Heimskringla*, he gets it wrong. He is familiar with Latin prose styles, such as the dialogue, but he wasn't impressed by them. His own writing style is refreshingly, even provocatively, different. Says a recent translator, "I think it would scarcely be possible for a writer trained in Latin grammar and rhetoric to write as Snorri does."

The school at Oddi certainly taught Latin. Snorri's foster father, Jon Loftsson, knew enough Latin to be ordained a deacon, one step below priest. Snorri's foster brother Pall Jonsson learned Latin at a young age, then went on to study at Lincoln Cathedral in England, surpassing his peers in singing, versifying, and the writing of books. While most were sacred books, Pall is believed to have written at least one saga, a history of the kings of Denmark. He became bishop of Skalholt, where he was responsible for the religious life of 220 churches and 290 priests.

To see why Snorri didn't turn out like Pall, we need to return to the boy who read the *Art of Love* at Holar—and who also became a bishop of Skalholt. Bishop Klaeng was known as a learned man, a good poet, and an eloquent lawyer. (He is the bishop whose oath Snorri's father, Sturla, sarcastically revered as he revered the Easter Mass.) Bishop Klaeng built an enormous church—archaeological excavations prove it to have been a wooden stave church 164 feet long, 39 feet wide, and an estimated 46 feet high, the wood all imported from Norway, since building timber was not to be found anywhere in Iceland—and "adorned the place with his bookmaking." He invited seven hundred guests to the church's dedication feast and was known afterward for holding crowded feasts and giving gifts of money to his friends.

Except for being an ascetic who wore monkish robes and went barefoot, Bishop Klaeng sounds very much like the man Snorri would become: a poet, a lawyer, a lover of books, flamboyantly rich, given to feasting and grand building schemes, not a warrior but a good negotiator and a canny businessman.

Why did Snorri not become a bishop? It seems that the rules changed between Klaeng's twelfth birthday at the school of Holar in about 1120 and Snorri's twelfth birthday at the school of Oddi in 1190. The archbishop of Trondheim decreed in 1190 that henceforth no priest in Iceland could be a chieftain and no Icelandic chieftain could be a priest. In the old days, according to the *Saga of Christianity*, "most respectable men were educated and ordained as priests, even those who were chieftains." For nearly two hundred years church and state in Iceland had been one. No conflicts arose about who should receive the tithe or which laws applied to clerics, as would occur in Snorri's lifetime.

Because of the archbishop's decree, someone—probably Snorri's foster father, Jon Loftsson, but perhaps Snorri himself—had to make a choice when
Snorri was twelve. Would he become a priest or a chieftain? As his nephew
Saga-Sturla later wrote, Snorri Sturluson was good at everything he put his
hand to.

A chieftain did not need Latin. A chieftain did need to know law, history, and genealogical lore and have mastery of several arts, especially the art
of poetry. A saga of the twelfth century expects an Icelander visiting Norway
to know how "to greet the king grandly" and to act as a skald, a Norse bard or
troubadour, entertaining the court with poems and tales.

According to a skald of the time, a cultured man knew nine arts:

I am eager to play chess,
I have mastered nine skills,
I hardly forget the runes,
I am interested in books and carpentry.
I know how to ski,
My shooting and sailing skills are competent,
I can both play the harp and construe verse.

Another accomplished Icelander in Snorri's day was a master craftsman in
wood and iron, as well as a poet. "He was the greatest of physicians and a man
of fine learning," his saga says. "He was knowledgeable in the law and spoke
eloquently. He had a great memory and was learned in all things. . . . He was a
good swimmer, agile in all that he did. He was a great archer and no one was
better at throwing. He traveled abroad as a young man and gained respect from
dignitaries in other countries."

Snorri may have learned all these arts growing up at Oddi (though there's
no mention of his being a physician or rune master). He certainly learned
how to read and write at Oddi but in Icelandic, not Latin. Unlike most medieval countries at the time, Iceland's learning was recorded in the vernacular.
Much of the writing was done during Snorri's lifetime, and he was at the
center of it.

Iceland's book culture began in the year 1000, when Iceland became
Christian by parliamentary decree at the Althing. Christians are "people of

the book": Christianity's most powerful symbol is not the cross but the Bible. Finding no books in Iceland, foreign priests introduced the technology in about 1030. A missionary bishop named Rudolf, from Normandy or perhaps England, ran a school in the West of Iceland until 1050. There, he and his fellows showed their Icelandic students how to make parchment. First they scraped the hair off a calfskin with a sharp blade. This was a more difficult task in Iceland, where limestone was unavailable, than in continental Europe; a bath in slaked lime made the hair simply fall off the skin. In Iceland the skins were washed in a hot spring, where the mineral-rich water loosened the hair, and scraped again and again. Another technique was to soak the skins in urine and leave them to rot until the hair came off. A third method involved tying a newly flayed skin to a heifer, with the hair side against the cow's skin. In a day or two the hair would be loose enough to pluck off. When suitably hairless, the skins were stretched on a frame and set in the shade to dry. After rubbing the skins smooth with pumice (plenty of that in volcanic Iceland), the parchment was made soft and pliable by twisting it and pulling it back and forth through a ring made from a cow's horn.

Quill pens were cut from swan, goose, or raven feathers (also easily come by in Iceland); left-wing feathers were best for right-handed writers because they bent away from the eye. Ink was made by boiling whole bearberry plants with a clay commonly used to dye wool black. A few shavings of green willow twigs were added to the pot, and the mixture was simmered until it turned sticky. "Let a drop fall onto your fingernail," says one recipe. "If it remains there like a little ball, then the ink is ready." A little bit of gum from the first milk of a young ewe or heifer was added to the ink to make it shiny. The result was ink that was black, glossy, and impermeable to water—important to people who often traveled by ship. Books are rarely mentioned in the sagas, but in one famous shipwreck a priest is desolate when his book chest is swept overboard. Learning a few nights later that it had washed ashore, he hurried to the spot to dry out his books; it took him six weeks. Mold is one thing a parchment book cannot survive.

The Icelandic alphabet was created early in the 1100s, based on the Latin and Anglo-Saxon alphabets, and sermons were the first texts written down. One of the oldest surviving scraps of manuscript in Icelandic contains the Stave Church Homily. Translations were made of parts of the Bible, and each church needed a copy of the life of its patron saint.

Next to be written down were the laws of the land, in 1117. That winter the lawspeaker and a cadre of experts met at the house of a leading chieftain. The lawspeaker recited a section, the experts debated the law, and a scribe recorded their final version. At the next Althing the laws were read out of the book by clerics—not by the lawspeaker, who presumably could not read. By the time Snorri took up the law, it may have become book learning, though eloquence and rhetorical skill must still have been taught orally. Jon Loftsson, the great negotiator himself, may have been Snorri's model. Jon's sons Orm and Pall, the bishop, were both good lawyers; Pall gets credit for reforming the laws on sales of cloth and establishing the official yardstick. But Snorri surpassed his foster brothers. He first appeared before the Althing in 1197, when he was nineteen, and won his case. He was elected lawspeaker—essentially, president of the Althing—in 1215 and retained the post, with a short break while he traveled abroad, until 1231.

Another of the oldest Icelandic manuscripts is mathematical: It contains an Easter table, calculations of the dates of Easter for many years in advance. Snorri might have learned how to make—or at least to interpret—an Easter table while he was at Oddi, since the lawspeaker was also responsible for keeping the calendar. The Christian calendar is based on the movable feast of Easter. Easter must fall on a Sunday, during certain days of the Jewish festival of Passover, after the vernal equinox, and during the right phase of the moon. Calculating the date was not trivial: You needed to integrate the lunar month (twenty-nine days, twelve hours) with the 365 and a quarter days of the solar year. To predict the equinox took skill in astronomy. An Icelander known as Star-Oddi devised a way to make accurate observations of the day-to-day variations in the sun's altitude; using his results, Bjarni the Mathematician reconciled the traditional Icelandic calendar with the church's Julian calendar. Snorri would have known of their work. Bjarni, a student at Bishop Jon's school at Holar, lived until 1173, five years before Snorri was born, and wrote a treatise in Icelandic about his almanac.

The correcting of Iceland's traditional calendar is also mentioned in the *Book of the Icelanders* by Ari the Learned, whom Snorri acknowledges as one of his sources for *Heimskringla*. The two bishops of Iceland commissioned Ari to write his history of the country shortly after the law books were completed. The *Book of the Icelanders* was also vetted by Saemund the Wise of Oddi. As a history it is dry, sketchy, and rather disappointing, given Ari's large reputation as Iceland's first historian. One scholar dubbed it "a collection of notes," another "a ten-page survey." Ari gave it a Latin title, *Libellus Islandorum,* as well as an Icelandic one, and it has a very Latin feel, with a preface, acknowledgments, table of contents, clear chapter divisions, and strict chronology. Even the sentence structure is Latinate, and the book is sprinkled with Latin words. But it—or others of Ari's works, now lost—impressed Snorri. As he writes in *Heimskringla,* "It is not strange that Ari knew the truth of old events both here and abroad, for he had got his knowledge from old and wise men, and he himself was eager to learn and had a good memory." Snorri concludes, "All his account seems to me most remarkable."

Next, books of family history became fashionable. Knowing genealogies at least five generations back was vital to a lawyer: Questions of inheritance, land-ownership, care of dependents, and compensation for killings all hinged on kinship. But memorizing chains of names was tedious. To enliven the task the names were attached to stories. Many were collected into a chronicle of Iceland's founders, the *Book of Settlements,* shortly after the *Book of the Icelanders* was finished. Ari the Learned may have been in charge of this project too, as it is equally well organized; it proceeds clockwise around the country and presents capsule portraits of 430 settlers and their kin. Snorri was familiar with the *Book of Settlements.* Both his friend Styrmir the Wise and his nephew Saga-Sturla wrote expanded versions, and it may be because of them that thirty-eight of the 399 chapters are devoted to Snorri's ancestors.

Before the end of the twelfth century the first saga was written. The *Book of the Icelanders* and the *Book of Settlements* were called books, not sagas, by their authors. A book is something to be read. A saga, derived from the verb *segja,* "to say," is something else. Exactly what has been debated for hundreds of years. One school of thought says the sagas existed, perfect, in oral form before being written down. We know now, from the study of oral literature in other cultures, that writers never take anything down verbatim, unless they use a voice recorder. Oral tales shift and change depending on the teller and the audience. But the sagas are too tightly structured to allow for this. Another school of thought says the sagas were created exactly the way authors of the twentieth century created novels. The truth is somewhere in between. Saga writers were not self-conscious authors. They did not sign their work, though Icelandic poets in this period did. The saga authors did not think of sagas as art. Stealing the best parts from each other's sagas was perfectly acceptable. Stealing a line from a poem, on the other hand, was either a vast compliment—because the audience would recognize the source—or an insult, a parody, as later happened to one of Snorri's verses.

One of the earliest sagas, written between 1180 and 1190, first in Latin and then translated into Icelandic, is the *Saga of King Olaf Tryggvason* by Odd Snorrason, a monk in the Benedictine monastery of Thingeyri in northern Iceland. For much of its 190 pages it is "a snarl of narrative contradictions," according to its modern translator. It is, he continues, "a particularly ill-assorted and ill-shuffled collection of anecdotes" with no apparent plot.

Odd the Monk also wrote the *Saga of Yngvar the Far-Traveler,* about two Viking expeditions into Russia. A note at its end explains Odd's method. He heard the saga told by three people: Isleif, Glum, and Thorir. Isleif had learned the story from a merchant, who in turn had heard it at the Swedish royal court. Glum learned the story from his father. Thorir heard it told by his older kinsmen. Of these three renditions, Odd "took what he thought to be most significant." He sent his saga to two people to review—Gissur Hallsson of Haukadale and Snorri's foster father, Jon Loftsson of Oddi—and made corrections based on their comments. Brother Gunnlaug, who described the school at Holar and recorded the tale of Saemund the Wizard, also wrote a *Saga of King Olaf Tryggvason* in about 1190. He too sent it to Gissur Hallsson for comments. Gissur, Gunnlaug complains, kept the book for two years.

An early collection of sagas about the kings of Norway and the Icelanders who visited their courts is known as *Rotten Parchment*—Icelandic parchment is generally dark and grubby, from either greasy-fingered readers or the lack of lime in the preparation of the skin. *Rotten Parchment* is striking for "the author's delight in storytelling" and his "rare narrative verve," say the experts, but it still lacks structure. Its author might have been Snorri's friend Styrmir and the date of composition as late as 1220.

A saga of the Danish kings, *Skjoldunga Saga,* may have been written at Oddi while Snorri was there, perhaps by his foster brother Pall Jonsson. When Pall was chosen bishop of Skalholt in 1195, the Norwegian archbishop had lost his eyesight. So Pall went to Lund in Denmark to be consecrated by the archbishop there. At Lund, Pall may have met the Danish cleric Saxo Grammaticus, who was writing his history of the kings of Denmark, the *Gesta Danorum,* at the urging of the same archbishop. In it Saxo praises the Icelanders for their "store of historical treasures" and "skill in ancient lore."

The author of *Skjoldunga Saga* blended history with myth and legend, with much of his material coming from poetry, just as Snorri would do in *Heimskringla,* his history of the kings of Norway. The outline of *Skjoldunga Saga* was provided by a genealogical poem in which the poet says, "Now I have counted ten rulers, each of whom sprang from Harald," the king whose unification of Norway in the ninth century prompted the settlement of Iceland by Vikings who had no taste for kings. Concludes the poet, "I narrated their lives according to the words of Saemund the Wise." This poem is thought to have been composed in 1194 to celebrate Jon Loftsson's seventieth birthday. It is eighty-three verses long and in a standard meter, competent but nothing special. In 1194 Snorri was sixteen. This "Tally of the Kings" may be his first effort as a poet, his entry into the world of the skald.

Whether he was the poet on this occasion or not, Snorri became a very skillful one. Skaldic poetry was a "game of puzzles," and Snorri mastered all its meters and rhetorical tricks. Few poems had been written down, so Snorri learned the way Icelandic skalds had for hundreds of years: by ear. He loved poetry and memorized a great deal of it. In his *Edda* he quotes 373 verses by more than sixty poets. *Heimskringla* includes nearly six hundred verses. Nor is that all the poetry he knew: Snorri quotes only single lines or half stanzas, not complete poems.

Skaldic poems are packed with mythological allusions. To understand them Snorri learned tales of the god Odin and the rest of the Norse pantheon. Who were his teachers? Odd the Monk gives us a hint in his *Saga of King Olaf Tryggvason.* He wrote the saga, he said, because "it is better to listen to such tales for entertainment than stepmothers' sagas, which shepherds tell even though no one knows whether they are true or not, and which always place the king in a diminished position in the story." (*Rotten Parchment* preserves a selection of these stepmothers' sagas, funny tales in which an Icelander goes to Norway and outwits the king.) Mothers and stepmothers were indeed an excellent source of ancient lore, since Icelandic women had long been responsible for keeping track of genealogies and family gossip. About the bishop Thorlak, who studied at Oddi a few years before Snorri, we read that when he was not busy with his books and prayers, he "learned what his mother taught him, genealogy and family history." When listing his sources for the *Book of the Icelanders,* Ari the Learned singled out an old woman named Thurid, who lived to be eighty-seven, for being both truthful and wise. Along with stories about kings and feuds, love affairs and lawsuits, old women like Thurid told stories about hills and islands—even today every rock in Iceland seems to have a story of its own. Ghost stories were popular, as were tales of trolls and dragons.

These stories were not sagas; they were the kernels of sagas—episodes told as the occasion warranted, not from beginning to end, chronologically, as written sagas generally are. The storyteller could assume her audience knew her characters and the overall plot. She could choose to zoom in on just one day, such as the day when Thorbjorg of Reykholt tried to stab Hvamm-Sturla in the eye.

Snorri, who would have heard that story umpteen times in the eighteen years he lived at Oddi, may eventually have taken up ink and parchment, for another saga thought to have been composed at Oddi while he lived there is the *Saga of Hvamm-Sturla*. The saga is biased toward the Oddi point of view, with Jon Loftsson as the hero, while Sturla is a bit of a rogue. But the fact that it was written at all suggests a connection with Snorri and his two older brothers, then making their mark as chieftains in the West of Iceland—and neither of Snorri's brothers was a writer.

On stylistic grounds too, the *Saga of Hvamm-Sturla* seems to mark Snorri's debut as a writer of prose. He may not have written the whole saga. Its end—including the anecdote about Odin's eye—is sharply different from the beginning. Instead of a jumble of events, the end is tightly plotted. The characters are well drawn, with clear motivations. In all this it resembles the later sagas attributed to Snorri, with their convincing dialogue, well-crafted scenes, dramatic action, and smooth shifts in point of view. Snorri's prose is terse and economical, easy to read aloud. His humor is light, ironic, and penetrating. He added realistic details of weather, landscape, or daily life that his predecessors skipped. He was not afraid of the fantastic but kept it in check, wavering on the margins of his sagas as it did in real life.

Finally, the story of Hvamm-Sturla's almost-lost eye calls to mind Snorri's characterization of the one-eyed wandering wizard-god, Odin, whose word was not to be trusted. Thorbjorg with her kitchen knife may well have meant to call Sturla the devil himself. But Sturla—and the writer of his saga—seem to take it as a compliment.

Two

THE UNCROWNED
KING OF ICELAND

And that age was known as the Golden Age, until it was spoiled by the
arrival of the women.

—Snorri, *Edda*

The gods had odd love lives.

According to Snorri, Odin traded a lonely giantess three nights of
blissful sex for three drafts of the mead of poetry. Another lucky giantess bore
him valiant Vidar, one of the few gods who survived Ragnarok, the terrible
last battle between gods and giants. The philandering All-Father coupled with
his daughter Earth to beget the mighty Thor, the thunder god. Odin's long-
suffering wife, wise Frigg, gave him Baldur the Beautiful, at whose death the
whole world wept. Frigg knew the fates of all men, though she revealed nothing.

Njord, god of the sea, married the giantess Skadi as part of a peace treaty.
She wanted to marry beautiful Baldur and was told she could have him—if
she could pick him out of a lineup by looking only at his feet. Njord, it turned
out, had prettier feet than Baldur. But Njord and Skadi didn't get along. He
hated the mountains, she hated the sea. He hated the nighttime howling of
the wolves, she hated the early morning ruckus of the gulls. So they divorced.
Afterward Skadi was honored as the goddess of skiing. She and Odin took up
together and had several sons, including Skjold, the founder of the Danish dynasty (Skjold was known to the writer of *Beowulf* as Scyld Shefing). Njord then
married his sister and had two children, the twin love gods Freyr and Freyja.

Beautiful Freyja is the goddess we honor on Fridays. Snorri keeps quiet about her infidelities, telling us only that her husband traveled often while she sat alone weeping tears of gold. Snorri says Freyja was fond of love poems and jewelry—she wore an expensive dwarf-forged necklace—and that she especially adored cats. Two giant ones drew her chariot.

Her brother, Freyr, fell head-over-heels for a giantess he saw from afar while illicitly sitting on Odin's high throne. "When she raised her arms to open the door, they illumined the sky and the sea, and the whole world grew bright from her," Snorri writes. Lovesick Freyr could not eat, he could not sleep, he thought he would die if he could not have her. Now, Freyr was the god who decided when the sun would shine and when it would rain. He governed peace and plenty. No one wanted him to be unhappy, so the gods deputized his servant to learn what troubled the god of love. Freyr extolled the charms of his giantess. He begged his servant to go to Giantland and woo her and bring her to him whether her father consented or not. His servant (also a god) bargained. Freyr must give him the sword that fought by itself. Freyr did so, and his servant went to woo the giantess. She eventually gave in to his threats and agreed to meet Freyr at a secret place nine nights later. Freyr could hardly wait. "One night is long, long is a second, how shall I three endure?" But he got his bright-shining giantess. And he died at Ragnarok because he could not defeat fiery Surt without his magic sword.

Then there's Loki, Odin's two-faced blood brother, whose love affairs led to so much trouble. Loki the Trickster, Snorri writes, was "pleasing and handsome in appearance, evil in character, very capricious in behavior. He possessed to a greater degree than others the kind of learning that is called cunning. . . . He was always getting the Aesir into a complete fix and often got them out of it by trickery." With his loyal wife, Loki had a godly son. In the shape of a mare (Loki could change himself into any creature of either sex), Loki was the mother of Odin's wonderful eight-legged horse, Sleipnir. But on an evil giantess he begot three monsters: the Midgard Serpent; Hel, the half black, half white goddess of death; and the giant wolf, Fenrir.

Odin sent for Loki's monstrous children. He threw the serpent into the sea, where it grew so huge it wrapped itself around the whole world. It lurked in the deeps, biting its own tail, until it took revenge at Ragnarok and slayed Thor with a blast of its poisonous breath. Odin sent Hel to the deepest underworld (renamed Hel in her honor), where she became the harsh and heartless queen over all who died of sickness or old age. In her hall, damp with sleet, they ate off plates of hunger and slept in sickbeds. The giant wolf, Fenrir, the gods raised as a pet until it grew frighteningly large. Then they got from the dwarfs a leash woven from the sound of a cat's footstep, a woman's beard, the roots of a mountain, the sinews of a bear, the breath of a fish, and the spittle of a bird. Fenrir would not let them tie him up until Tyr, the brave god of war for whom Tuesday was named, put his hand in the wolf's mouth as a pledge of the gods' good faith. The wolf could not break free of this leash no matter how hard he struggled, and the gods refused to let him loose. It had been a trick all along. "Then they all laughed except for Tyr," Snorri writes. "He lost his hand." At Ragnarok the wolf swallowed Odin. Valiant Vidar avenged his father's death by ripping the wolf's jaws apart.

The gods were a lusty bunch. They had wives and mistresses and casual mates. They divorced and remarried. They stole their brides at swordpoint. (Or picked their husbands for their pretty feet.) Even incest was not forbidden. They acknowledged all their children. Some were paragons of strength (Thor), beauty (Baldur), or faithfulness (Vidar). Others were monstrous—though they might have turned out better if raised right. Eight-legged Sleipnir, after all, was not a normal child, and he became Odin's favorite horse. As parents the gods were pretty dysfunctional.

Snorri and his kin had odd love lives and dysfunctional families, too, or so it seems today. The archbishop of Trondheim thought so as well. He sent numerous missives to Iceland's two bishops, ordering them to clean up the island's morals, but to no avail.

Snorri's foster father was one of the worst offenders. Though married with two children, Jon Loftsson openly kept the bishop of Skalholt's sister as his mistress. When that bishop, the soon-to-be-sainted Thorlak, threatened him with excommunication, Jon shrugged. He would not part from the woman he loved, he said, "until God breathes it into my breast" to do so. She gave him two sons of whom he was vastly proud (one was Pall, who became a bishop himself). But Jon's affection for his mistress did not stop him from having four children with three other women. He acknowledged them all, paid for their upkeep and education, and ensured that after his death his estate would be divided equally among his legitimate and illegitimate offspring. He was not ashamed of his potency.

Nor was Snorri's father. Hvamm-Sturla sired fourteen children: seven legitimate and seven illegitimate. As a young man he took a fancy to a "wise and able" widow. They had five children but didn't marry. Instead Sturla allied himself with a powerful chieftain by marrying his daughter, who happened to be "the fairest woman in Iceland at that time." They had two daughters before she died. Sturla then had two more children out of wedlock before marrying his second wife, Gudny, Snorri's mother, when she was about sixteen and he was forty-five. She gave him three sons and two daughters.

In her brief appearances in the *Saga of Hvamm-Sturla*, Gudny organizes a ring dance to raise people's spirits. She orders her husband to stop harrassing one of her friends (Sturla gives her a chance to patch things up, but ends up killing her friend anyway). And she calls up reinforcements when Sturla rides off half-cocked after a band of sheep thieves.

The *Saga of Hvamm-Sturla* is part of the long *Sturlunga Saga* collection, the "Sagas of the Sturlung Age." The next part, which begins with Sturla's death in 1183, was written by Gudny's grandson, Saga-Sturla. In it Gudny comes across as independent and doughty, a true *skörungur*. A great compliment, *skörungur* is a word translators have trouble with. In modern Icelandic it is a fireplace poker. In modern English translators have tried "high-spirited," "forceful," "noble," "fine," "remarkable," "superior," "of great magnificence," and "a very stirring woman." All these might apply, but when a man is called a *skörungur,* the translation is usually "a good leader." Gudny, the daughter of a chieftain, was descended from the great Viking and poet Egil Skalla-Grimsson of Borg, hero of *Egil's Saga.* Egil's troll-like father, Skalla-Grim (Bald-Grim), was one of Iceland's founders. Skalla-Grim's father, Kveld-Ulf (Evening-Wolf), was a chieftain in Norway and reputed werewolf. It was not a family to trifle with.

When Hvamm-Sturla died, Gudny was only thirty-five. Within a year she had taken as a lover the chieftain Ari the Strong, grandson of Iceland's first historian, Ari the Learned. No shame attached to a woman for taking a lover. If her menfolk did not like it, her liaison might provoke a feud, but in this case Gudny's sons and brother had no complaints. Ari the Strong already had a wife and daughter, though, so he and Gudny decided to travel to Norway. Their adventure did not end well. It seems Ari bragged too much about his great strength. One day he and some others were carrying a ship's beam when the other men ran out from beneath it. Ari held the heavy load up alone, rupturing himself in the process. He died a few days later, and broken-hearted Gudny took the next ship back to Iceland and home to Hvamm; she lived the rest of her long life alone or as housekeeper for one of her sons.

Before they went to Norway, Gudny and Ari had married her eldest son, Thord, then twenty-one, to his daughter, Helga. With his young wife Thord got Ari's chieftaincy and a rich farmstead. When Ari died, the rest of his wealth went to Thord and his wife, but, as the saga says, "Thord was not lucky enough to feel for Helga the love he should have." After four years of marriage and no children, they divorced. Thord kept the farm, most of Ari's wealth, and the chieftain's title. He took up with a married woman, Hrodny, the estranged wife of Bersi the Rich of Borg—the farm of his famous ancestor Egil Skalla-Grimsson—but though "they enjoyed a lasting love," Thord and Hrodny didn't marry. Instead Thord married a rich widow named Gudrun, who "brought a great deal of money with her," the saga says. "Thord then became a great chieftain." He and Gudrun had a son, Bodvar, who was his father's only legal heir, and a daughter. Later in life Thord fell in love again, taking as his mistress Thora, who gave him six children; her son Sturla, born when his father was fifty, wrote the saga. In it Saga-Sturla paints his father as a pious and peace-loving man, self-controlled, wise in counsel, even a bit of a seer, since his warnings to his brothers (as reported) often do come true.

Gudny's second son, Snorri's brother Sighvat, was five years younger than Thord and almost monogamous in comparison. Sighvat inherited a good farm from their father and—since Thord already had Ari's chieftaincy—took over Hvamm-Sturla's title, with the approval of his mother and older brother. Little Snorri's opinion was not sought. Sighvat cemented his status by marrying Halldora, daughter of the most powerful chieftain in the North Quarter of Iceland. "They had a happy marriage," we're told, even though Sighvat kept a mistress who made him "a very rich man" and gave him a daughter. Sighvat was grasping and stubborn, with a streak of cruel humor and none of his brother's religious feeling, but Sighvat and Halldora "won the respect of everyone," the saga says. They had nine children, including Snorri's nemesis, another Sturla. Dreaming of the birth of this grandson, Gudny named him Vigsterk (Battle-Strong).

By the time Snorri came of age, his mother had wasted his small inheritance from his father, Hvamm-Sturla: the value of forty cows. Snorri inherited only a book or two (if anything) from his foster father, Jon Loftsson, who died in 1197 when Snorri was nineteen. Jon Loftsson not only had many children of his own, both legitimate and illegitimate, but in his last years the bishop's fire and brimstone finally got to him—or else God breathed in his heart. Jon saw his mistress responsibly married and spent much of his wealth building a new church and monastery (it was never completed). Snorri's prospects for becoming a rich chieftain like his brothers looked dim.

Then a woman stepped in. For some unknown reason Hrodny, the mistress of Snorri's brother Thord, took an interest in young Snorri. She had a marriageable daughter, Herdis, the only legitimate child of the chieftain and priest Bersi the Rich, whose estate at Borg was worth eight hundred cows. With the help of Snorri's foster brother Saemund Jonsson of Oddi, Thord and Hrodny arranged the match. The wedding was to be held at Hvamm in the summer of 1199; afterward Snorri's mother would turn over the family estate to Snorri and Herdis as the bride-price.

If Snorri met his bride before their wedding day, it was only briefly. Marriages in Iceland had long been business transactions, arranged by the couple's families. Though love matches were not unknown, the lovers needed their families' approval, and formal procedures had to be followed. Before witnesses the bride's and groom's fathers (or other representatives) announced the wealth they were giving the couple. The bride's family supplied a dowry, the groom's family a bride-price of land, livestock, and other goods that the couple would jointly own while their marriage lasted. The fathers then shook hands on the deal. It was the same way they sold a plot of land or an ocean-going ship or transferred a chieftaincy. The bride didn't even need to be present—much less agree to the deal. Nor was the groom expected to be monogamous.

The church was trying to change that. From the time of Snorri's birth the archbishop of Trondheim had sent letter after letter explaining that marriage was a sacrament, "a bond comparable to the mystical union between Christ and his Church." In a Christian wedding not only did the bride have to consent, audibly, but the bride and groom vowed to be faithful to each other for life. That was not an idea the Icelanders embraced: Witness Bishop Thorlak's long argument with Jon Loftsson about his mistress. Nor were all the bishops as keen to enforce the rules as the soon-to-be-sainted Thorlak. Thorlak's successor, Bishop Pall, who was the result of Jon's adulterous love, was notably lax.

Snorri may have hoped for love in marriage. But more important were the wealth and power his new family connections would bring him. In these Snorri was not disappointed.

Snorri's family estate of Hvamm (Grassy Slope) was tucked into a lush green bowl at the inward tip of a deep island-studded fjord in the West of Iceland. Sheltered by jagged hills, it was one of the few great estates without a sweeping view. Its first settler was a woman, Aud the Deep-Minded, the only female chieftain Iceland ever had. Once a queen in Dublin, Aud was a grandmother ruling Caithness with her son when he was betrayed and killed by the Scots. She rounded up the rest of their kin, had a ship secretly built, and sailed off to Iceland. As the *Book of Settlements* tells us, twenty freeborn men chose to accompany her (including everyone's favorite Viking, Eystein Foul-Fart). Aud claimed the Dales, an enormous swath of land surrounding Hvamm and bisected by the river Laxa (Salmon River), and parceled it out among her followers. A Christian, she erected a cross on a prominent hilltop at the edge of the fjord.

When she felt death coming on, Aud arranged a match for her grandson and heir. She was very old by then, we are told, and "would give an irate reply if anyone asked about her health." Still, she insisted that all her kinsmen come to the wedding. It was held at Hvamm at the end of summer, "the best time for getting all the necessary provisions," and lasted three days, with three nights of feasting and ale drinking, during which Aud parceled out both fine gifts and "sound advice" to her many guests. On the final evening, while the ale was still going around, she turned over the keys of the household to the young couple and went to bed. In the morning she was found dead, sitting regally upright, having "kept her dignity to her dying day," as *Laxdaela Saga* says.

This saga was written in the mid-1200s, and readers have wondered if it wasn't the wedding of Snorri Sturluson and Herdis of Borg, held at Hvamm in the late summer of 1199, that the writer was actually describing. Some scholars have even suggested that *Laxdaela Saga* was written by another of Snorri's nephews, Thord's son Olaf White-Poet. He might have heard the story from his grandmother Gudny, who lived until 1221, when Olaf was nine or a little older. Whoever wrote the tale, what he thought important to record was not the food or drink, not the beauty and enormous wealth of the bride, or even the sagas told around the fire. Instead he stressed how dignified the hostess was. She was tall and stout and walked briskly down the hall. She spared no expense, inviting "many eminent people far and wide," so that the wedding was "attended in great numbers." And everyone "marveled at the magnificence of this feast."

Everyone except perhaps Snorri himself, who declined to accept the keys to Hvamm from his mother. He took his bride home to Oddi, where they lived with his foster brother Saemund Jonsson until Herdis's father died three years later, and they inherited Borg. At Oddi they had a daughter, Hallbera. Soon after they moved to Borg, their son Jon (probably named for Jon Loftsson) was born; Jon was so small as a boy he acquired the nickname *Murtr,* or Trout. He was his father's favorite child.

Why did Snorri not take Hvamm? His interest in his father's estate may have waned when he learned that no part of his father's title as chieftain went with it. Chieftaincies were often split, not passed down whole. Snorri should have received at least a third. Instead his brother Sighvat held on to the honor, while his brother Thord ruled a different chieftaincy, courtesy of his mother's deceased lover. At Hvamm Snorri would have lived in their double shadow. That didn't suit. Instead Snorri made himself useful at Oddi.

When Jon Loftsson died, he left a power vacuum. Many men felt qualified to fill the shoes of the uncrowned king of Iceland; first among them was Saemund, Jon's heir. But Saemund was soon mired in a petty feud. It had to do, as most feuds did, with the inheritance of property. The quarrel eventually came before the Althing, and Saemund graciously offered to settle, but his enemy snubbed him. Saemund's opponent was backed by Snorri's brash older brother Sighvat and Sighvat's even more obstreperous brother-in-law, Kolbein Tumason, the leader of the North Quarter and another candidate for uncrowned king. Saemund had not his father's patience or political touch. That winter he called up a posse and killed the man living on the farm at the center of the dispute. Then Saemund had Snorri summon the man's chieftain, Sigurd Ormsson, to the spring assembly.

Sigurd sent a boy hurrying north for reinforcements. But Kolbein and Sighvat demurred. The roads were too bad, they said. They couldn't ask their men to ride through ice and snow. Wait for the Althing come summer, they promised, and we will back you there.

Snorri, meanwhile, mustered men for Saemund in the West Quarter, around Borg. Even at twenty Snorri had a persuasive tongue and could convince men of the justice in his case—he was a born salesman. Snorri came to the spring assembly in Oddi's part of the South Quarter at the head of an army of seven hundred fighting men. Sigurd Ormsson had two hundred. Bishop Pall (Saemund's half brother) offered to negotiate. "Because of the superior numbers on the other side," the saga says, "Sigurd had but one choice." He agreed to let Bishop Pall decide the case, and Pall gave all the property to Saemund. Sigurd got nothing. "Kolbein Tumason liked this outcome little but Sighvat liked it less," says *Sturlunga Saga*. Snorri had sent his older brother Sighvat a message: *Think your title of chieftain counts for something? Let me show you what I can do without one.*

No one yet mistook Snorri for the uncrowned king of Iceland. But his marriage to rich Herdis of Borg, and his legal drubbing of his older brother and his friends, were the first steps on his road to becoming the richest and most powerful man in Iceland. It would take him fifteen years.

Snorri's first chieftaincy came to him in 1202, when Bersi the Rich died and Snorri moved his young family west. Borg was more storied even than Hvamm, for Borg was the home of Egil, irrepressible poet and irresponsible berserk, and his father, the troll-like Skalla-Grim.

Egil's Saga is one of the best, as well as one of the earliest, of the Icelandic sagas. Many scholars believe Snorri wrote it, perhaps while he lived at Borg, more likely toward the end of his life. Not only does it center on his kinsman Egil, ancestor of his mother, Gudny, it depicts the landscape surrounding Borg in a way that only someone who lived there could. The author is an expert on the lives of the kings of Norway, the subject of Snorri's *Heimskringla,* and his grasp of Norwegian geography is excellent. Stylistically too, *Egil's Saga* shares many quirks with *Heimskringla,* according to computer-based comparisons of word choices, as well as the keen eyes of literary critics who see Snorri's fingerprints in the plotting and pacing and precisely drawn characters. Both works use the same words to signal irony; this tic can be found in Snorri's *Edda,* too.

Then there's the poetry, Snorri's obsession. *Egil's Saga* is full of poetry. Presumably the historical Egil wrote the poems, though it's possible that Snorri wrote some of them as well as the prose. Egil's poetry is rich and complex. He writes about love and grief, battle and friendship. He chronicles, with wicked humor, the hardships of growing old. For him poetry is a weapon and a wonder and a form of therapy. And because he is a poet, Egil is the only saga character to declare his allegiance to the god Odin, Snorri's favorite, patron of poets; all other non-Christian Icelanders in the sagas worship Thor the Thunderer or the fertility god Freyr.

Portrait of Snorri's ancestor Egil Skallagrimsson of Borg, from a seventeenth-century manuscript, AM 426. Snorri is thought to have written Egil's Saga *either while he lived at Borg or toward the end of his life. Copyright © The Árni Magnússon Institute, Reykjavík. Photo by Jóhanna Ólafsdóttir.*

Many themes of *Egil's Saga* seem to reflect Snorri's own life and relationships: the conflicts between brothers or between fathers and sons, coping with loss and disappointment, loving inappropriately, what it means to be a king (crowned or uncrowned), and the importance of liberty. In the words of one Icelandic scholar, by writing *Egil's Saga* Snorri was "expressing his own identity."

Egil's Saga begins in Norway in about 860. King Harald the Shaggy "had sworn a solemn oath never to cut or comb his hair until he'd made himself sole ruler" of the land, which until then had had many petty kings and independent chieftains. King Harald taxed every farmer, forester, hunter, and salt maker. All free men had to choose: swear loyalty to Harald, leave the country, or face his wrath. The chieftain Kveld-Ulf did not care for that choice. "Every day, as it drew towards evening, he would grow so ill-tempered that no one could speak to him, and it wasn't long before he would go to bed. There was talk about his being a shape-changer," a werewolf. He had two sons. Thorolf was the perfect Viking: tall, blond, and blue eyed, a great fighter, cheerful and popular, but more than a little dense. His brother, Skalla-Grim, was ugly and bald and bad tempered, much better at shaping cold iron or catching fish than at making friends, but quick witted. Thorolf decided to swear loyalty to the king now politely called Harald Fair-Hair.

Kveld-Ulf was not pleased. "This king will be the death of us all."

Thorolf insisted he would win great honor as a king's man. He could not see the danger.

"Do as you see fit, Thorolf," said his father. "Just take care not to be too ambitious. Never try to compete with men greater than yourself, but never give way to them either."

Thorolf rose to great heights—so high that the king became jealous. Believing the lies of slanderers, King Harald ambushed Thorolf and killed him.

Kveld-Ulf and Skalla-Grim packed up two ships and set sail for Iceland. On the way they took their revenge. Recognizing a dragonship that Thorolf had owned, they attacked. Kveld-Ulf leaped into the stern, Skalla-Grim into the bow, and both went berserk. They cut down every man in their way, until the deck was cleared. Kveld-Ulf fought with a halberd, a kind of long-handled axe with a spike on it. He hewed at the ship's captain, we're told, "slicing through both helmet and head and burying the weapon right up to the shaft. Then he gave it a hard tug towards himself, lifted [the captain] into the air and tossed him overboard."

If *Egil's Saga* was written before *Heimskringla,* with this passage the Viking hero was born. Kveld-Ulf's deck-clearing, axe-swinging, bloodthirsty berserk rage has been reenacted countless times in novels and films and comic strips. He and Skalla-Grim didn't even know whose men they were butchering. Only after more than fifty men died did they catch two and ask who was on the ship: Among the dead were the king's young cousins, boys of ten and twelve, they learned. Thorolf's death was fully avenged. Skalla-Grim composed a poem and told the two lucky captives to go to the king and recite it, telling him "precisely what happened and who was responsible." Then they turned their ships toward Iceland.

Kveld-Ulf died on the way (berserk rages take a lot out of you). His men threw his coffin overboard, and it floated to land in western Iceland. On the spot where it washed ashore, Skalla-Grim raised his farmhouse, calling it Borg (Fortress), for a blocky hill that rose protectively behind the house. He claimed a huge tract of land, bordered by rivers on north and south and stretching from the glaciers in Iceland's center all the way to the sea. In one version of the story it was exactly the tract of land Snorri Sturluson ended up ruling three hundred years later. One theory about the writing of *Egil's Saga* is that Snorri was creating a "symbol of unity" for the people of what is now called Borgarfjord. With a common history and hero they would see themselves as a political unit—and be amenable to being ruled again by one man.

Skalla-Grim gave land to his relatives and set up his friends as tenant farmers. His wealth, the saga says, "walked on many feet." His land claim included marshes and brushland, where the few livestock he had brought on his ships grew fat and proliferated. There was ample seal hunting and salmon fishing, swans and ducks to snare, seabirds to net and their eggs to collect, driftwood to gather along the sandy shoreline, and occasionally a whale became stranded. In some sheltered areas barley would grow. The bogs had iron deposits, and Skalla-Grim set up a smithy, where he went to work so early each morning that his assistants complained. Skalla-Grim composed a poem about it, mocking them for their laziness.

Like his father, Skalla-Grim had two sons, one handsome and cheerful, whom everyone loved; he was called Thorolf, after his dead uncle—and he was just as dense as that uncle when it came to seeing through the fair words and fine promises of kings. The other son, Egil, was "as black-haired and ugly as his father." Big and strong, he was brooding and irritable, clever and quick tongued. He killed his first enemy at age six. They were playing a rowdy ball game, and the bigger boy knocked him down and jeered at him. Egil got an axe and drove it into the boy's skull. Egil's father was not pleased when he heard about it, but his mother said Egil "had the makings of a real Viking."

At another ball game, when Egil was twelve, Skalla-Grim went berserk (these were rough games). He killed a friend of Egil's plus an old woman who tried to break up the fight. When Egil returned home, he took revenge by killing the capable man who managed Skalla-Grim's estate. "For the rest of the winter, father and son spoke not a single word to each other."

Meanwhile Egil's handsome brother had gone off to Norway and made friends with the king's heir, Eirik Blood-Axe. On his next voyage Egil insisted on going along, and, not surprisingly, he made a mess of things. Egil showed up at a farm where Eirik, now king, and his queen were being feted, got swinishly drunk, insulted the farmer with slanderous verses, and finally killed him. Despite the king's best efforts, Egil got away. He made a poem about it:

I made a mockery of
Their Majesties' mastery,
I don't deceive myself
As to what I dare.

Eirik Blood-Axe and his queen became Egil's enemies for life, and the next thirty chapters of *Egil's Saga* are a rollicking Viking adventure, ranging through Norway, Finland, England, and the Baltic, with glorious battles and drinking bouts, pillaging and burning, vast quantities of silver and gold and other booty, duels with berserks, a little fondling of beautiful women, a poignant love scene in which Egil woos his brother's widow, some tricky sailing, occasional rune magic and outfoxing of spies, and always looming in the wings Eirik Blood-Axe and his witchlike queen. When they finally catch Egil helpless, he is not friendless. Through the intercession of Eirik's own righthand man, Arinbjorn, Egil is allowed to trade a poem—which he has one night to compose—for his ugly head. Egil's "Head Ransom" is a marvel of tongue-in-cheek punning, set within the rigid form of rhyme, rhythm, and alliteration required of a skaldic poem in the meter fit for a king. If we ignore the double entendres, it could be taken for a praise poem, and Eirik Blood-Axe chose to accept it that way (he couldn't afford to lose Arinbjorn's support). Egil went free and, after a few more adventures, sailed home to live out his long days in Iceland.

Back at Borg, Egil married his daughters well and took pleasure in the prowess of his sons. Then two of his beloved sons died. Distraught, Egil himself lay down to die, but one of his daughters craftily revived his will to live by getting him to make a poem about it, the beautiful "Lament for My Sons":

My mouth strains
To move the tongue,
To weigh and wing
The choice word:
Not easy to breathe
Odin's inspiration
In my heart's hinterland,
Little hope there.

The poem is as much about poetry, the "purest of possessions," the "word-mead," as it is about Egil's sons. "Now I feel it surge," he says, "swell / Like a sea, old giant's blood." As he created this long poem, the saga says, "Egil began to get back his spirits." When it was finished, he took his seat in the hall and declaimed the lament before all the family.

Egil made do for an heir with a third son for whom he cared little. He went back to bullying the neighbors and twisting the law when that son found himself in difficulties. Egil grew very old. His sight and hearing failed, and he stumbled. Women laughed at him. He made a poem about it:

My bald pate bobs and blunders,
I bang it when I fall;
My cock's gone soft and clammy
And I can't hear when they call.

His last act was to sink two chests of silver in a bog (so his blasted son couldn't enjoy them) and kill the slaves who had carried them there. What an ancestor for man of learning!

Though Egil and his father are larger than life, they share several traits with Snorri Sturluson, their direct descendant. They're poets, but more than that they're perceptive, observant readers of men. They're willing to match wits with anyone and are not cowed by titles or family ties: They "never try to compete with men greater" than themselves, but they "never give way to them either." On top of this, they are skillful farmers and hard workers.

Like Skalla-Grim, Snorri ran the estate of Borg well by diversifying its sources of income. Dairying was the foundation of every Icelander's wealth in the thirteenth century, but while a typical family farm had seven milk cows and as many as thirty milking ewes, an estate like Borg had twenty to fifty milk cows and as many as two hundred ewes—not to mention bulls, heifers, steers, calves, rams, wethers, lambs, and horses of all ages. Some farms also had pigs and geese. For every forty-five milking animals, the estate needed forty acres of hay fields; most of the other animals would graze year-round, herded to the highlands, where the farm owned grazing rights, in the summer. The estate held the right to fish, collect driftwood, cut brushwood, and make charcoal on other lands. It had tenant farms that paid rent in hay, butter, or wool cloth. It had workers to cut the hay and plow the barley fields, milk and herd the animals, train the horses, repair the buildings, buy and sell supplies, cook and clean and sew and weave, brew ale and beer, make butter and cheese, burn seaweed to gather salt, and craft iron tools from horseshoes to scythes. It was like a small village. All this, Snorri, as chieftain, organized and managed, and his neighbors took note of how capably he did so.

While he lived at Borg, Snorri bought or was given several other farms, though he didn't always fulfill his side of the bargain. He gained the rich churchstead of Stafholt (Stave Wood)—with its twenty milk cows, 120 milking ewes, 120 other sheep, 6 tenant farms, driftwood rights, fishing rights, and grazing rights—by promising to see the old man's son, who had leprosy, taken care of and his daughter wed. But the girl was a halfwit; she never married.

Nor did Snorri always get his way as chieftain. An early dispute involved a merchant from the Orkney Islands, Thorkel Walrus, who landed at the harbor Snorri owned on the river Hvita. Snorri invoked the chieftain's traditional right to set the prices for a merchant's goods. That rule had long been disregarded in the West of Iceland, though Jon Loftsson had insisted on it at Oddi. Snorri's prices must have been low, for Thorkel Walrus accused Snorri of stealing. Before he set sail the next summer, he killed one of Snorri's men in revenge. Snorri gathered a war party—including his two brothers, this time—and tried to capture the merchant's ship, but Thorkel Walrus slipped away. Unfortunately for him, Thorkel suffered from bad weather-luck: As Snorri soon learned, the Orkney ship made it only as far as the southern coast of Iceland, where Thorkel Walrus sought refuge for the winter with Snorri's foster brother, Saemund of Oddi. The men of Oddi had enjoyed close ties with Orkney for generations, but Snorri took no account of that, nor did he take into consideration his kinsman Saemund's honor before sending assassins east to Oddi—three times that winter—to kill Thorkel Walrus. All failed. Snorri got no redress for the death of his man.

But on the whole Snorri was so successful as the chieftain of Borg that several other chieftains in the vicinity asked him to take over a share of their duties, either permanently or while they traveled abroad. Like Egil, Snorri was charismatic, good at getting men to do his will. Like Egil, he was a master of the law—and willing to twist it to his own or his clients' advantage. He was a hard bargainer and, like Egil, had a reputation for being tight fisted. Though he never buried chests of silver to keep them from his family, he did vigorously dispute the ownership of farms and valuables. Saga-Sturla, for example, accuses his uncle Snorri of stealing the money his grandmother Gudny gave him when he was seven, and both of Snorri's sons later fought with their father over the ownership of the farm at Stafholt.

Publicly, on the other hand, Snorri was generous, in keeping with his idea of how a chieftain—or king—should act. According to that same nephew, Saga-Sturla, Snorri gave elaborate feasts and was a cheerful host. Snorri himself writes often and at length about eating and drinking: Reading *Heimskringla,* you might think a nobleman's major duty was organizing feasts.

In both Iceland and Norway feasts followed the same pattern. First the great hall was decked with tapestries and the floor strewn with fresh rushes or juniper tops. Tables were set up and extra benches brought in. The table service could include golden bowls, silver bowls, wooden bowls, and cow horns fixed with silver rims and stands and studded with gemstones. In Iceland, at least, a dip in the hot tub occurred at some point during the evening. The meat was always boiled—meat was roasted only if a kettle couldn't be found—and might be beef, sheep, pork, horse, or various birds (swan was preferred). Fish was not on the menu at a feast.

For entertainment there could be fiddlers, harpists, or other musicians. Sometimes there was dancing or chess matches—one of Snorri's men was called Dancing-Berg, another Chess-Berg. Sometimes there were wrestling matches or other rough games—another of Snorri's men was said to be the strongest man in Iceland. Sagas were told and poems recited, some rather insulting. At one Icelandic feast two chieftains traded lampoons about whose belches smelled fouler:

Whence comes this stink?
Thord is breathing at table.

When the laughter let up, Thord replied,

Ingimund's breath
Brings no boon to the bench.

Afterward a good host handed out gifts: silver bowls filled with coins, silk-lined cloaks or scarlet gowns, lengths of leaf-green cloth or russet homespun, blankets, coats of ring mail, shields, spears, swords, halberds, axes, gold rings, silver belt buckles or cloak pins, quantities of malt or meat or corn, sometimes a well-grown ox or a horse with a painted wooden saddle.

But the real purpose of a feast was to drink oneself into a stupor. "The horn does not get to dry out too much," Snorri writes in his *Edda*, complimenting a feast held by the king of Norway. Later in the same work Snorri devotes a whole section to different drinks: "The king gives currents of yeast (that is what I adjudge ale to be) to men. Men's silence is dispelled by surf of horns (that is old beer). The prince knows how speech's salvation (that is what mead is called) is to be given. In the choicest of cups comes (this is what I call wine) dignity's destruction." In another stanza he notes, "Mead keeps back men's miseries."

Writing about the kings and earls of Norway in *Heimskringla*, Snorri praises Earl Erling for serving his drink "unmeasured" and King Frodi for having a mead vat big enough for a man to drown in (and one did). Earl Sigurd, Snorri says, hosted feasts in honor of the gods Odin, Njord, and Freyr at which "all men should have ale." He describes King Olaf the Quiet as "merry at his ale, a great drinker in company, fond of conversation, happy and peaceful."

From all the feasting Snorri probably grew stout over time. (*Stout,* in Snorri's lexicon, was a compliment. Dignified men and women in his books are stout.) He was probably a hard drinker: Revelers in his books are often described as "very drunk" or "dead drunk." Egil too was a hard drinker. When he was three years old, his father, Skalla-Grim, refused to take him to a feast, telling him, "You don't know how to behave yourself when there's company gathered and a lot of drinking going on. You're difficult enough to cope with when you're sober." Later Egil was known for imbibing more than any two or three other men could—and, when provoked, vomiting spectacularly in his host's face.

There are no stories of Snorri vomiting.

The biggest difference between Snorri and his ancestors at Borg, however, is that Snorri was in no way a berserk. He avoided fights unless he and his men vastly outnumbered his enemies, according to his nephew Saga-Sturla, who recounts such episodes in excruciating detail in *Sturlunga Saga.* An early one involved a widow who had taken a lover against her brothers' will. The two parties made up slanderous rhymes about each other, and tempers flared. As chieftain of most of the men, Snorri was expected to make peace among them. He arranged a meeting, but it turned into a brawl. Snorri ordered them to stop, but no one listened. A man was killed. A bystander urged Snorri to intervene, "but Snorri said he hadn't enough men for that, what with their folly and their fury." The bystander reproached him harshly. Thinking quickly, the man ran to where the horses were tethered, untied them, and stampeded them at the fighters. The battle stopped while everyone ran to catch his mount, and the losers took the opportunity to slip away.

Given that Saga-Sturla wasn't yet born when this incident occurred, we have to wonder who told him the story—and why—and if he recorded it accurately. It would make more sense if quick-witted Snorri, not the other man, thought to stampede the horses. But that's not the story we have. And other episodes in *Sturlunga Saga* show Snorri running from a fight when the odds were against him. That could be cowardice or it could be wisdom. The English king Richard the Lionheart was famous for avoiding battle, as was the French king Philip Augustus. They followed the advice of the most popular military handbook of the time, Vegetius's *Art of War,* which advised a commander to consider every plan and try every expedient before bringing matters to that last extremity. To Snorri, who likely did not read Vegetius, it was the difference between the god Thor's approach and the god Odin's. Rather than attempt to fight giants twice his size, Odin outwits them or simply outruns them; later he sends Thor back to Giantland to do the fighting. It's the difference between an aristocrat—a king—and a Viking.

We can gain more insight into how Snorri saw himself as a chieftain by returning to his books, especially *Heimskringla*. As any writer can tell you, the narrator of a book is not its author. But authors unintentionally reveal themselves in what and how they choose to write. Some kings and noblemen Snorri describes in *Heimskringla*, like Olaf Tryggvason, are true Vikings: good at all sports, nimble, strong, able to juggle three swords and throw two spears at once, bold, "gruesome when he was wroth," passionate, "playful and blithe," generous, and a good host.

But others are not so typical. King Olaf the Saint was "deft with his hands and had skill in all smith's work." Earl Erling managed his estates well. Snorri goes into great detail about how Erling gave his thralls land and seed and so allowed them to buy themselves out of slavery; he then set them up in fishing or other trades. King Sigurd Sow is praised for personally overseeing his farms. Snorri portrays him out in the field taking care that the corn was cut and stacked properly in the barns. "He was a very enterprising man and eager for his goods and his estate, and he himself managed the business of the place." King Harald Hard-Ruler is called "deep-thinking" and of "good counsel." Snorri writes, "King Harald never fled from any battle, but he often sought clever ways by which to escape when he had to do with great odds. All men who followed him in battle or in warfare said that when he was placed in great peril and when a quick decision depended on him, he always chose that plan which all men afterwards saw was the most likely to succeed." Perhaps what Saga-Sturla portrayed as Snorri's cowardice, Snorri thought of as being clever like King Harald.

Snorri reveals more of his values in a lengthy episode in *Heimskringla* in which he compares King Sigurd Jerusalem-Farer (Jon Loftsson's great-grandfather) to his brother, King Eystein. The two kings were attending a feast, and the ale was sour. People were glum. "Why are the people so silent?" asked Eystein, the concerned host. "It is more usual in drinking parties that people are merry, so let us fall upon some jest over our ale that will amuse people."

The jest Eystein chose was the game called man balancing, in which the qualities of two men were compared, with the audience chose who won.

"I could throw you on your back whenever I pleased," began Sigurd, "even though you are a year older."

"But you were not so good at games that required agility," said Eystein.

"I could drag you underwater, when we swam together, whenever I pleased."

"But I could swim as far as you, and dive as well. And I could ice-skate so well that nobody could beat me. You could no more do that than an ox."

"I think you could scarcely draw my bow, even if you used your foot to help."

"I am not as strong at the bow as you are, but I hit the target just as often. And I can ski much better."

"It seems to me," said Sigurd, "that a king must be tall, so as to be conspicuous in a crowd."

"It is no less important that a man is well-dressed, so as to be easily known on that account, because the best ornament is beauty. Besides, I know more about the law than you, and on every subject my words flow more easily than yours."

"It may be that you know more law-quirks. I have had something else to do." Sigurd then listed his exploits on his epic voyage to Jerusalem and back: his battles, his booty, the velvet sails on his longship, his chip off the True Cross, the knot he tied in a willow branch on the banks of the Jordan River that he dared his brother to go and untie. "You have only a home-bred reputation."

So far, most of this story appears in Snorri's source, the collection known as *Rotten Parchment*. But in that version, Eystein has no answer to Sigurd's boast. He has no way to match his brother's crusade.

In Snorri's version Eystein says, "I would not have brought up this conversation if I had not known what to reply on that point." Eystein had equipped the entire Jerusalem expedition, and he accomplished many useful things at home while Sigurd was off a-Viking. Eystein settled the laws, "so that every man can obtain justice." He built a harbor and a shipbuilding station and fish houses "so that all poor people could earn a livelihood." He built churches and monasteries and houses for priests. He built a road over the fells and set up hostels along the way: "All travelers know that Eystein has been king in Norway," he claimed. In Bergen he built a royal hall, "so that all kings who come after me will remember my name." He annexed the Swedish province of Jemteland "more by prudence and kind words than by force and war." Norway, he concluded, had been better served by his public works "than by your killing bluemen [the Vikings' term for Africans] in the land of the Saracens and sending them to hell."

With that the game came crashing to an end, leaving both kings angry. But the winner—in Snorri's eyes, at least—is Eystein the Builder, not Sigurd the Crusader. Snorri favors Eystein so strongly that one reader has suggested he was painting his own self-portrait: a man agile and athletic, handsome and well dressed; an attentive host who is concerned that his guests are merry and well entertained; a smooth talker, learned at law; someone who values good harbors, roads, buildings, and churches, and who cares that poor people can make a living; someone who sees more ways than brute force to make a name for himself—or even to expand the borders of his realm.

Snorri may even be describing himself when he tells us that Eystein had wide-set blue eyes and curly blond hair, and he stood a little under average height. All these particulars he added to the king's description in *Rotten Parchment.* He also added Eystein's debate point that, for standing out in a crowd, being beautifully dressed was just as effective as being tall.

When Snorri had been chieftain of Borg for about four years, he decided to move inland to Reykholt.

A man in his household who was named Egil had a dream. He dreamed that Egil Skalla-Grimsson himself came to visit. The old berserk was frowning terribly, perhaps like he did in *Egil's Saga,* "with one eyebrow sunk down right to the cheek and the other lifting up to the roots of the hair."

"Does our kinsman Snorri intend to leave this place?" Egil Skalla-Grimsson asked.

"So men say," replied Snorri's man.

"If he means to leave, then he does ill," warned the dream-Egil. He should not scorn this land, he said, then spoke a verse:

A man spares with sword to strike,
Snow-white is blood to behold,
An age of quarrels we are able to relate,
Sharp blade got land for me,
Sharp blade got land for me.

Snorri's a coward, the poem says—his blood runs white, not red—and bad times are coming because he spares the sword. If Snorri did indeed write *Egil's Saga* to give the people of his district a common hero, he may have done too good a job. His portrait of the lovable, vicious Viking was too popular. By the time his nephew Saga-Sturla recorded this dream verse in the 1270s, the comparison of the two chieftains of Borg did not favor Snorri. On the other hand, Saga-Sturla knew by then that Snorri had failed in his bid to become the uncrowned king of Iceland. And the times had become very bad indeed: An "age of quarrels" is an understatement.

But in 1206, when Snorri moved his base of operations to Reykholt, it seemed a logical step up for the young chieftain. Reykholt was one of the largest church estates in Iceland, with an enormous income from the tithe. It encompassed extensive lands, including some thirty tenant farms, along with grazing rights in the mountains and rights to collect driftwood and beached whales by the sea. Fifteen miles from the coast, it lay in a broad farming valley, one of several parallel valleys that ran inland east from Borg. The valley was flanked by long, gentle hills. Two rivers cut through the estate, with the most fertile land in the floodplains. Salmon and trout could be netted in the rivers. In the vast bogs and marshlands—nearly 50 percent of the estate was wetlands—ample grass could be cut for the livestock's winter hay. Nor was there any shortage of turf for building house walls and fences or of peat for cooking and firing the smithy. Some barley (for beer) was grown on Reykholt's fields, but, unlike the owners of the similar church estate in the South at Skalholt, Snorri and his predecessors made little effort to manure their fields. They could afford to buy barley if they needed more.

To the east of Reykholt the soil became thin until it petered out altogether in wasteland under the eye of the glaciers. A main route from the North of Iceland to the assembly plains at Thingvellir ran along the edge of this wasteland, meeting a route to the sea near Reykholt. Travelers and trade were thick along both routes—one saga tells of a man who became rich peddling such things as chickens. Archaeological research has shown that the chieftains of Reykholt in Snorri's time imported fish, seal meat, and seaweed, as well as driftwood, from the coast, and lumber, glass, ceramics, and grain from farther away. Artifacts have been found from Germany, England, and France, including a beautiful gold ring engraved with a Romanesque design.

The estate's name, Smoky Wood, derives from two important natural resources. The hillsides to the north and south of the valley were thickly wooded with scrubby birch and willow, useful for making charcoal, though the forests were in decline and wood would become scarcer by the end of the thirteenth century. As elsewhere in Iceland, the trees never grew tall or straight enough to use in shipbuilding—the wind saw to that—and even the post-and-beam frames and interior paneling of most houses had to be imported, though drift-wood could sometimes be used.

Smoky referred to the steam from the hot spring on the property. The spring had long ago been plumbed: Conduits ran downhill to supply warm water for a large stone-lined hot tub. Mornings, the women would use the hot water for laundry and cooking. Evenings, the men would gather and soak, sorting out the day's troubles, telling stories, and talking politics. Some priests, according to one saga, even heard confession while men lounged in the bath.

When Snorri cast his eye on this rich church estate—the saga says he "had a strong hankering" for it—Reykholt was owned by the priest Magnus Pallsson.

Snorri's bathing pool at Reykholt. The reconstruction follows the archaeological evidence, though the doorway shown does not open into the actual tunnel that led, by a spiral stone stair, up into Snorri's living quarters. Photo by the author.

Magnus was the son of Pall Solvason, whose wife had tried to stab Snorri's father in the eye. One theory explaining Snorri's hankering is that he was avenging his father, who was cheated of his right to self-judgment by Pall and Jon Loftsson twenty-five years before. Snorri could apparently be quite patient when it came to revenge.

Magnus, like his father, was a scholar as well as a priest. Reykholt had a good library and an active scriptorium where books were produced (another reason Snorri wanted the property). Either Pall or Magnus is thought to have written there the book of sermons that contains the Stave Church Homily.

Along with its church and scriptorium, Reykholt was the site of a chieftaincy. As owner of the estate Magnus was technically the Reykholt chieftain, though he did not meet the requirements. First, the archbishop of Trondheim had declared in 1190 that no priest could be a chieftain (or vice versa). Second, Magnus was not a good manager. He took over Reykholt upon his father's death in 1185, says *Sturlunga Saga,* and "gradually used up all the wealth as he began to grow older." Third, Magnus's father, Pall, was illegitimate. Legally, according to Snorri's (somewhat twisted) interpretation of the law, Pall had never been the rightful owner of Reykholt, and Magnus therefore had not lawfully inherited it from him.

Snorri's uncle Thord Bodvarsson, on the other hand, was a legitimate son of the legitimate daughter of Pall's uncle. This uncle should have inherited Reykholt instead of the bastard Pall, making Thord now the rightful owner of the estate. Thord was not inclined to press his rights; he'd had enough trouble from churchmen already, as we will see. By 1206 he had already given Snorri half his chieftaincy, and he now sold his kinsman his title to Reykholt. Snorri searched out all other potential heirs and bought their titles, too. He gained the support of influential men, including an abbot, a priest, and the powerful chieftain Gissur Hallsson from Haukadale in the South of Iceland. Then Snorri suggested that he and Magnus have a talk.

Magnus knew better than to face Snorri in the law courts. And Snorri's offer was surprisingly generous: Magnus could remain at Reykholt as the priest, in charge of all church functions. He and his wife could live comfortably on the property, and Snorri would see their young sons provided for. He would build a bigger church and outfit it splendidly. In exchange Snorri would become the chieftain of Reykholt. He would manage the vast estate, collecting the church tithes and giving the priest an allowance. Snorri would have all the responsibility—and all the honor.

Magnus agreed. He—or perhaps Snorri himself—recorded their contract in the Reykholt church inventory, a single sheet of calfskin that, though tattered and nearly unreadable, still exists; it is the oldest surviving document written in Icelandic. There we learn that Snorri and Magnus sealed their bargain by jointly giving to the church a saint's reliquary, or shrine. Gissur and the other witnesses showed their support by donating the value of sixty cows to the church.

Writes Saga-Sturla, "Snorri Sturluson moved his household to Reykholt. He became a great chieftain, for he was not short of money. Snorri was a very good businessman." Later, Saga Sturla adds, Snorri "became a good poet and showed himself skillful in everything he set his hand to; he always gave the best advice about what should be done."

At the age of twenty-eight Snorri owned three valuable estates: Borg, Stafholt, and Reykholt. He controlled all or part of six chieftaincies, and he was soon given a seventh to look after while its owner went to Norway. When we next hear of him in *Sturlunga Saga*, he is thirty-seven and has been chosen lawspeaker, the only elected position in Iceland's government. Snorri was not the uncrowned king of Iceland, but as a lawspeaker he was quite influential. No wonder if he began to throw his weight around.

Trouble began at the Althing in 1216. Snorri stayed in a tent-roofed booth he nicknamed Gryla, for a mythical giantess who sometimes appears as a fox with fifteen tails. (Later, as his head swelled more, Snorri renamed his booth Valhalla, equating himself with the god Odin.) Among Snorri's followers at this Althing was a German named Herburt who was a master at fighting with the buckler, a small round shield then coming into fashion. The buckler protected the sword hand, not the whole body, as the heavy Viking shields did, and so the fighting style was quite different. Herburt was asked to give a demonstration. He and a few of Snorri's men went to a neighbor's booth and took some sticks of firewood to use as swords, fighting with weapons being banned at the assembly site.

An ale brewer who was watching cried, "Thief!" He ran after them to take the wood back—he would need it before the assembly ended to brew his chieftain more ale. A shouting match ensued. More men gathered around, and

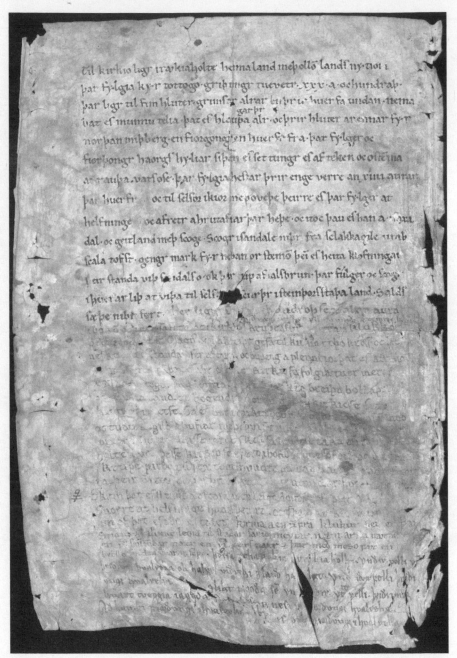

The inventory of the church at Reykholt is a double-sided sheet of calfskin. Part of it dates back to 1206, when Snorri took over the estate, and it mentions him several times. He may have even written that part. The inventory is the oldest extant document in Icelandic. Kept in the National Archives of Iceland, Þí Kirknasafn Reykholt, AA/1.

fists flew. Herburt drew his real sword and was about to strike the ale brewer when the man's chieftain burst through the crowd and grabbed the blade bare handed. His palms, the saga says, were badly scored.

The injured chieftain, another Magnus, was the nephew of Saemund Jonsson of Oddi. Saemund was reluctant to get involved, but his hot-tempered son Pall egged him on. The Althing broke into two factions: Saemund and Magnus on one side, Snorri on the other, and this time the men of Oddi had more backers. A truce was brokered, and both sides sent home for more fighting men, but before the backup troops could arrive, Saemund made peace with his foster brother. Snorri was fined a large sum, which he paid on the spot.

He was not pleased. Magnus's hands got bloodied because he was an idiot, Snorri may have thought. He could have halted Herburt with a word—or a sword. Nor did the ale brewer need to make such a fuss about two sticks of wood.

Snorri held a grudge.

The next winter brought him an opportunity to get his money back. An old woman named Jorunn the Rich died. Her chieftain, Magnus, took over her property, as was his right since she apparently left no heirs. Snorri sent a man south, and when he returned he brought a vagrant named Kodran with him. This Kodran, Snorri claimed, was the old woman's legal heir. Acting as Kodran's lawyer, Snorri accused Magnus of stealing Kodran's inheritance and summoned Magnus to the spring assembly—but not to the one Magnus usually attended. This assembly was full of Snorri's friends, and Magnus was sentenced to outlawry. He appealed the ruling to the Althing, and both sides gathered their forces.

Snorri rode to the Althing at the head of six hundred men, including eighty Norwegians, all with shields—most likely not bucklers but big Viking shields. These were rather expensive items of armor at the time. No one knows where Snorri found eighty armored Norwegians. His two brothers backed him with additional men.

The bishop of Skalholt stepped in and negotiated a compromise. The old woman's farm would continue to be worked by her former overseer, who would pay Snorri rent in grain. "Snorri gained in prestige from this case," *Sturlunga Saga* says. "His status grew considerably throughout the country." He was not a man to cross.

One person was not cowed: Snorri's wife, Herdis of Borg.

When Snorri moved his household to Reykholt in 1206, Herdis and their two children, Hallbera (born in 1201) and Jon Trout (born in 1203), did not come along. They stayed at Borg, where Herdis would remain until her death in 1233. We don't know if Herdis found solace with a lover, as her mother had, but she and Snorri did not formally divorce. They did not divide their property, and neither she nor Snorri remarried.

The church did not recognize divorce, though it had been routine in Iceland in the old days. In a famous scene from *Njal's Saga,* written in the mid-1200s about events three hundred years earlier, a woman divorces her husband because he is impotent: "He is unable to consummate our marriage and give me satisfaction, although in every other way he is as virile as the best of men."

"What do you mean?" asked her father. "Be more explicit."

"Whenever he touches me, he is so enlarged that he cannot have enjoyment of me, although we both passionately desire to reach consummation. But we have never succeeded."

"You have done well to tell me this," said her father. "I can give you a plan."

She needed to declare herself lawfully divorced in front of witnesses: once beside the bed and once at the door of the house. Her father then announced the divorce at the Law Rock and sued not only for the return of her dowry but also for her husband's bride-price, since he was the guilty party.

According to laws still on the books in Snorri's time, a couple could divorce for reasons of poverty, domestic violence, if a man tried to take his wife's money out of the country against her will, if he failed to sleep with her for three years (Snorri was probably guilty of that), or simply because of incompatibility, provided they had a bishop's consent.

The bishop was the sticking point: Iceland had only two, one in the North at Holar and one in the South at Skalholt. When Snorri's oldest brother, Thord Sturluson, obtained a divorce from his first wife, Helga, in about 1190, the bishop of Holar was relatively easygoing; Thord probably appealed to him, not to the stricter Thorlak, bishop of Skalholt. The year Snorri left Borg, 1206, his foster brother Pall Jonsson was bishop of Skalholt. But because Snorri and the men of Oddi were then quarreling about his treatment of the Orkney merchant Thorkel Walrus, Snorri could not appeal to Pall. The bishop of Holar at the time was the miracle-working Gudmund the Good. Gudmund was not easygoing. On the contrary, he was unyielding when it came to church rules and rights, with a "stiff, moody, and violent temper" and a "narrow and fanatic mind." He and Snorri were kinsmen, as kinship was defined in those days: Snorri's father's first wife, Ingibjorg, "the most beautiful woman in Iceland," was Gudmund's aunt. Gudmund had watched over Hvamm-Sturla's deathbed and probably gave him the last rites. He had attended Snorri and Herdis's wedding at Hvamm, where he probably officiated. He was not likely to dissolve their marriage, especially when the reason Snorri and Herdis were breaking up their household was so obvious.

It was not simply incompatibility. It was not that she hated the mountains or he hated the sea. While he lived at Borg, Snorri wrote a love poem in which he described walking into a house and seeing a girl just letting her long hair down to comb it. One stanza of the poem remains, mellifluous, with lush repetitions of the sounds *ann* and *arth,* in which the word for *girl* is *svanni:* It could have come from the Icelandic words for either *swan* or *slender* and seems to have overtones of each.

That slender long-haired girl, lovely as a swan, was Gudrun. She was the illegitimate daughter of Snaelaug, who had been happily married to Snorri's uncle Thord Bodvarsson—until Bishop Thorlak of Skalholt intervened. Snaelaug had given birth to Gudrun quite young, saying the baby's father was a cowherd. Her own father, a priest, forgave her, but sent her away to live with a relative. There she met young Thord, who was the future chieftain of Gard and brother to Snorri's mother, Gudny. Thord and Snaelaug fell in love. Thord sued for her hand in marriage, and with their families' approval they were wed. They were happy and had three sons.

In 1183, when Snorri was five and Gudrun at least three, news came from Norway that a young man named Hreinn had died, and Snaelaug let it slip that Hreinn, not the cowherd, was really Gudrun's father.

Hreinn and Thord were third cousins: They shared a great-great-great-grandfather. Even in a culture as obsessed with genealogy as medieval Iceland's, this did not worry Snaelaug. Yet according to the church's byzantine incest laws, it meant that she and Thord could not be married. Their relationship was incestuous because of her long-ago one-night stand with her husband's third cousin.

Snaelaug's father, a priest who should have known these laws, did nothing about it. For this he was chastised by Bishop Thorlak—the same bishop who had thrown fire and brimstone at Jon Loftsson for living openly with his mistress. The soon-to-be-sainted Thorlak "was so inspired by faith in God," a saga says, that he marched up to the Law Rock during the Althing "with all his clergy and swore in public that this marriage contract was contrary to the Law of God. He then named witnesses, declaring the union null and void." He excommunicated "all the parties to the contract" and declared that any children Thord and Snaelaug had after that moment would be illegitimate.

They argued. They pleaded. They ignored the bishop. But finally they had to part. Thord went home to his family farm of Gard, while Snaelaug raised her children at her family farm of Baer. From Baer to Snorri's Borg was about ten miles. Since his uncle Thord had given Snorri half his chieftaincy, the two men were in close contact. Snorri had ample occasion to travel to Baer to meet with his uncle—and to be smitten with love one day when he walked in upon slender Gudrun combing her hair.

Gudrun brought Snorri not only love but more wealth—the two seem always entangled in Snorri's life. When Snorri got his hankering for Reykholt, his legal maneuvering hung on his uncle Thord's claim to be the legitimate heir. Of the four men who witnessed the transfer of Reykholt from Magnus to Snorri, three were linked to Gudrun: Thord was her mother's lover, the abbot was Gudrun's uncle, and the priest was Gudrun's grandfather.

Gudrun's family gave Snorri the estate of Stafholt, too. The halfwit girl and the boy with leprosy were Gudrun's cousins; their father had married Snaelaug's sister. Snaelaug suggested her elderly brother-in-law turn the estate over to Snorri, who would see his troubled children taken care of.

Finally, Snorri gained yet another chieftaincy through Gudrun. Gudrun's father, Hreinn—though he never acknowledged her before he died in Norway—had been its only heir.

Knowing this, it comes as no surprise that when Snorri moved to Reykholt in 1206, Gudrun came with him. Officially she was his housekeeper, in charge of the weaving and clothes making, the laundry and housecleaning, the dairying and cheese making, ale brewing and cooking, and overseeing the multitude of female chores involved in running a large household. She and Snorri had several children but only one lived past childhood: their daughter Ingibjorg, who was born in 1208.

It is a bit of a surprise, though, to learn that Snorri had at least two other mistresses during these years. His son Oraekja was born in 1205 to a woman named Thurid, while his daughter Thordis was born in 1207 to a woman named Oddny.

Nor did Snorri's love for Gudrun last (she may have died; the sagas do not say). In 1218 Snorri brought his mother to Reykholt to be the housekeeper there. In 1226 Hallveig Ormsdottir, then the richest woman in Iceland, moved to Reykholt as Snorri's partner. Though they had no children, Snorri was very fond of Hallveig. He had no children with any other woman while Hallveig lived, and when she died in 1241, all the fight seemed to go out of him. He was killed a few months later, having taken no precautions to protect himself against an attack he knew was coming.

Like his favorite god, Odin—and his two father figures, Jon Loftsson and Hvamm-Sturla—Snorri was proud of his virility. But he also simply enjoyed the company of women. Of the young woman who married his nephew and nemesis, Sturla Battle-Strong, we learn that Snorri "found it altogether delightful to converse with her." He was, says the saga, "a man of many pleasures."

Three

ON THE QUAY
AT BERGEN

I cut the ice-cold wave with oak—the pale planking was put to the test—to meet the powerful ruler. I am renowned for such.

—Snorri, *Edda*

*T**he gods were braggarts. They were tricksters and cheats, no* good at keeping oaths, greedy and niggling, always eyeing a bargain but always wanting the best: the fastest horse, the finest ship, endless meat and drink. Odin was one of the worst, in Snorri's telling, though occasionally he did remember his manners.

One day while Thor was off fighting trolls in the East, a giant entered the gods' city of Asgard. He was a stonemason, he said, and offered to build the gods a wall so strong it would keep out any ogre or giant or troll. All he wanted in return was the sun and the moon and goddess Freyja for his wife.

The gods talked it over, wondering how they could get the wall for free.

"If you build it in one winter, with no one's help," the gods said, thinking that impossible, "we have a deal."

"Can I use my stallion?" the giant asked.

Loki replied, "I see no harm in that." The other gods agreed. They swore mighty oaths.

The giant got to work. By night the stallion hauled enormous loads of stone, by day the giant laid them up. The wall rose, course upon course. With three days left of winter, it was nearly done.

"Whose idea was it to spoil the sky by giving away the sun and the moon—not to mention marrying Freyja into Giantland?" the gods shouted. They wanted out of their bargain. "It's all Loki's fault," they agreed. "He'd better fix it."

Loki transformed himself into a mare in heat. That evening, when the mason drove his stallion to the quarry, his horse was uncontrollable. It broke the traces and ran after the mare. The giant chased after them all night, and, needless to say, he got no work done.

Nor could he finish the wall the next day with no stone. His always edgy temper snapped. He flew into a giant rage.

The gods' oaths were forgotten. Thor raised his terrible hammer and smashed the giant's skull.

Eleven months later Loki had a foal. It was gray and had eight legs. It grew up to be the best horse among gods and men.

Odin claimed the horse, Snorri says in another tale, and named it Sleipnir. One day Odin rode Sleipnir into Giantland, where a giant named Hrungnir complimented him on his marvelously good horse.

"There's none in Giantland to match it, I'll bet," Odin snootily replied.

Hrungnir took that badly. His horse Gullfaxi had a much longer stride, he said. He leaped into the saddle and raced off after Odin. Sleipnir galloped so fast that Odin was over the hill in no time. But "Hrungnir was in such a great giant fury," Snorri writes, "that the first thing he knew was that he had rushed in through the gates of Asgard." The giant reined his horse to a halt before the doors of Valhalla. Odin hospitably invited him in for a drink.

Like a later visitor to Valhalla, Hrungnir may have noticed the hall's 540 doors and its roof tiled with golden shields. He may have marveled at a juggler tossing seven knives or at the fire whose flames were swords. He may have watched courtiers playing chess with golden chessmen and armed warriors fighting furiously without being killed. These were the fallen heroes whom Odin's shield maidens, the Valkyries, fetched from battlefields; these fighters would make up Odin's army for the last battle, Ragnarok. When not polishing their fighting skills, the heroes in Valhalla feasted on the boiled meat of a magic boar. Every morning it was butchered, every night it came back to life. A magic goat chewed on the leaves of a magic tree. The goat gave not milk but bottomless vats of mead.

Odin on Sleipnir, from the eighteenth-century manuscript known as Melsted's Edda, *SÁM 66, 80v. Only Snorri tells stories of Odin's marvelous eight-legged horse. Copyright © The Árni Magnússon Institute, Reykjavík. Photo by Jóhanna Ólafsdóttir.*

The Valkyries poured mead for the heroes, but Freyja gave the giant ale. (Odin drank only wine, which was the most expensive.) "The goblets that Thor normally drank out of were brought out," Snorri writes, "and Hrungnir drained each one. And when he became drunk, there was no lack of big words." He was going to level Asgard—except for Odin's great hall. Hrungnir would carry Valhalla back to Giantland as booty. He'd kill all the gods—except for beautiful Freyja and Sif of the Golden Hair. They could be his bed slaves. But first the giant meant to drink up all the gods' good ale. He hollered for more.

The gods hollered for Thor. He entered Valhalla with hammer raised. "Who let a giant into Asgard?"

"Odin did," the giant answered, with a level stare. "I am his guest. Besides, you'll win no honor killing me unarmed."

Instead Hrungnir challenged Thor to a duel on the frontier of Giantland. Thor agreed. No one had ever had the audacity to challenge him to a duel before. Hrungnir galloped home to get ready, and his journey was "very widely talked of among the giants."

Hrungnir, of course, hadn't a chance. Thor arrived at the duel site in a storm of thunder and lightning. "He was traveling at an enormous rate and swung his hammer and threw it from a great distance." The giant also threw his weapon—a whetstone—and the two collided in midair. The whetstone shattered. "One piece fell to the ground," says Snorri, "and from it have come all whetstone rocks." Another piece pierced Thor's forehead and he collapsed. But Thor's hammer split the giant's skull. The giant came crashing down dead— and landed with a leg across Thor's neck. The mightiest god could not get up until his little three-year-old son (whose mother was a giant) arrived and lifted the leg. In thanks Thor gave the boy Hrungnir's fine horse.

Odin was not pleased. Thor was wrong to waste that fine horse on the son of a giantess. Odin wanted Gullfaxi for himself.

Odin could never get enough. And neither could Snorri, though he probably did not recognize, when he was writing this tale, how very much like the god he was: impulsive, proud, not a fighter, hospitable, rich but still greedy, and a little petulant.

By the time he was forty, in 1218, Snorri had plucked all the prizes Iceland had to offer. He had wealth, lands, and the love of women. He wielded more power than any Icelander before him, as he was not only the lawspeaker but held seven chieftaincies, with the ability to tax and call to arms thousands of men. He wanted more.

In the old days, the sagas say, ambitious Icelanders had gone to Norway to seek their fortunes. They joined the king's retinue and fought in his wars against the oath-breaking Swedes and Danes or wrested tribute from the troll-wise Finns. Icelanders sailed on Viking voyages, harrying the coasts of the Baltic, Atlantic, and Mediterranean and raiding Normans, Saxons, Saracens, and fellow Scandinavians. Icelanders traded peacefully in Kiev or Dublin. Icelanders joined the Varangian Guard of the emperor of Constantinople, fought as mercenaries for the king of England or the Holy Roman Emperor, and joined the Crusades.

They brought home to Iceland finger-rings and arm-rings of gold; chests full of silver; damascened swords; decorative shields like the one Egil of Borg received, "painted with illustrations of heroic legends" and "inlaid between the pictures with spangles of gold and set with jewels." They brought home glittering pendants and brooches and earrings and beads; fancy bridle mounts, stirrups, and spurs; sturdy coats of ring mail; and iron axes inlaid with silver. They brought home bright-colored cloaks and tunics and hose in the brilliant scarlets and leaf-greens of the alum-fixed dyes that were all the rage in twelfth-century Europe; an ell of scarlet wool sold for six times the equivalent length of undyed gray. Icelanders also favored silk from Spain. And they were terribly fashion conscious. Snorri writes about a king who dressed sumptuously in cordovan hose, gilded spurs, and a scarlet cape; another wore a red silk jacket over his mail shirt on which a lion was embroidered in golden thread. King's men sported "fine hose laced to the leg," "long kirtles with cords on the side and sleeves five ells long and so tight that they had to pull them on with hand cords and tie them tight up to the shoulders." (An ell at the time was eighteen inches; no one could wear this costume while riding a horse.) Their high shoes "were silk-sewn and some overlaid with gold." Egil of Borg was inordinately proud of a long silk gown tailored specifically for him, with gold buttons all the way down the front. He was quite miffed when his son, shorter than he, wore it to the Althing and got the hem all muddy. A more practical (or pious) Icelander who was given a white fur cloak lined with purple silk had it resewn into a church's altar cloth.

A chieftain like Snorri would give away such treasures (after wearing them once or twice) to the guests at his feasts, enhancing his reputation for magnificence and generosity. But the heroes of the sagas were in their teens and twenties when they sold their swords into the king's service or became raiders, traders, or crusaders. Snorri was now forty, and we have already established that he was not much of a Viking. He was not tall, strong, or recklessly brave, and he was tending toward fat from all that feasting and ale drinking. (Stout, he would have said. Dignified.)

Another long-established way in which an Icelander could impress a king and gain treasure and an aristocratic title was as a king's skald, or court poet. This was the route Snorri took. When he was in his early twenties, the king of Norway was the colorful King Sverrir. A priest born in the tiny Faroe Islands, Sverrir claimed to be an illegitimate son of King Sigurd Jerusalem-Farer (a lot of those were scattered about). He waged a long civil war against King Magnus Erlingsson, the last king Snorri chronicled in *Heimskringla* and the first to be crowned by the church, not the chieftains. King Sverrir, rallying the chieftains against the church, took the throne of Norway in 1184, when Snorri was six. In addition to being a good tactician, Sverrir was a cultured man: He commissioned an Icelandic abbot, Karl Jonsson of Thingeyri, to write a saga about him, the lively and well-drawn *Saga of King Sverrir,* which probably inspired Snorri to write *Heimskringla* (and to end it when he reached Sverrir's reign). Several years before it occurred to Snorri to begin his kings' sagas, he composed a praise poem for King Sverrir. He sent it to Norway before the king died in 1202, but he got no response.

Sverrir was succeeded by his son, Hakon, whose reign was cut short by his death in 1204. Hakon left an illegitimate infant son (also named Hakon) as heir. But Sverrir's sister had two grown sons: The elder (a third Hakon, nicknamed "the Mad" for reasons that are not clear) was rejected as king because his father was Swedish. His half brother, Ingi, whose father was Norwegian, was chosen instead. Hakon the Mad was given the title of earl and served as his half brother's war leader until his death ten years later.

Rather than choose sides, Snorri wrote poems to honor both King Ingi and Earl Hakon. He sent them to Norway in about 1211, most likely not on parchment but by way of an eloquent traveler who had memorized them. Earl Hakon replied by sending Snorri a sword, a shield, a coat of ring mail called a byrnie, and—a rare distinction—a poem. Snorri's countrymen were impressed. The poem, by a skald named Mani, was remembered for many years. In the 1270s Snorri's nephew recorded it in *Sturlunga Saga:*

These well-intended gifts,
The noble earl then sent,
All these would treasures prove,
The wealth of wealthy love,
To Snorri, valiant lord,
Came sword, and shield, and byrnie,
Showers of honors,
As I, the poet, have learned.

Earl Hakon commissioned another poem from Snorri in praise of his wife, Lady Kristin. He invited Snorri to visit them in Norway, "promising to show him great honor," Saga-Sturla reports. "That was much to Snorri's liking, but the earl died at that time, so Snorri delayed his journey for some years. Still, he had set his mind on going as soon as there was an opportunity."

A summons was not an opportunity. Snorri and five other Icelandic chieftains received one of those in 1211 from the archbishop of Trondheim. It concerned the case of Gudmund the Good, the moody, violent, and fanatical bishop of Holar.

Snorri's fate and Gudmund's were entangled. The crises of the Sturlung Age—the abrupt shifts of power, the breaking of old alliances—were catalyzed by Gudmund's intransigence as much as by Snorri's ambition. As the church's influence waxed, that of the chieftains waned. A key issue was who controlled a church's money. When Iceland became Christian in the early eleventh century, the chieftains vied with each other to see who could build the biggest church. Many also became priests—as the *Saga of Christianity* says, "Most respectable men were educated and ordained as priests." They supported the tithe, when it was introduced by law in 1096, for purely selfish reasons. In Iceland the tithe was a 1 percent property tax assessed on every neighboring farm, rather than the usual 10 percent income tax; the church farm itself was exempt. The money was divided into four parts, one each for the bishop, the priest, the church owner, and the poor—which meant that many chieftains, as both priest and church owner, received half.

When Snorri was twelve years old, the archbishop of Trondheim ruled that chieftains could no longer be priests. But the tithe laws were not amended. As chieftain of Reykholt Snorri collected the tithe and from his half gave the priest an allowance. A good businessman, Snorri could outfit the church, run the scriptorium, and still turn a profit, which legally he was allowed to pocket. To Bishop Gudmund, that Snorri should keep this money was anathema—contrary to the set of international church laws known as canon law. These laws divided the tithe only among the priest, the bishop, and the poor. Gudmund made it his crusade to rewrite Iceland's tithe laws. Snorri must have been aghast: Canon law would severely cut into his income. But his position was complex. Gudmund was not only a holy man, he was Snorri's kinsman; they may also have been friends.

Before his election as bishop of Holar in 1201, Gudmund was "a popular man and easygoing," if a bit strange. His childhood was scarred by the loss of his father, a valiant courtier who took a spear thrust intended for the Norwegian king. Gudmund did not inherit his father's property. Instead his uncle educated him for the priesthood, rather against his will: He had to be "beaten to his books." When he was nineteen, he and his uncle set off for Norway but were caught in a storm and blown back to Iceland. In the wreck Gudmund's foot was crushed, "the toes twisted around to where the heel should be," like the foot of the devil. After some painful medical treatments involving protruding bones and rebreaking the foot with tongs, Gudmund could walk again—something he did quite a lot of as a bishop, as we will see.

He was ordained a priest at twenty-four. Soon after, he was "separated from the two men he loved best," one by death, the other by distance. In his grief he "devoted himself so completely" to prayers and ascetic living that his parishioners thought he would die. From then on rumors circulated: Gudmund could work miracles. He called up a favorable wind for some boys in a boat. He healed an old woman's arthritic hand by making her massage his bad foot. He calmed a turbulent river so people could safely cross. He blessed springs that forever after healed the sick—or at least never ran dry. He killed trolls and chased ogres away from cliffs where people liked to collect birds' eggs. For this he was given the name Gudmund the Good.

Not everyone believed in Gudmund's saintly powers. At a church festival, when he brought out holy relics to be kissed, one farmer said he "wasn't sure whether they were the bones of saints or simply horses' bones." Another man pissed in a spring Gudmund had blessed: "After that no one was healed any longer by that spring." But enough people did believe, including some influential churchmen. When Gudmund visited the monastery of Thingeyri in 1199,

Abbot Karl Jonsson (author of the *Saga of King Sverrir*) led the welcome procession. The monks chanted a response honoring Gudmund the Good as a
saint in the full grace of God.

Saints were on people's minds in Iceland then. Gudmund and Snorri had
met, maybe for the first time, the year before at the glorious translation of
Bishop Thorlak—the ceremony by which the bishop was officially recognized
as Iceland's first saint. It was a spectacle not soon forgotten: The bishop's coffin,
buried for five years, was dug up, dusted off, and carried into Skalholt Cathedral.
Saint Thorlak's holy relics (his bones) were taken from his coffin, washed, and
encased in a golden shrine. Gudmund, then thirty-eight, was a coffin bearer,
a signal honor; he chanted the Te Deum in his unforgettable voice. Twenty-
year-old Snorri probably accompanied his foster brothers Saemund and Orm,
whom the saga says attended the ceremony. During the mass that followed, he
would have marveled at the 130 expensive beeswax candles twinkling on the
altar (all imported, since honeybees do not survive in Iceland).

Spectacle—a vision of heavenly glory—was one thing Icelanders wanted
from the church. Another was supernatural help for their hard lives. Thorlak
had not been terribly helpful when he was alive. He was the bishop who
climbed the Law Rock and excommunicated Snorri's uncle for loving his wife.
He was the one who threatened Snorri's foster father with eternal hellfire for
loving his mistress (who was Thorlak's sister). But soon after Thorlak died in
1193, people began reporting miracles that occurred when they called on him
for aid. These miracles, like those attributed to Gudmund (who was never officially sainted), provide a digest of the common Icelander's woes in Snorri's
day: Saint Thorlak cured stiff hands, sore throats, burning eyes, and distended
stomachs. He found lost hobbles, lost sheep, a sledgehammer, and a ring. He
healed a horse ridden "unwarily where there was volcanic heat"; its legs "got so
burned that people thought it would die." He healed a woman who "fell into a
hot spring in Reykholt and got so severely burned that her flesh and skin came
off with her clothes." He stemmed the flow of blood when a chieftain, soaking
in his hot tub, cut himself with a razor. Thorlak calmed storms and floods,
resuscitated a drowned boy, quenched a house fire, and mesmerized a seal so a
starving woman could kill and eat it.

Faced with accounts of Thorlak's miracles, Bishop Pall—who was the illegitimate son of Jon Loftsson and Thorlak's sister—"was flexible and open-
minded . . . in his handling of this joyful news," says *Thorlak's Saga* in the usual

understated Icelandic way. Declaring the miracle worker a saint was completely up to Bishop Pall. The pope in Rome had nothing to do with it in those days. Not even the archbishop in Norway had to be consulted. Sainthood was a local matter—and Iceland had no saints of its own. Instead Icelanders in trouble made vows to Saint Olaf, the former king of Norway, or to the English saint Thomas Becket. A chieftain named Hrafn, for instance, went out hunting walrus in a small boat. He speared a nice one but was having difficulty landing it, so he vowed to give Saint Thomas the valuable ivory tusks if he would assist. The walrus was secured. Hrafn went on pilgrimage to England, presented the tusks to Canterbury Cathedral in Saint Thomas's name, and gave the monks money to remember him in their prayers.

Such vows—and the money promised—convinced Bishop Pall to be open-minded and label Thorlak's miracles authentic. Saint Thorlak changed the economics of sainthood in Iceland's favor. "Because of the holy Bishop Thorlak's good deeds," his saga says, "much money was given to the see in Skalholt from all the lands in which his name was known, mostly from Norway, much from England, Sweden, Denmark, Gautland, Gotland, Scotland, the Orkneys, the Faroes, Caithness, the Shetland Islands, and Greenland; but most came from within Iceland." Sainthood was a money-making proposition. Skalholt Cathedral and the other thirty-two Icelandic churches dedicated to Saint Thorlak received an immediate influx of funds from individuals hoping the new saint would help them catch walrus, find lost sheep, or recover from a burn or shaving cut.

The money Saint Thorlak brought in, however, exacerbated the debate then destabilizing Icelandic society: Who controlled a church's money? The priest (or bishop) or the chieftain whose ancestors had built the church and on whose land it stood?

On orders from Norway, Bishop Thorlak had broached that question with Jon Loftsson shortly after 1190, when the archbishop had declared chieftains could no longer be priests. The uncrowned king of Iceland refused to discuss it. The old laws would stand. "I may hear the archbishop's mandate," Jon said, "but I am minded to hold him at nought, and I think that he neither wills nor knows better than my forebears Saemund the Wise and his sons. And I will not also condemn the conduct of our bishops here in the country who conform to that custom of the land, that laymen should rule those churches which their forefathers gave to God."

So the matter stood until Gudmund the Good became bishop of Holar in 1201. He was no longer easygoing but even more righteous than Saint Thorlak. Gudmund had not wanted to be bishop, but his family would not let him turn the honor down. "I have never heard of such a thing," said an uncle, "as to flip your fingers at your own advancement and that of your family as well."

Gudmund had warned everyone he would take his duties seriously. "Would you yourself obey me if I were to find fault with your way of life?" he asked one chieftain.

"For whose evil ways ought you to feel a greater responsibility," the chieftain replied suavely, "than for mine?" He had no idea what Gudmund really meant.

Bishop Gudmund's crusade to control the church's money was bad enough. But he didn't stop there. The tithe laws were not the only Icelandic laws that contradicted canon law. "Archbishop Thorir sends this message of lamentation and sound advice," began the letter from Norway in 1211; it was addressed to Snorri and five other Icelandic chieftains. After the obligatory Bible verse, it continued: "From here we learn of the deplorable and extraordinary cruelty, contrary to God and all God's laws, visited upon Bishop Gudmund." If the bishop had erred, the chieftains should have sent him to Norway, not taken matters into their own hands, the archbishop of Trondheim wrote, for "no man has the right to judge him except the Pope (and we on his behalf)."

The key phrase is "no man has the right to judge him." Until now the law courts at Iceland's spring assemblies and summer Althing had the right to judge everyone in the country, from chieftain to slave. That the law applied to all people, rich or poor, high or low, was the basic truth of Icelandic society since the founding of the Althing in 930: "With laws shall our land be built up, but with lawlessness laid waste."

But Bishop Gudmund insisted—and the archbishop in Norway agreed—that Icelandic clergymen were exempt from Icelandic laws. They could not be served with a lawsuit or summoned to the Althing. They could not be fined or exiled—no matter what they did, including rape, theft, and murder. They could be judged only by canon law, which established a clergyman's bishop, and above him his archbishop and the pope, as his only legal judges. This strict separation of church and state had indeed been church doctrine since the reforms of Pope Gregory VII in the mid-eleventh century, but no Icelandic clergyman in the succeeding 150 years had even hinted that such a rule should be followed.

Then in 1206 Bishop Gudmund came to court in full episcopal regalia and broke up a lawsuit between the chieftain Kolbein Tumason and a priest who owed him money. It was a little, everyday lawsuit. No one could have predicted the cataclysm it unleashed.

The bishop "forbade them to pass sentence on the priest," the saga says. "But they passed sentence on him just the same."

The priest was outlawed—exiled from Iceland.

The bishop took the outlawed priest into his own household at Holar (which made the bishop an outlaw, too) and banned Kolbein from church. When Kolbein protested, Bishop Gudmund formally excommunicated him.

Kolbein was taken aback. He considered himself a pious Christian. He had long been the bishop's firm supporter. Gudmund was a cousin of Kolbein's wife and had been chaplain of the family's church before the chieftain pushed for Gudmund's election as bishop in 1201. True, Kolbein's support may not have been entirely selfless. Notes *Sturlunga Saga,* "Many men commented that Kolbein had wanted Gudmund chosen bishop because he thought he himself would thus control both laymen and clergy in the north." The writer of a later *Life of Gudmund the Good,* adds, "As soon as they got to Holar, Kolbein assumed full control both of household affairs and of finances." It was like Snorri's arrangement with the priest Magnus concerning Reykholt, except that Gudmund had not agreed to it.

Historians blame Gudmund the Good for much of the strife that enveloped Iceland during the Sturlung Age—strife that would climax with Snorri's murder at the request of the king of Norway in 1241 and result in Iceland becoming a colony of Norway in 1262. When Gudmund denied the universality of Iceland's laws, "the fate of Iceland's independence was ultimately sealed." But Gudmund was not thinking about Iceland's independence. If he thought about anything other than the rights of the church, it was the martyrdom of Saint Thomas Becket, murdered in Canterbury Cathedral when Gudmund was a stubborn boy of ten. Saint Thomas's dispute with King Henry II hinged on the punishment of "criminous clerks," churchmen who committed crimes, just as Gudmund's dispute with the Icelandic chieftains did. In the *Life of Gudmund the Good,* written by one of his pupils, a woman dreams that Gudmund will "rank as high in Iceland as Thomas in England." The saga quotes a verse by Kolbein himself. Gudmund, Kolbein says,

> *Keeps firm his wish*
> *To wield such power*
> *As Thomas Becket.*
> *This bodes danger.*

The first time Gudmund insisted that churchmen were above the law—when Kolbein sued the priest who owed him money—Kolbein backed down. The chieftain offered the bishop self-judgment and settled for a fine of twelve cows. Kolbein got six. The next time Kolbein sued some clerics (for theft), he said there was no use making an agreement, since the bishop wouldn't honor it. A scuffle broke out. Someone threw a stone. It hit Kolbein in the forehead and killed him.

God's will be done! Gudmund fined some of Kolbein's men and excommunicated others. "Now there was grumbling and ill-feeling among the farmers, for it seemed to them that they had lost their chieftain, had themselves fallen into disgrace . . . and now they had to pay fines into the bargain. They said it was all pillage and robbery."

In the North people no longer thought Gudmund was so good. They turned to Kolbein's brother Arnor and his brother-in-law, Sighvat Sturluson, for help. Sighvat called on his brothers, Snorri and Thord. Snorri agreed to back him, though he and Gudmund had always been friendly. Their brother Thord refused outright. He was the most pious of the three. Unable to convince him, "Sighvat became angry and leapt on his horse and they parted. Thord said that after that their relationship was never again what it had been." The disagreement among the three Sturlung brothers over Bishop Gudmund was another cause of the strife of the Sturlung Age. In Snorri's *Edda* the end of the world is presaged by the Axe Age, when brother fights brother. In Snorri's own life the most harmful feud he fought was with his brother Sighvat and Sighvat's son Sturla Battle-Strong. Sturla would attack Snorri ruthlessly, forcing him eventually to flee to Norway for asylum, leaving everything behind.

But that was nearly thirty years in the future. Now in 1209 Snorri and five other chieftains answered Sighvat and Arnor's call. They rode to Holar seven hundred strong, surrounded the buildings, and waited. All night men slipped out of the bishop's houses, deserting him. The chieftains' army let them go. At dawn they attacked. Six of the bishop's men died, as did six on the chieftains' side. The rest of the bishop's men took refuge in the cathedral. The chieftains gave the bishop two choices: He could lift all the excommunications and leave Holar, in which case they would let most of the people in the church go free, though they would deal with the outlaws according to the law—which meant they could be killed. Or, if the bishop refused to lift the excommunications, they would drive him away all the same and kill everyone in the church, sparing none. The bishop refused to choose. He was ready to become a martyr like Saint Thomas Becket.

Snorri broke the impasse. He politely convinced Bishop Gudmund to come to Reykholt and stay with him as his honored guest. Snorri called out a cleric named Vigfus and gave him quarter. Then, with the two churchmen, Snorri and his men rode away.

What followed inspired the archbishop of Trondheim to write deploring the "extraordinary cruelty . . . visited upon Bishop Gudmund" and summoning Snorri and five other chieftains (though, oddly, not Snorri's brother Sighvat) to Norway to explain themselves. The chieftains ordered everyone in the church to come out or they would starve them out. The bishops' men came out. Three outlaws were executed—one in quite grisly fashion, piece by piece. He was said to sing the Ave Maria while his hands and feet were cut off. The other people were let go, some taken into the chieftains' followings, others ordered to leave the country.

We don't know if Gudmund and Snorri debated law at Reykholt that winter. They probably discussed books, which the bishop had grown to love. According to his saga, "Wherever he went he scrutinized thoroughly the books and information which he had not seen before." But the life of a scholar did not satisfy him, and in the spring he tried to return to Holar. When the chieftain Arnor barred his way, Gudmund turned west instead and began his many years of wandering around Iceland, trailed by a troop of hundreds of hungry beggars and devoted servants. He blessed springs, banished trolls, healed the sick, ate his hosts out of house and home, and then looted the neighbors' storehouses to feed his flock.

The archbishop's letter in 1211 had no effect. No archbishop in Norway had the right to summon an Icelandic chieftain to appear before him. Neither did the king—though Snorri would soon give him that right. Bishop Gudmund, who was in fact answerable to the archbishop, tried three times to respond, but his ship was blown back to Iceland twice. By the time he reached Norway in 1214, the archbishop who had summoned him was dead. The new one kept Gudmund with him for four years, then sent him back to Iceland in 1218 with the kindly advice to start a school.

Gudmund's ship and Snorri's may have crossed on the high seas, for in 1218 Snorri finally sailed to Norway. He had no invitation—or summons. He seized an opportunity: a new king had been crowned, Hakon, the illegitimate son of the short-lived Hakon Sverrisson. The new king was an impressionable fourteen. The regent, Earl Skuli, was half brother to the former King Ingi, who was half brother to Snorri's erstwhile patron, Earl Hakon the Mad, and thus perhaps susceptible to poetry. There might be an opening for a king's skald.

Beyond garnering a fancy title, it's not clear what Snorri hoped to accomplish in Norway. Like his foster father, Jon Loftsson, Snorri was simply fascinated by kings and kingship. He knew that in ancient times the kings of Norway had greatly honored poets. He was a fine poet. He saw no reason why the world should have changed. Snorri could not know that this impulsive trip to Norway would be the turning point of his life. He could not know that one quick, persuasive speech to the young king, along with one colorful poem pronounced on the quay at Bergen, would mar his reputation—and seal his doom. When Snorri sailed to Norway in 1218, he was, by most calculations, the uncrowned king of Iceland: lawspeaker, holder of seven chieftaincies, and the richest man in the country. When he returned in 1220, he was a suspected traitor.

To prepare for his voyage he gave up his post as lawspeaker, with the intention of resuming it upon his return. He transferred his property temporarily to his brother Thord. He called his mother to Reykholt to be housekeeper. He married off his eldest daughter, seventeen-year-old Hallbera, against her will to Arni the Quarrelsome, the thirty-eight-year-old cousin of the Magnus whose palms had been bloodied in the altercation at the Althing, when Snorri's man Herburt wanted to show off his skill in fighting with a buckler. That feud was now ended. Arni the Quarrelsome supplied a rich estate as his bride-price, but the wedding took place at Reykholt and Hallbera refused to leave, so the newlyweds lived there instead. It would not be the last time Snorri failed to consider his children's happiness when spinning his web of alliances.

Snorri sailed from his own harbor on the river Hvita and landed, after an uneventful trip, in Bergen. He knew something about the city. His foster father had been there, as had his foster brother, Bishop Pall. But the information Snorri gathered here and elsewhere in Norway and Sweden during the next two years proves he was a keen observer. He must have sought out the most knowledgeable tour guides and grilled them mercilessly, for the trivia and touches of whimsy he added to his written sources are what make *Heimskringla,* his history of Norway's kings, so lively. His grasp of geography was astonishingly good, given his map-less culture. His memory was robust, though he might have taken notes—medieval notebooks have been found. But notes would be arranged by place, according to his travels. Back home in Iceland during the next fifteen years, Snorri shuffled the details, showing a tremendous ability to organize, and delivered them chronologically, by king. As the sagas in *Heimskringla* progress, we watch towns, as well as kings, rise and fall.

Bergen, a market town on Norway's rocky western shore, Snorri tells us, was founded by King Olaf the Quiet, who reigned from 1067 to 1093. He laid the foundations of "the great stone church," Christ Church, and erected a wooden stave church for use until the masons were finished (which was not in his lifetime). Once the town was established, "many rich men began to reside there, and merchants from other lands came sailing to the place." Olaf the Quiet "was also the first to have rooms furnished with stoves, and have the floor covered with straw in winter as well as in summer." In the old sort of Viking king's hall, with an open fire running lengthwise down the center, floor coverings were fire hazards.

In 1110 King Eystein built "a splendid stone minster" in Bergen. He established a monastery on North Ness. He built another stave church and a great hall that Snorri calls "the most magnificent wooden structure that has been built in Norway," though he never saw it: Bergen burned to the ground in 1198. Snorri doesn't describe the fire; he ends *Heimskringla* in 1177, before his own birth and the terrible Norwegian civil wars that burst out periodically until 1240, when the young king he had come to meet would triumph—and call for Snorri's death.

When Snorri arrived in 1218, archaeologists have found, Bergen had one main street running parallel to the wharf on the north side of the wide sheltered bay. Along it were compact rows of wooden houses "two and two together, with a passage between." The narrow ground floor of each house was used for storage, with the living quarters in a wider loft upstairs; the overhang sheltered the passageway between neighbors. The docks stretched from the wharf at least a hundred feet into the sea. Since the townsfolk dumped their refuse off the ends of the docks, the harbor kept getting shallower and the docks, built on pilings, longer. Still, two hundred ships at a time could tie up at the wharf or anchor in the bay.

The town held eleven churches in various stages of construction in 1218. There were shops of shoemakers and leatherworkers, carvers of bone, wood-workers and toolmakers of all kinds. Among the imported goods that might have caught Snorri's eye were green-glazed jugs molded to look like human faces—an early version of what is known as a Toby mug—from England. He could not have escaped noticing how inexpensive the wine was. King Sverrir had complained about that in 1186. He says in his saga: "We desire to thank the Englishmen who have come here, bringing wheat and honey, flour and cloth. We desire also to thank those who have brought here linen or flax, wax or cauldrons. . . . But there are Germans who have come here in great numbers, with large ships, intending to carry away butter and dried fish, of which the exportation much impoverishes the land; and they bring wine instead." Public drunkenness was a problem.

It was thrilling to visit such a town—there were none in Iceland. But Snorri's goal in Norway was to impress the young king, and Hakon was in Tunsberg, four hundred miles east. Before autumn set in and the seas grew dangerous, Snorri again took ship. At first he followed an inland passage, past countless islands (one modern tour company counts 667). Some were wooded: Snorri would have marveled at the mast-high spruce and pine. Others were sheep meadows.

He sailed past Moster, where Olaf Tryggvason came ashore in 995 on his return from exile. This king forceably Christianized Norway and directed the conversion of Iceland. Olaf "had mass sung in a tent" on Moster, Snorri writes. "In after times a church was built in that same place"—apparently Snorri didn't visit it.

Snorri did take a look at the gravesite of King Harald Fair-Hair, who united Norway in 885. "At Hauga Sound," Snorri writes in *Heimskringla*, "there stands a church, and close by the churchyard, to the northwest, lies the mound of King Harald Fair-Hair." At some point the barrow was emptied—Snorri does not tell us by whom, only what's left. "West of the church there is the gravestone of King Harald—the one which lay over his resting place inside the burial mound, and that stone is thirteen and a half feet long and nearly two ells broad. The grave of King Harald was in the middle of the mound. There, one stone was placed at his head and another at his feet. The slab was placed above him, and loose stones were piled up around the grave. The gravestones which were inside the mound and have just been described, now stand there in the churchyard."

On the island of Karmoy, where the North Way—the shipping lane that gave Norway its name—strategically narrows, Harald Fair-Hair had an estate called Avaldsnes. He was not the first king to live there: The island sported rows of burial mounds. Under one that was 141 feet in diameter and sixteen feet high, archaeologists found the richest Roman-period grave in Norway. This king, who died before 300 A.D., wore around his neck a torc of pure gold weighing nineteen ounces. Buried with him were weapons and casks of silver and bronze. Surprisingly no Viking had plundered this rich grave, though a number of barrow break-ins are recounted in the sagas. Even Odin the wizard-king, in Snorri's *Heimskringla,* was a grave-robber. He knew where treasure was hidden, Snorri writes, "and knew such songs that the earth and hills and rocks and howes opened themselves for him, and he bound with spells those who might be dwelling therein, so that he could go in and take all that he wished."

Snorri did not go treasure hunting but spent his time on Karmoy sharing stories. Hakon the Good (who reigned from 934 to 961) fought a great battle here, winning the kingdom from the sons of Eirik Blood-Axe. Olaf Tryggvason (995–1000) drowned a pack of sorcerers there by chaining them to rocks that became submerged at high tide. Here the god Odin came to visit him. "One evening when King Olaf was being entertained at Avaldsnes, an old and very wise-spoken man came in," Snorri writes. "He wore a hood coming low down over his face and was one-eyed. This man had things to tell of every land . . . and the king found much pleasure in his talk and asked him about many things."

"Who was Avaldsnes named for?" Olaf asked.

For King Ogvald, said one-eyed Odin. This king had an odd habit, the god confided: He worshipped a cow. He took that cow with him wherever he went and found it "salutary always to drink her milk." Ogvald was buried in one of the mounds on the island, "'and in another place close to here the cow was buried.' Such tales he told, and many others, about kings and other stories of olden times." And such tales Snorri gathered or double-checked, if, like this one, he'd learned it before from an Icelandic monk.

Judging from one tale, Snorri's tour guide must have taken him on a lengthy hike. This was the story of Asbjorn and the second King Olaf, Olaf the Stout (1015–1030), who after his death became Saint Olaf. Asbjorn came south from

Halogaland to Avaldsnes to buy grain when there was famine in the North. But King Olaf had forbidden anyone in the South to sell grain or malt or flour, said Thorir, the king's steward. Asbjorn sailed on to his kinsman Erling's estate. Erling too would not sell, but he thought they could get around the king's prohibition if Asbjorn bought from Erling's slaves. Asbjorn loaded his ship. On his way north he stopped again at Avaldsnes—and Thorir promptly confiscated his cargo. He also took Asbjorn's fine striped sail, exchanging it for a plain one. Asbjorn sailed home, shamed. He returned in the spring with a warship.

Just before Easter he reached Karmoy. "That is a large island, long and for the most part not broad, and it lies on the outside of the fairway," Snorri writes. "On the land side there is a large settlement, but most of the island on the side facing the sea is uninhabited." Asbjorn landed on the sea side. He disguised himself and went alone to scout things out. "He went up on land and crossed the island. And when he came to a hill," Snorri says, "he observed a great stir of men both on sea and land and he noticed that all the people were going toward the farm on Avaldsnes. That seemed strange to him." He went up to the farm and mingled with the servants. "Very soon he gathered from their talk that King Olaf had arrived." He sneaked into the hall. Thorir the Steward was standing before the king telling a story—the very story of how he had confiscated Asbjorn's grain. Asbjorn "thought Thorir plainly was one-sided in his account. Then he heard a man ask, 'How did Asbjorn bear it when you cleared his ship?'

"Thorir said: 'He bore that with some composure . . . but when we took his sail he blubbered.'

"When Asbjorn heard that, he drew his sword quickly and rushed into the hall and straightway dealt Thorir a blow. It fell on his neck, the head dropped on the table before the king, and the body before his feet. The table cloths were all spattered with blood."

Asbjorn's kinsmen saved his life with difficulty. They convinced the outraged King Olaf to wait until Easter was over before executing him, and by then Erling had arrived with reinforcements.

The outline of this story appears in one of Snorri's sources, but it contains none of the sense of place that makes Snorri's version so suspenseful. It says only that Asbjorn anchored in a concealed harbor, went up on land, walked into King Olaf's feast, and lopped off Thorir's head, filling the king's plate with blood. In adding the details, Snorri transformed a chronicle into a saga. *Heimskringla* is not just a history of the kings of Norway but an exploration of what it means to be a king.

From Avaldsnes, Snorri continued south, passing the inlet where Olaf the Stout took his revenge for Asbjorn's outrageous action: The king lay in wait there for Asbjorn's kinsman Erling and caught and executed him.

Snorri also passed the hammer-shaped Hafrsfjord, where Harald Fair-Hair won the battle that united Norway in 885. Snorri sailed along the treacherous seacoast of Jaeren, where the winds were capricious and no offshore islands offered shelter to a ship. "Now there is surf off Jaeren," a tenth-century skald had warned his prince on a stormy winter's day. The boy sailed anyway and drowned.

Snorri probably tucked into Egersund, a stopping place often mentioned in *Heimskringla*. There he saw his first oaks—great, spreading, leafy trees so different from the spindly, wind-twisted birches of Iceland, which rarely rose higher than one's head. The name of the harbor comes from the Old Norse for oak, *eik*. This part of Norway was famous for its ship timbers.

Next Snorri rounded Lindesnes. Its name comes from an Old Norse verb that means "to go to the end." It marked the southernmost part of Norway, the turning point into the Skaggerak and the inlet known as the Vik; our word *Viking* might originally have meant "man from the Vik."

Sailing north from the old kingdom of Agdir into Westfold, Snorri would have noticed the beech forests and the many barrows, though he did not know what treasures they hid. He probably sailed right by the strand at Larvik, where archaeologists have found the palace of the Yngling kings, the earliest Scandinavian royal dynasty. At the beginning of *Heimskringla* Snorri traces their line to Yngvi-Freyr, companion to the wizard-king Odin. Excavations have revealed a stone-paved hall with massive boat-curved walls. One hundred feet long by thirty-six feet wide, it sits on a forty-foot-high cliff atop a man-made platform constructed from ten thousand cubic feet of stone and packed earth. It is the only such platform building in Norway. But to Snorri, though he might have learned some tales of the Yngling kings nearby, the palace seemed just another burial mound.

Snorri did take note of the barrow a little farther north at Geirstadir—the modern Gokstad, where the iconic Viking ship was discovered in the 1880s. The man buried in the Gokstad ship, whose leg bones show signs of gout, could be Olaf the Elf of Geirstadir, who, Snorri says, "succumbed to a disease of his leg and is buried in a mound." The Elf was king of Westfold in the early 800s. His stepmother, the vengeful Queen Asa, of whom Snorri tells a bloody tale, could be one of the two women buried in the Oseberg ship discovered in 1903, its beautifully carved prow another icon of the Viking Age. Oseberg may mean "Asa's Fortress." Snorri likely walked over the queen's rich grave while he stayed with the king and Earl Skuli in nearby Tunsberg during the winter of 1218. Though he does not link the Oseberg mound to Queen Asa, he mentions several other barrows around the town. Eirik Blood-Axe, Egil Skalla-Grimsson's enemy who reigned from 930 to 935, was responsible for three of them, having killed his brothers at Tunsberg to claim the throne. A fourth, called Haugar Hill (*haugr* means "grave mound"), was the meeting site for assemblies.

North of Tunsberg was a natural fortress; it was fortified by King Magnus and besieged by King Sverrir for twenty weeks in the winter of 1201. Snorri would have heard that tale but chose not to tell it. He did mention how Olaf Tryggvason invited all the Tunsberg locals suspected of practicing magic to a feast. He "entertained them well with strong drink. And when they were drunk he had the house fired, and it burned down with all those inside, except that Eyvind Kelda escaped through the louver." Eyvind was later drowned on the rocks at Avaldsnes.

In all, Snorri has disappointingly little to say about Tunsberg. If not for his nephew Saga-Sturla's insistence in *King Hakon's Saga* that the king and Earl Skuli spent the winter of 1218 there, we would think Snorri had met them elsewhere. He mentions no church building. He ignores the royal hall (except for its indoor toilet, which impressed him). He tells one funny story in the *Saga of Saint Olaf* about and Icelander, known for his very ugly feet, who is tricked by the king. But mostly he harps on the town's fine market. In the *Saga of Harald Fair-Hair* he writes, "Many merchant ships frequented Tunsberg, both such from Vik and such from the northern part of the country, as well as ships from the south, from Denmark and Saxland." In the *Saga of Olaf Trygvasson*, "Many merchant ships came to the town, both Saxons, Danes, and men from Vik in the east and from the northern parts of the land. There was a great multitude there. Harvests had been good that year and there were many drinking bouts."

Snorri may not even have met the young king of Norway that first winter—certainly, he was not welcomed to court with the pomp due a king's skald. In *Sturlunga Saga,* Saga-Sturla writes only, "The earl was very well disposed toward Snorri, and Snorri stayed with him." Snorri's companions from Iceland kept going, heading south for Rome.

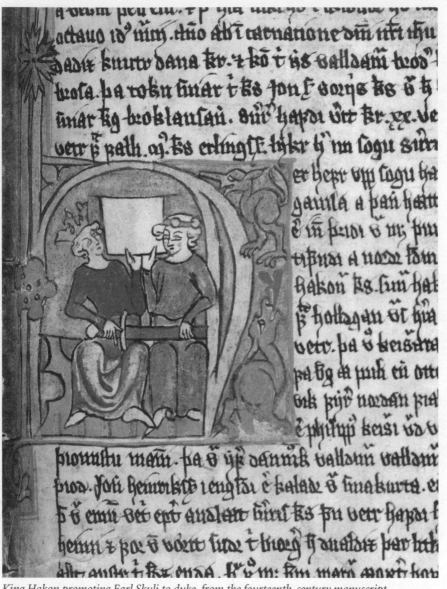

King Hakon promoting Earl Skuli to duke, from the fourteenth-century manuscript,
Flateyjarbók, GKS 1005 fol. Snorri and Skuli became great friends. The king was less
impressed with the Icelandic poet and later grew to distrust him—probably with reason.
Copyright © The Árni Magnússon Institute, Reykjavík. Photo by Jóhanna Ólafsdóttir.

In the spring, rather than accompany the king and court back to Bergen, Snorri traveled east into Sweden, where he had a poem to deliver: the love poem Earl Hakon the Mad had commissioned years before for his wife, Lady Kristin. Its title alone remains, "Andvaka," loosely "Sleepless Nights," a reference to how Kristin's beauty kept her husband awake.

Lady Kristin had remarried; her new husband was Askell, the lawspeaker of West Gautland, a large province in the South of Sweden. To visit them Snorri may first have sailed to Sarpsborg, on the border of Norway and Sweden. In his time the town was known as Borg, for the moated fortress Olaf the Stout had built beside the Sarp waterfall. Inside the walls Olaf had erected Saint Mary's Church. "He had also sites for other buildings marked off and got other men to build there," Snorri writes. (City planning was one of his favorite subjects.) Olaf stayed there in 1016 while negotiating to marry the Swedish princess Ingigerd. When talks broke down, he "forbade all movements of herring and salt from Vik to Gautland. And these wares the Gautar could ill do without." The Swedish earl of Gautland was eager to end the embargo. King Olaf had an Icelander with him, Sighvat the Skald, who volunteered to travel to Sweden as Olaf's ambassador to "see if any agreement could be brought about. The king was pleased with this proposal," Snorri writes.

Sighvat the Skald wrote a series of poems about his journey east into Gautland, and Snorri includes many in *Heimskringla*. When he went to see Lady Kristin and her husband, Snorri may have followed the same route the skald describes, through "trackless forest wastes" and "over steep rocks." It was not like crossing Iceland. "The steed runs in the gloaming, famished, over long paths," Sighvat wrote. "My swift one caught his leg in a ditch—day and night converge."

One river crossing in an old boat was almost disastrous:

Almost we upset it.
May trolls take that crazy
Tiller-horse: there was not
Ever seen a sorrier
Sea-buck. I was lucky.

Some paths were too rough for horseback:

Wearily we went our
Way—and that is certain—
Through Eithar forest onward,
All of thirteen miles then.
Blisters and sores, I swear, were
Seen on the soles of us king's men.

Often Sighvat found no farm that would let him in overnight. As he writes in a sequence of verses:

Doors were barred; so outside
Stood I, knocking, and stoutly
Stuck my nose in, plucky . . .
"Wreak his wrath will Odin,
Wretch," said a witchlike gammer.
"Keep out," quoth she, "nor further
Come; for we are heathen."

Travel in Sweden was no picnic, Sighvat complained:

Aye, missed we in the east, in
Eith-wood yonder wandering,
The ale that all had drunk at
Asta's farm, without asking.

Finally Sighvat the Skald reached Gautland. The earl gave him a gold ring for his trouble. Better yet, the poet wrote, a serving maid flirted with him, admiring his "bonny Icelandic black eyes."

Unfortunately Snorri does not describe his own arrival in Sweden—no gold ring, no flirtations. But he did deliver the love poem that the long-departed Earl Hakon the Mad had commissioned him to write for Lady Kristin. In return Kristin gave Snorri something he must have prized: the war banner of her grandfather, the Swedish king. A king's banner was carried by his most trusted companion, the one he wanted always by his side. Owning one was quite an honor.

Snorri spent the summer of 1219 in West Gautland with Lady Kristin and her new husband, Askell the Lawspeaker, learning about Swedish history and, especially, its law. Snorri reports that Sweden was divided into seven parts, of which West Gautland was one; as a measure of its size, he notes that it alone had eleven hundred churches. Each of the seven districts of Sweden had its own laws, he writes, and over each "is a lawspeaker, and he has the greatest power among the farmers, because whatever he decides to be the law stands. And whenever the king or an earl or bishop travel about the country and hold an assembly with the farmers, then the lawspeaker makes answer for them. . . . Even the most powerful chieftains hardly dare to come to their meetings unless the farmers and the lawspeaker permit them."

It was Thorgny, lawspeaker of Uppsala, who told the king of Sweden he must marry his daughter Ingigerd to Olaf the Stout, the king of Norway. Before Thorgny intervened, the king would not even discuss it. Norway and Sweden were at war, and he had no mind for peace.

Thorgny was a huge old man, with a beard "so long that it came down to his knees and spread over his whole chest," Snorri writes. Thorgny stood up at the assembly and reprimanded the king: "Different is now the disposition of the Swedish kings from what it was before." The king in his grandfather's day, Thorgny said, "was not so haughty that he did not listen to men who had important business to discuss with him. . . . But the king whom we now have lets no one presume to talk to him except about what he himself wants done." He wants to rule Norway as well as Sweden, but "it is the will of us farmers that you make peace with Olaf the Stout, the king of Norway, and give him your daughter. . . . If you will not do as we say, we shall set upon you and kill you, and not tolerate from you lawlessness and hostility." At that, all the people at the assembly "clashed their weapons together and made a great din. Then the king arose and said that he would follow the will of the farmers in all matters."

Of course he reneged. Princess Ingigerd was married off to the king of Kiev. But through the intercession of Sighvat the Skald, her illegitimate half-sister, Princess Astrid, was induced to elope to Norway. The earl of Gautland and a hundred Swedes escorted her across the border to Sarpsborg, where King Olaf "had made all preparations. The choicest beverages obtainable were held ready, and everything else was of the best. He had also summoned to his court many men of influence from the surrounding districts. And when the earl arrived there with his company, the king made him most welcome. They were given roomy and good quarters, with excellent furnishings and with servants and others who saw to it that nothing was lacking."

The king of Sweden disowned his daughter until, again, a lawspeaker brought him around. Emund of West Gautland was noble, rich, and eloquent—but also "a guileful person and not to be relied on," Snorri notes. Emund told the king a funny story about a squirrel hunter and another one about an unlucky Viking. In both cases the fool loses a great treasure by chasing after a little one. The king didn't get it. "What is your errand here?" he asked.

"I come, sire, to seek a solution of the difficulties arising through our laws differing from the Uppsala laws," Emund the Lawspeaker said. Two noblemen had quarreled about land. Each did damage to the other until their quarrel was settled in the assembly. "'Then he who was the most powerful had to pay a fine. And as a first payment he substituted a gosling for a goose, a pig for a hog, and instead of a mark of burnt gold he paid out half a mark of gold and the other half in clay and mud, besides threatening retribution on him who got this payment for his debt. How would you judge this case, sire?'

"The king replied, 'Let him pay in full what he was ordered to.'"

Emund called for witnesses and referred the king's decision to the Uppsala Assembly. Then "he saluted the king and went his way"—leaving town posthaste, before the king figured things out.

The king of Sweden was rather slow. He feasted. He enjoyed his jesters and harpers. He drank away the remainder of the day and slept through the night. But in the morning he thought about Emund's tales and the judgment he had given. His advisers confirmed that the nobleman who had paid a gosling for a goose was the king, who had substituted the illegitimate Princess Astrid for the legitimate Ingigerd. The Swedish king met Olaf the Stout on the border and made good on the rest of his promises.

We can imagine the two lawspeakers—Askell of West Gautland and Snorri of Iceland—chuckling about clever Emund and proud Thorgny. A year after Snorri left Sweden, the laws of West Gautland were written down for the first time. Scholars see Snorri's hand in that, since Iceland's laws had already been in writing for a hundred years. For Snorri the powerful Swedish lawspeakers were a model of how things should go when he resumed his post as lawspeaker of Iceland.

Snorri also collected in Sweden some of the mythological tales he tells in his *Edda,* as well as the folktales in *Heimskringla*—such as the time the Swedish king vowed to find Odin. "One evening after sunset," Snorri writes, King Svegdir came upon a dwarf sitting beside a large stone. The stone had a door in it. "Svegdir and his men were very drunk, and ran towards the stone. The dwarf stood in the door, and called to Svegdir and bade him go in, if he wished to meet Odin. Svegdir leaped into the stone, and it straightway locked itself, and Svegdir never came back."

At summer's end Snorri returned west to Norway, perhaps by rowing down the Gota Elf River to the harbor town of Konungahella, where Snorri's foster father, Jon Loftsson, grew up. Snorri credits King Sigurd Jerusalem-Farer with establishing the town. He "had so many buildings erected in Konungahella that there was no more richly provided market town in Norway." He built a fortress with a moat, a royal hall, and Holy Cross Church: "That was a wooden church, very carefully built both as to material and workmanship." To the church Sigurd gave his souvenirs of the Crusade. "He placed the Holy Cross in Konungahella"—the elaborate silver processional cross containing a splinter of the True Cross, which Jon's foster father later saved from the pirates. "In front of the altar he placed the altar-piece he had had made in Greece. It was of bronze and silver, beautifully gilded, and set with enamel and jewels." This the pirates took. They burned down Holy Cross Church. Writes Snorri, "The merchant town of Konungahella never afterwards rose again to the affluence it had before." His descriptions were based not on his own observations but likely on his foster father's recollections.

From Konungahella, Snorri sailed to the royal town of Trondheim. The first leg of his trip took him back to Bergen; from there north, all was new. He passed Herle Island, where Snorri's ancestor Egil Skalla-Grimsson killed the young son of Eirik Blood-Axe, then erected a *niðstöng* (insult pole). As Snorri writes in *Egil's Saga,* Egil took a horse head, set it on a hazel pole, and proclaimed, "'I direct this insult against the guardian spirits of this land, so that every one of them shall go astray, neither to figure nor find their dwelling places until they have driven King Eirik and Queen Gunnhild from this country.' Next he jammed the pole into a cleft in the rock and left it standing there with the horse head facing towards the mainland, and cut runes on the pole declaiming the words of his formal speech."

The hard going on this sea route came at Stad, a high plateau topped by a distinctive mountain peak. Stad is the windiest promontory in Norway and one of those few places along the west coast where no outlying islands shield the shipping channel. Many ships wrecked at Stad, and even kings took it seriously: "King Harald and his men agreed that he was not to sail south around the promontory of Stad so late in fall," Snorri writes. Stad marked the boundary of four districts, and in 997 the missionary king Olaf Tryggvason called an assembly there. "He bade people to be baptized, as he had in other places. But because the king had the support there of a large army, they were alarmed. In the end the king offered them two alternatives: either to accept Christianity and be baptized, or else fight it out with him. But since the farmers saw no chance to fight the king they decided on having all the people christened." Much of Norway became Christian the same militant way.

The gateway to Trondheim Fjord was a place called Agdanes. Because of the tricky currents, travelers often disembarked there and rode horseback the remaining twenty-five miles to Trondheim. Agdanes was also the first port of call for Icelanders sailing from the North of their island. They waited there for a wind—or for news. In one story a pagan skald learns that Olaf Tryggvason is in residence. He vows three measures of beer to the god Freyr if a wind blows up that will take him to Sweden and three measures to Thor or Odin if the wind takes him back to Iceland. But he gets no wind at all, so he has to row in to Trondheim and be baptized.

The royal town of Trondheim, or Nidaros (the old name means "mouth of the River Nid"), was the seat of Norway's kings. Surrounded by farmland, it controlled the luxury trade in furs and walrus ivory from the far north. Land routes linked it with Oslo and the Vik area, as well as with Sweden. It was rich in fish and forests—famous ships were built here, such as Olaf Tryggvason's *Long Serpent*. This ship was "larger than any other ship then in the country, and the stocks on which it was built still exist and can be seen" below the cliffs at Lade, just outside of town, Snorri writes. "It was constructed as a dragon ship, on the model of the *Serpent* which the king had taken along from Halogaland; only it was much larger and more carefully wrought in all respects. . . . The *Long Serpent* had thirty-four compartments. The head and the tail were all gilt. And the gunwales were as high as those on a seagoing ship. This was the best ship ever built in Norway, and the most costly." Connoisseur of ships that he was, Snorri tells a long story about the shipwright who systematically defaced one side of the *Long Serpent*. He was wagering his head that the king would agree the strakes had been cut too thick.

Snorri spent the winter of 1219 in Trondheim; in *Heimskringla* he says more about this town than about any other part of Norway. He writes about Trondheim's founding by King Olaf Tryggvason and how his successor, Earl Eirik, preferred his estate at nearby Lade. Eirik "neglected the buildings which Olaf had erected on the banks of the Nid River, so that some had collapsed and others still stood but were rather uninhabitable." When Olaf the Stout made his claim to the kingship, he rebuilt Trondheim. His enemy Earl Svein burned it down. Olaf built it back up. "He had the royal quarters erected there and laid the foundations of Saint Clement's Church at the place where it now stands. He marked out sites for homes and gave them to farmers and merchants and others he liked and who wanted to build there. He kept many men about him, for he did not trust the Tronders to be loyal to him" (and rightly so, for they turned on him in 1030).

We learn that the River Nid freezes over in winter and that Trondheim boys make pests of themselves throwing snowballs. We learn that dense deciduous forest grows in places along the banks of the fjord. Earl Svein, fleeing Olaf's wrath, "moored the ship so close to the wooded slope that the leaves and branches of the trees hung down over the ship. Then they felled trees and placed them in the water on the outside so that the ship could not be seen for the leaves." The king rowed right past.

Snorri must have wanted to visit Stiklastadir, sixty miles up the fjord, to see the rock against which Olaf the Stout made his heroic last stand in 1030. Snorri may not have made it. When he describes the battle, his stage directions are vague: "The king had stationed his men on a certain hillock." We get more detailed information about Trondheim's many churches—perhaps Snorri's tour guide this time was a cleric. Saint Nicholas's church, for example, "is very richly adorned with woodwork and all kinds of artistry." Snorri's admiration is plain, while his later renovations at Reykholt show he paid careful attention while touring the bishop's palace.

Snorri probably arrived in Trondheim in time for the royal wedding on September 29 of fifteen-year-old King Hakon and Margret, Earl Skuli's daughter. Snorri was made a retainer at King Hakon's court, but his title was not the one he coveted, king's skald. Instead he became a *skutilsveinn* (trencher bearer).

The origins of this name are obscure; perhaps such men served at, or ate at, the king's table. Later a *skutilsveinn* would be called a knight: It was an honor but not as high as Snorri's ambitions reached. Most visiting Icelanders from good families would be made knights. They did not even have to be chieftains.

As Hakon's knight a disappointed Snorri traveled south with the king and Earl Skuli to Bergen in the spring of 1220. There he begged leave to return to Iceland.

Only then, it seems, did Snorri come to the full attention of the young king. The merchants of Bergen were in an uproar about injustices inflicted upon them in Iceland. The quarrel had begun several years earlier when the men of Oddi, led by Snorri's foster brother Saemund, had insisted on exercising the Icelandic chieftain's traditional right to set the prices on imported goods, no matter what the Norwegian traders thought their goods were worth. In 1216 Saemund's son Pall had come to Bergen. He was not treated well. "The men of Bergen mocked him greatly and said that he probably intended to become king or earl over Norway," says *Sturlunga Saga*. Pall was haughty and hot-tempered. He was also descended from King Magnus Bare-Legs and may have bragged about it—at a time when illegitimate claimants to the throne were causing political unrest in Norway. Annoyed, Pall left Bergen for Trondheim. His ship sank while rounding treacherous, windswept Stad.

When the news reached Iceland, Saemund (quite irrationally) accused the men of Bergen of plotting his son's death. He gathered six hundred men and rode to Eyr—a trading station on the southern coast of Iceland—"where he brought charges against the men from Bergen. There was no choice for the Norwegians but to pay him as much as he demanded," since they were so outnumbered. Saemund seized the value of three hundred cows, an outrageous sum.

Later that summer a Norwegian merchant ship arrived in the Westman Islands off Iceland's southern coast. Saemund fined its owners, too, what seemed to them "an exorbitant loss of goods." Saemund's half-brother Orm tried to make amends. He invited the Norwegians to spend the winter with him and bought timber from them at a good price. But when he and his son went out to the islands to pick up the wood in the spring, the Norwegians killed them both. "Men thought this a portentous and terrible event." Orm's son-in-law Bjorn rode in a rage to the North of Iceland, where he "dragged a Norwegian out of the church and had him killed." No Norwegian ships at all came to Iceland in 1219—the men of Bergen had imposed a trade embargo.

Until he arrived in Norway in 1218 Snorri had not known of the murder of his foster brother Orm. While visiting Bergen, Snorri may have been alarmed to hear that the Norwegians thought the killing justified by Saemund's extortion of goods. Two years later, when Snorri wanted to sail home from that same town, "the Norwegians still felt most unfriendly toward the Icelanders, particularly the men of Oddi." They convinced Earl Skuli to send a "harrying force" to Iceland—and he had already chosen ships and men for this army.

A determined leader with a handpicked attack force could quickly take over Iceland. The island had no defenses. Few Icelanders owned decent weapons. About one of the battles of the Sturlung Age, we read that "each man did the best he could," but this was hard "because they were so short of weapons. The men of the East Fjords had some shields, but the men from the west had only one." The most deadly weapons in many of these fights were stones.

An Icelandic retainer of Earl Skuli's composed a poem to dissuade him from attacking: "What's in it for me?" he complained,

> *What's to be gained*
> *O my prince?*
> *Harrying*
> *In home harbor*
> *Kills honor for me.*

That skald was not Snorri.

His role in the dispute was crucial, everyone agrees, but what Snorri did is unclear. Saga-Sturla wrote twice about Earl Skuli's plan to attack Iceland, once in *King Hakon's Saga* in 1264 and later in *Sturlunga Saga*, written sometime between 1271 and 1284. We don't know why his two accounts differ, only that one saga was written under royal commission and the other for an audience of Icelanders. In *King Hakon's Saga* Snorri was among several Icelanders in Bergen who appealed to Dagfinn the Lawspeaker, a close confidante of the king's. At Dagfinn's urging King Hakon nixed Earl Skuli's plan. In *Sturlunga Saga*, on the other hand, Snorri speaks to the earl directly:

> Snorri strongly advised against this expedition, and said that his advice would
> be to make friends with the best men in Iceland, and claimed that as soon as he
> could reach them with his advice, his countrymen would think it best to turn to

the Norwegian rulers for protection. He also said that there were no greater men in Iceland than his brothers, except for Saemund, and claimed that they would follow his advice entirely when he reached home. By such persuasions as these the earl's intentions softened, and he advised that the Icelanders ask King Hakon to intercede for them.

The Icelanders did so, and "even as the king decreed, no harrying force was sent out. But King Hakon and Earl Skuli then made Snorri their landed man." This was a great step up from *skutilsveinn*. No Icelander had ever borne the exalted title of landed man before—it was equivalent to baron. There were only fifteen barons in all of Norway. A landed man received lands—a fief—from the king, which gave him an income. In return he supplied warriors to swell the king's army. The landed man was, above all, the king's noble ally and sworn to do his lord's bidding. For the first time in history a king of Norway did have the right to summon an Icelandic chieftain to court.

The question of what lands Snorri held in fief from King Hakon has disturbed Icelanders ever since. A fiefdom in Norway would have been a great boon to an Icelandic chieftain, providing a constant free source of lumber for ships or house building, grain for bread (or beer), and well-armed men for a bodyguard. After Snorri returned to Iceland, *Sturlunga Saga* mentions that he received a shipment of lumber but does not say whether he paid for it. According to the *Annals of Oddi,* on the contrary, Snorri received no Norwegian lands. Instead he gave his Icelandic estate of Bessastad and one other to King Hakon, who returned them as his fief—but this witness dates from the sixteenth century.

Equally disturbing is the question of what Snorri promised to do for the king of Norway—and did he intend to keep his promise? Did Snorri, as lawspeaker of Iceland, accept King Hakon's judgment in the single legal case of the men of Oddi versus the Bergen merchants? Or was Snorri selling out his country's independence, offering to become the king's deputy in Iceland, collecting the king's taxes and forcing his countrymen to accept Norwegian laws? Saga-Sturla says in *Sturlunga Saga* that Snorri would convince the Icelanders to "ask King Hakon to intercede for them." But in *King Hakon's Saga,* Saga-Sturla says, "This was the first time that the earl brought up the idea that Snorri should bring the country under King Hakon's rule." Saga-Sturla later adds that "Snorri made no headway with his countrymen, but he also did not press the issue. Nonetheless the merchants enjoyed peaceful conditions at this time in

Iceland." Was the issue that Snorri did not press the lawsuit between Oddi and Bergen or Iceland's independence? We cannot be sure. We also have to wonder at Saga-Sturla's source. Snorri himself is unlikely to have discussed with his six-year-old nephew the full implications of his negotiations with the king.

On the quay at Bergen, as he was leaving Norway in the autumn of 1220, Snorri declaimed a poem he had composed in honor of Earl Skuli. In response Skuli gave him the ship he was to sail in and fifteen other magnificent gifts. Snorri's poem, Saga-Sturla acknowledges, was skillful, but he quotes only the refrain: "Hard-mouthed was Skuli, created the very greatest of earls" (says another translator, "a stallion of power among earls"), "with the high-country's strongbeam," meaning gold. It's a difficult verse to figure out. The negative adjective *hard-mouthed*, when applied to gold, was apparently intended to mean generous. The choice was unfortunate.

After a rough voyage in which his new ship was dismasted, Snorri reached the Westman Islands. He and his eleven followers—all well equipped and displaying "great self-confidence"—were ferried to the mainland. They borrowed horses and rode to the bishop's seat at Skalholt, where Snorri clearly expected to be welcomed as the savior who had warded off Norway's "harrying force" and kept Iceland safe from Earl Skuli's warships. He was not.

Snorri's bargain with the king was widely discussed. His countrymen were leery of his new rank. No Icelander had ever held the title of landed man. What did it mean? Was the fief Snorri had received from King Hakon Iceland itself? Was he to be the baron of Iceland? The carl of Iceland?

The men of Oddi were the most suspicious. Even if Snorri's promise to advise his countrymen to "turn to the Norwegian rulers for protection" applied only to their feud with the merchants of Bergen, they felt he had gone too far. Bjorn, who had dragged the Norwegian out of the church and killed him, rushed to Skalholt. He "walked straight up to Snorri and asked him if he intended to usurp their rights," Saga-Sturla writes. "Snorri denied this. Bjorn said that he couldn't believe this, and they exchanged threats with one another."

The bishop of Skalholt was no longer Pall, Snorri's foster brother. Pall had died just before Snorri left for Norway and had been replaced by Bishop Magnus, a member of the powerful Haukadale family—and Bjorn's uncle. Bishop Magnus was able, with some difficulty, to keep his nephew under control, but Bjorn and Snorri "parted pretty coldly."

Snorri went home to Reykholt. As winter came on he heard squawks from the South: Parodies of the poem he had composed for Earl Skuli were circulating. One anonymous wit had been paid a sheep to write this one:

> *To us it seems ill to kiss an earl,*
> *That one who rules a country,*
> *The lip is too sharp on the lord,*
> *Hard-mouthed is Skuli.*
> *Never has more mud of a*
> *Carrion-vulture of the sea*
> *Come before wise lords—*
> *People find fault in the poems.*

Bad enough that this paid hack turned *hard-mouthed* from *generous* into "ill to kiss." The "carrion-vulture of the sea" was an eagle, so its mud was eagle's shit. As Snorri himself would explain in his *Edda*, when Odin stole the mead of poetry and was flying in eagle's form back to Valhalla, he expelled some of the mead backward in order to clear the walls of Asgard. That eagle's shit was left on the ground for the makers of ditties to lick up. Snorri could not have been more grossly insulted than to have his royal praise poem described as eagle's shit.

Four

NORSE GODS
AND GIANTS

Most poets have composed poetry based on these stories and have used various elements in them.

—Snorri, *Edda*

*T*he Norse gods are not omnipotent. They're not even always dignified. Sometimes their job is not to rule the universe but just to make us laugh, as in the story of the god Thor's encounter with the giant Utgard-Loki. No other source tells this tale. Snorri might have made it up.

We can imagine him regaling his listeners with it, as they sat around the feast hall sipping horns of ale. He might have read aloud from his work in progress, the *Edda*. Or he might have told the tale from memory, like an ancient skald.

Thor the Thunder God and Loki the Trickster, he would begin, sailed east across the sea to Giantland. With them was Thor's servant, a human boy named Thjalfi, who carried Thor's food bag. They trudged through a dark forest—it had a very Swedish feel (as Giantland often does in Snorri's tales).

At night they found no lodgings except one large, empty house. It had a wide front door, a vast central hall, and five side chambers. Thor and his companions made themselves comfortable in the hall. At midnight came a great earthquake. The ground shuddered. The house shook. They heard scary grumblings and groans. Loki and the boy fled into one of the little side chambers, and Thor guarded the doorway, brandishing his hammer against whatever monster was making that noise.

Nothing more happened that night. At dawn Thor saw a man lying asleep at the edge of the forest. Thor clasped on his magic belt and his strength grew. He lifted his hammer—but then the man awoke and stood up. He was so huge that even the mighty Thor didn't dare to strike him. Instead he politely asked the giant's name.

The giant gave a fake one. "I do not need to ask your name," he said in return. "You are the mighty Thor. But what were you doing in my glove?"

Snorri pauses while laughter fills the room. He refills his ale horn.

The giant, Snorri continues, suggested they travel together and offered to carry their food bag in his giant knapsack. After a long day of keeping up with giant strides, they camped for the night under an oak tree. The giant settled in for a nap. "You take the knapsack and get on with your supper."

Thor could not untie the knot. He struggled. He fumed. And—giant-like?—he flew into a rage. He grasped his hammer in both hands and smashed the giant on the head.

The giant awoke. "Did a leaf fall on me?"

Pause for laughter.

He went back to sleep.

Thor hit him a second time.

"Did an acorn fall on me?"

Pause for laughter.

He went back to sleep.

Thor took a running start, swung the hammer with all his might—

The giant sat up. "Are you awake, Thor? There must be some birds sitting in the tree above us. All sorts of rubbish has been falling on my head."

Pause for laughter.

The giant showed Thor the road to the castle of Utgard, then went on his way.

Thor and Loki and little Thjalfi walked all morning. They reached a castle so huge they had to crane their necks all the way back to see the top. Thor tried to open the gate but couldn't budge it. They squeezed in through the bars. The door to the great hall stood open. They walked in.

King Utgard-Loki (no relation to the god Loki) greeted them. "Am I wrong in thinking that this little fellow is Thor? You must be bigger than you look."

The rule of the giant's castle was that no one could stay who was not better than everyone else at some art or skill. Hearing this, Loki piped up. He could eat faster than anyone.

The king called for a man named Logi. A trencher of meat was set before Loki and Logi. Each started at one end and ate so fast they met in the middle. Loki had eaten all the meat off the bones, but his opponent, Logi, had eaten meat, bones, and wooden trencher, too. Loki lost.

The boy Thjalfi was next. He could run faster than anyone. The king had a course laid out and called up a boy named Hugi. Thjalfi lost.

Thor could drink more than anyone, he claimed. The king got out his drinking horn. It did not look terribly big, though it was rather long. Thor took great gulps, guzzling until he ran out of breath, but the level of liquid hardly changed. He tried twice more. The third time he saw a little difference.

He called for more contests.

"Well," said the king, "you could try to pick up my cat."

Thor seized it around the belly and heaved—but only one paw came off the ground. "Just let someone come out and fight me!" he raged. "Now I am angry!"

The king's warriors thought it demeaning to fight such a little guy, so the king called out his old nurse, Elli.

"There is not a great deal to be told about it," Snorri writes. "The harder Thor strained in the wrestling, the firmer she stood. Then the old woman started to try some tricks, and then Thor began to lose his footing, and there was some very hard pulling, and it was not long before Thor fell on one knee."

Utgard-Loki stopped the contest but allowed them to stay the night anyway.

The next day the king treated Thor and his companions to a feast. When they were ready to go home, he accompanied them out of the castle and said he would now reveal the truth. He himself had been the giant they had met along their way; he had prepared these illusions for them.

When Thor swung his hammer—the leaf, the acorn, the rubbish—Utgard-Loki had placed a mountain in the way. It now had three deep valleys. At the castle they had competed against Fire (the name Logi literally means "fire"), Thought (Hugi), and Old Age (Elli). The end of the drinking horn had been sunk in the sea—Thor's three great drafts had created the tides. The cat? That was the Midgard Serpent, which circles the entire earth.

Outraged at being tricked, Thor raised his mighty hammer once more. But he blinked and Utgard-Loki and his castle disappeared.

Did Snorri get a chuckle out of young King Hakon with this tale? Or did he relate it first to gales of mead-laced laughter in his new feast hall at Reykholt, where he gathered to himself a sort of royal court?

For Snorri spent the winter of 1220 planning, not sulking. In the spring he began a vast building project that transformed the houses and halls of Reykholt into ones better suited to a Norwegian baron. Snorri had taken notes in Norway, not just on history and mythology but on the latest fashions in architecture. He had arranged for lumber to be delivered; in 1223, Saga-Sturla notes in passing, Snorri's overseer met with an accident on his way to the harbor in northern Iceland to fetch the wood.

Over the next several years Snorri built huge timber houses with stone foundations and wooden floors and paneling: a great hall with a turf roof for his henchmen to sleep in, another hall for feasting and entertaining (this one decorated with woven wall hangings), and a little parlor for a private chat or to use as a writing studio. These rooms were connected to each other (and to the kitchens and storehouses) by a maze of hallways, but Snorri's bedroom was a freestanding wooden cottage. Next to it was a two-story house with a small ground floor and an overhanging loft like the townhouses Snorri saw in Bergen. One door opened into the feast hall, another into the parlor, and a third—perhaps a trapdoor—into the fateful cellar where Snorri would meet his end.

But that dark night was still some years off. Now Snorri, the richest and most powerful man in Iceland, was busy building a sauna with stone walls and floor. Steam was piped to it from the nearby hot spring through stone-and-clay conduits. Steam pipes may also have run under the floor of the parlor and feast hall, like a Roman hypocaust; the archbishop's palace in Trondheim had a similar heating system. Another Norwegian idea Snorri might have mimicked was the indoor toilet he had admired in the king's palace at Tunsberg.

Snorri enlarged the hot spring–fed bathing pool to the south of the houses. His circular stone-lined pool was twelve feet in diameter and had a ledge to sit on. The hot water was piped 350 feet from the spring in a buried stone-lined channel. A hidden door in the hillside opened onto a convenient tunnel that led from the pool to the basement below Snorri's parlor or writing studio. A curved stone stairway, perhaps concealed in a wall, led up to his room.

Finally, around the whole complex Snorri built a wall of enormous stones and turf blocks topped by wooden stakes. It had drawbridges facing north and south, making Reykholt a seemingly impregnable fortress. Later events would prove its defenses were showy but easily breached. Snorri had paid more attention to comfort and prestige than safety.

The spiral stair leading from Snorri's writing studio to the cellar that was connected to his bathing pool by tunnel. Discovered by archaeologists in 2002. Used by permission of Guðrún Sveinbjarnardóttir and the National Museum of Iceland.

A few of the men who joined Snorri's "royal court" at Reykholt in the 1220s and '30s are known by name. Extrapolating from church records, we can assume Snorri supported five clerics at Reykholt: three priests, a deacon, and a subdeacon. Another five lived at nearby Stafholt. All were educated men who could read and write in both Latin and Icelandic. In addition to saying mass, their primary job was writing and copying books. One priest, Styrmir the Wise, lived with Snorri for some time. His son seems to have been the overseer at Reykholt (the one killed while riding to the harbor to fetch the wood for Snorri's building projects). Styrmir was twice elected Iceland's lawspeaker and stood in for Snorri on at least one occasion. His known works include an expanded version of the *Book of Settlements* about Iceland's founding and a *Saga of Saint Olaf.* He made a copy of Karl Jonsson's *Saga of King Sverrir*—maybe the copy that inspired Snorri to write *Heimskringla.* Styrmir may also have written the collection of kings' sagas known as *Rotten Parchment*—again, an inspiration for Snorri. After Snorri and some other chieftains established

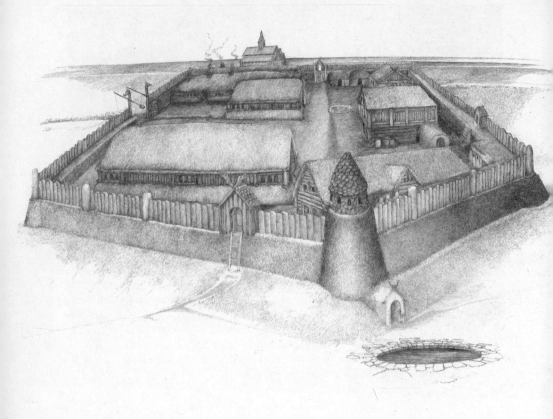

A reconstruction of Reykholt in Snorri's days, based on archaeological research and descriptions from Sturlunga Saga. *Illustration by Guðmundur Oddur Magnússon from* Snorri: Ævisaga Snorra Sturlusonar 1179–1241, *by Óskar Guðmundsson (2009). Copyright © GOddur. Used by permission.*

an Augustinian monastery on the island of Videy in 1226, Styrmir became the prior; he died there in 1245.

One of Snorri's friends was his neighbor Eyjolf Brunason, who was once belittled in Snorri's presence as "a good poet and farmer, but not rich." Snorri's response came in the form of a verse that said, "Bring to Eyjolf a greeting most fit for his ears: for I praise him, the most excellent of candid poets; may he live the richest of all truly rich men under the sun." To Snorri, Eyjolf was truly rich because he *was* a good poet.

Poets, even moody types like the hero of *Egil's Saga,* were always welcome at Reykholt. Like Odin's other companions, the berserks, poets were expected to be provocative, even dangerous to have around. Gudmund Galtason lived with Snorri after his patron, Hrafn Svcinbjarnarson, was murdered in a feud in 1213. Gudmund is described in *Hrafn's Saga* as "a fine poet and an unruly man and rather difficult to deal with. Hrafn had said that he thought Gudmund the skald and the dog Rosa most alike of those in his household, and this angered Gudmund."

Another of Hrafn's poets, Sturla Bardarson, also joined Snorri. Sturla, a deacon in the church, was Snorri's nephew, the son of his half-sister, and a friend of Bishop Gudmund the Good's. Deacon Sturla had only one leg. The other had been chopped off after he'd been captured while defending Hrafn. He was a bitter man, and his poems have an acid taste.

Jatgeir Torfason, skald to kings Ingi and Hakon and Earl Skuli, as well as the Danish king Valdimar, came to Reykholt from Norway with Snorri's son Jon Trout in 1224 (Snorri had sent his favorite son to spend three winters with Earl Skuli). Jatgeir was Skuli's spy; we know little about him except that he was brave and loyal to his lord. In 1240, during the civil war in Norway between Earl Skuli and King Hakon, Jatgeir put his life on the line while trying to slip messages to Sweden for Skuli.

A brash young man named Ingjald Geirmundarson is mentioned several times in *Sturlunga Saga* as visiting Reykholt. He later became an adept poet— did he learn the art from Snorri? He was a friend of Snorri's illegitimate son, Oraekja, and good with a spear. Ingjald would help avenge Snorri's death in 1241.

Gudmund Oddsson was the skald who tried to dissuade Earl Skuli from attacking Iceland—*What's in it for me? What's to be gained, O my prince?* He may have sailed home with Snorri in 1220, though he didn't stay with him long. He became the private poet of Snorri's nephew and nemesis Sturla Battle-Strong. When Sturla fought Bishop Gudmund the Good in 1222, the poet Gudmund crafted a fight song—though he himself was no fighter. When Sturla's house was attacked in 1229, the poet crawled up into the rafters. In a verse he confessed, "In terror I trembled above, / Narrowed myself on the board overhead." In another battle the poet was hit by a stone "so that he fell to the ground with his feet thrown up higher than his head," says *Sturlunga Saga*. "Some of the men wanted to pick him up. Sturla said, 'Let him lie quiet. He won't do any harm. He behaves like that in every fight,' and he burst out laughing." A coward could earn his keep in Iceland if he was a poet.

Sturla Battle-Strong and his uncle Snorri were often at odds during these years. They periodically traded barbs in verse form, with Gudmund Oddsson mostly writing for Sturla and Snorri answering for himself. But Sturla also had an artistic side. He was known to have dashed off a poem or two. (In Iceland a way of calling someone stupid was to say he couldn't even string a verse together.) And Sturla appreciated his uncle's sagas. During the winter of 1230, when it seemed Snorri and his nephew had settled their differences, "Sturla spent some considerable time at Reykholt and gave much thought to having copies made of the saga books which Snorri was writing." It is the only direct mention *Sturlunga Saga* makes of Snorri's rich literary life.

Sturla's younger cousins, the illegitimate brothers Saga-Sturla and Olaf White-Poet, became accomplished writers. When Snorri returned from Norway in 1220, Saga-Sturla was six and Olaf a few years older. They spent much of their youth at Reykholt, living there off and on, and were heavily influenced by Snorri. Saga-Sturla, who seems not to have liked his uncle much, wrote the only accounts we have of Snorri's life, in *Sturlunga Saga* and *King Hakon's Saga*. Saga-Sturla wrote a saga about King Magnus Hakonarson (now lost) and an expanded *Book of Settlements*. He may have written the *Saga of Christianity* about Iceland's conversion. He is named as a source in *Grettir's Saga,* the story of a famous outlaw. Some people credit Saga-Sturla with that masterpiece of all sagas, *Njal's Saga,* which captures the legal environment of Iceland like no other. He was also a poet: His sagas contain more than a hundred of his own stanzas, fifteen by his brother Olaf, and a handful of Snorri's.

Olaf White-Poet wrote the *Third Grammatical Treatise*. Highly technical, it uses the Latin principles of rhetoric, found in Priscian and Donatus, to analyze traditional Icelandic poetry. As examples Olaf quotes 123 poems by thirty-four poets, including Snorri's love poem to his swanlike mistress. Olaf also wrote about the ancient runic alphabet, saying he learned rune lore at the Danish court. Olaf took charge of Borg at Snorri's request and traveled with his uncle to Norway in 1237. Later Olaf established a school at Stafholt. He may be the author of a history of the kings of Denmark and possibly even the classic *Laxdaela Saga,* which is in many ways a response to *Njal's Saga.* He wrote praise poems for King Hakon, Earl Skuli, Earl Knut (the son of Hakon the Mad), King Valdimar of Denmark, and King Eirik of Sweden. Olaf wrote an elegy for his friend Aron, a long poem about Saint Thorlak, one about Saint Thomas Becket, and many occasional verses, lines from which he uses in the *Third Grammatical Treatise* to explain figures of speech. For instance, defining *ambiguity,* he says,

My friend, be clever and enjoy
Well his handsome wife
Boy, the lack of girls
Will certainly not last long.

He may also have been the one—if not Saga-Sturla—who gathered up Snorri's *Edda* after his uncle's murder, when it was left lying loose, a sheaf of random parchment pages, in Snorri's writing studio at Reykholt.

Poetry had real power in medieval Iceland. In the law courts the poet's skill at twisting meaning was taboo: "Every word is to be as it is spoken. No word is to be taken according to the language of poetry," says an Icelandic law. Poetry was also restricted in everyday life: "A man has no right to compose defamation or praise of anyone." Poetry was never neutral. A man could be outlawed and killed for composing a love poem (the woman's husband or father was shamed). Lampoons—*To us it seems ill to kiss an earl . . . hard-mouthed is Skuli*—ignited feuds.

Legality aside, poetry was the way Icelanders shared news and opinions. When Bjorn, who had dragged the Norwegian out of the church and threatened Snorri upon his homecoming from Norway, was killed in a fight with his kinsman Loft in 1221, the poem that flew around the country was suspected to be Snorri's. (Gudlaug was Bjorn's killer; Grasida is the name of his spear.)

Bjorn's been stroked
By a sharp caress—
Grand touch was that,
Gudlaug's, grim.
The rich man struck dumb
By Grasida's kiss,
Harsh her tongue—
Hard-mouthed was Skuli.

Poems were also the basis of the prose writings just coming into fashion. Snorri's *Edda* is based on mythological poems, while poems were both source and outline for some of his kings' sagas. A late ninth-century poem called "Tally of the Yngling Kings" names thirty ancient kings, citing how they died and where they are buried. It provided the skeleton for the first saga in Snorri's *Heimskringla,* the *Saga of the Ynglings,* about the kings who ruled from the time of Odin the Wizard down to the ninth century. The information in this poem Snorri amplified, he says, with that from "Tally of the Halogaland Chieftains," written by a tenth-century poet, as well as with "information given to us by learned men."

Poems, Snorri argues in *Heimskringla,* are more trustworthy than prose, if "correctly composed and judiciously interpreted." Often the poets were eyewitnesses to events—or at least pretended to be. King Harald Fair-Hair, who united Norway and prompted the settlement of Iceland in the late 800s, kept several poets at court. More than three hundred years later, Snorri notes, "men still remember their poems and the poems about all the kings who have since his time ruled in Norway." King Olaf the Stout made sure the three poets in his retinue were safe behind the shield wall at his last battle in 1030, so they could record his courageous death for posterity. (Despite his efforts all three died; the poet who composed Olaf's elegy was in Rome when the battle was fought.)

To write his kings' sagas, Snorri says, he sought out poems that were recited in front of the kings themselves or their sons, even though he was well aware that court poetry was propaganda. Poets always "give highest praise to those princes in whose presence they are," he acknowledges. "But no one would have dared to tell them to their faces," he argues, "about deeds which all who listened, as well as the prince himself, knew were only falsehoods and fabrications." That, he says, would be mockery, not praise. Comments his latest translator, "I think Snorri underestimated kings' appetites for flattery and their facility in self-deception."

He may also have overestimated the kings' ability to interpret what their poets were saying. Viking court poetry, or skaldic poetry, was a sophisticated art form. The rules are more convoluted than those for a sonnet or haiku. In the most common form for a praise poem, a stanza had eight lines. Each line had six syllables and three stresses. The rhythm was fixed, as were the patterns of assonance and alliteration. The musicality of a line was of utmost importance: A skaldic poem was designed to please the ear. It was first a sound picture, though in a great poem sound and meaning were inseparable. Each four-line half-stanza contained at least two thoughts—and these could be braided together so that the listener had to pay close attention to the grammar (not the word order) to disentangle subject, object, and verb. Especially since nothing was stated plainly. Why call a ship a ship when it could be "the otter of the ocean"?

The rules made it easy to memorize a poem—change a word and it simply won't work. (The rules also make skaldic poems impossible to translate well, which is why many of the poems in this book are translated into prose.) As Snorri wrote, "The words which stand in verse are the same as they were originally, if the verse is composed correctly, even though they have passed from man to man." For this reason they were considered trustworthy historical sources, even if hundreds of years old.

But being intricate did not make a skaldic poem more understandable. After Saga-Sturla had declaimed a praise poem about King Hakon in front of Hakon's son King Magnus and his queen in 1263, the queen said, "I think this poem is well written."

The king said, "Can you understand it clearly?"

She replied, "I want you to believe that is so, sir."

To some people the opaqueness of skaldic verse was part of its appeal. A poem was a cross between a riddle and a trivia quiz. The riddle entailed disentangling the interlaced phrases so that they formed two grammatical sentences. The quiz part was the kennings. Snorri defined kennings in his *Edda* (he may also have coined the term). "Otter of the ocean" is an easy one. As Snorri explained, there are three kinds of kennings: "It is a simple kenning to call battle 'spear clash' and it is a double kenning to call a sword 'fire of the spear-clash,' and it is extended if there are more elements."

Kennings are rarely so easy to decipher as these. Most kennings refer—quite obscurely—to pagan myths. Here's a literal translation of one of Snorri's own verses: "The noble hater of the fire of the sea defends the woman-friend of the enemy of the wolf; prows are set before the steep brow of the confidante of the friend of Mimir. The noble, all-powerful one knows how to protect the mother of the attacker of the worm; enjoy, enemy of neck-rings, the mother of the troll-wife's enemy until old age." Who are the enemy of the wolf, the attacker of the worm, and the troll-wife's enemy (not to mention their various friends, confidantes, and mothers)? As the translator of this stanza notes, the audience needs to know five myths and the family trees of two gods or it's nonsense. What does it mean? "A good king defends and keeps his land."

Kennings were the soul of skaldic poetry. One modern reader speaks of the "sudden unaccountable surge of power" that comes when she finally perceives in the stream of images the story they represent. She imagines listeners memorizing a verse and picking at it over time, until rewarded with "the sudden glory of fused metaphor."

Once the puzzle was solved, the meaning was often a letdown. Praise poems are repetitive, uninformative, tedious, banal, bewildering, even alienating, with their "grotesquely tortured word order," according to the experts who study them. One sighs, "When one has unravelled the meaning behind the kennings, one finds that almost a whole stanza contains only the equivalent of the statement 'I am uttering poetry.'"

Some kings acknowledged they had no taste for the stuff. When the Icelander Sighvat the Skald first brought a praise poem to Olaf the Stout, "the king said he did not want to have poems composed about himself and that he did not understand skaldship." Sighvat the Skald answered him in verse (of course):

> List to my song, sea-steed's—
> Sinker thou, for greatly
> Skilled at the skein am I—
> A skald you must have—of verses;
> And even if thou, king of
> All Norway, hast ever
> Scorned and scoffed at other
> skalds, yet I shall praise thee.

A skald you must have. Throughout *Heimskringla* it is a point Snorri stresses. Who would remember a king's name if no poems were composed about him? In a world without written record—as the Viking world was—memorable verse provided a king's immortality. In fact the only king known today from Viking Age York in England is Eirik Blood-Axe, courtesy of Egil Skalla-Grimsson's poem "Head Ransom." It may have been insincere and ironic, but it did the trick.

We know the names of more than two hundred skalds. We can read (or experts can) hundreds of their verses: In the standard edition they fill one thousand two-column pages. What skalds thought important enough to put into words provides most of what we know today about the inner lives of people in the Viking Age, what they loved, what they despised. The big surprise is how much they adored poetry. Vikings were ruthless killers. They were also consummate artists.

Skalds were a fixture at the Norwegian court for more than four hundred years. They occasionally were swordsmen. But more often in *Heimskringla* Snorri shows them as a king's ambassadors, counselors, and keepers of history. They were part of the high ritual of his royal court, upholding the Viking virtues of generosity and valor. They legitimized his claim to kingship. Sometimes skalds were scolds (the two words are cognates), able to say in verse what no one dared tell a king straight. They were also entertainers: A skald was a bard, a troubadour, a singer of tales—a time-binder, weaving the past into the present.

By the tenth century it was a commonplace that the best skalds were Icelanders and, conversely, that any Icelander had a bit of skald in him. When he entered the court of King Magnus in the late twelfth century, Mani looked like a vagabond. But he knew how to "greet the king grandly," the saga says. The king asked who he was. Mani gave his name, said he was Icelandic, and that he had just come from Rome. The king, keying in on the Icelandic part, said, "You must know some lore. Sit down and recite me some verse." Mani recited a long poem composed by another poet about Magnus's grandfather, King Sigurd Jerusalem-Farer. "The poem was highly acclaimed and people thought this was good entertainment."

Being a skald had for generations been a way for an Icelander—even one who looked like a vagabond—to get a foot in the door at the court of Norway. It was a mark of distinction, and Snorri had fully expected it to work in his case. It did—a little. When Snorri declaimed his praise poem about Earl Skuli on the quay at Bergen in 1220, the earl gave him a ship and fifteen magnificent gifts.

But King Hakon didn't acknowledge the poems Snorri composed for him—he may have declined to hear them. The sixteen-year-old king didn't like skaldic poetry. He didn't understand it. Worse, it was old-fashioned.

Hakon was the best-educated king Norway ever had. According to Matthew Paris, the French ambassador to Norway in 1248, Hakon was *bene literatus*. At the cathedral school in Trondheim, Hakon learned Latin, sacred chant (his favorite subject, he once said), and at least a little French. From the earliest years of his reign, his look was outward. He sent Icelandic falcons to the young king of England, Henry III. Later Hakon would send some to the sultan of Tunis. Hakon corresponded with Pope Innocent IV, the German emperor Frederick II, and King Louis IX of France, who invited Hakon on crusade. After negotiations with the Russian grand duke Alexander Nevsky broke off, Hakon married his daughter to the brother of Alfonso the Wise, king of Castile in Spain.

Chivalry came to Norway during Hakon's long reign, 1217 to 1263. He had clerics translate for him the stories of King Arthur and his Round Table; the first, in about 1226, was the tragedy of Tristan and Isolde. The translations were not very good, from our point of view. According to one modern critic, "Friar Robert's translation of the story of Tristan has very nearly ruined that great love story." But the attitude came through. The old Viking ideals of generosity and valor were replaced by the new chivalric ideals of courtesy and high-mindedness. The life of a Christian knight in the French romances is one of idleness and luxury punctuated by gallant adventures in which he succors the weak while showing his deep-seated contempt for anything practical. No chivalrous king could, like Olaf the Stout, be praised for being "deft with his hands" and skillful "in all smith's work."

But could a king of Norway turn his back on his country's lore, choosing a foreign culture over his native one, King Arthur over King Olaf? The concept would have shocked Snorri. It also hit him in the pocketbook. Poetry was Iceland's cultural capital, to use a term popularized by sociologists. It was all Snorri had to sell on the international market. Iceland's other exports were wool and dried fish. The bright-colored cloth from England and Flanders was more highly prized, and Norway had ample fish.

Perhaps, Snorri thought, Hakon was just poorly educated. He simply needed a good introduction to the lore of the North. He needed a Sighvat the Skald to say, "Listen, King, *a skald you must have.*" Snorri decided to be that skald. At Reykholt, shortly after he returned from Norway in 1220, Snorri wrote his poem "Hattatal" ("Tally of Verse Forms"). It's a showpiece, a virtuosic praise poem of 102 stanzas, each stanza in a different form, some so tricky they may never have been tried before. Hedging his bets, Snorri addressed it to both the king and Earl Skuli (with Hakon only sixteen, it wasn't clear who ruled Norway). The first thirty stanzas praise Hakon, the next group praises Skuli, while the final third praises poetry itself. Each stanza is accompanied by a prose commentary.

"Tally of Verse Forms" is a skald's how-to. The commentary is written in the form of a dialogue between pupil and teacher, like the Latin textbooks Hakon studied in the cathedral school. "What is variation of tense?" Snorri's imaginary pupil asks. "There are three kinds," the teacher answers. "How?" asks the pupil. "That which was, that which is, and that which shall be."

"Tally of Verse Forms" is well organized, adding difficulty step by step. We learn how to use all of a skald's tools: syllable length, line length, stress, alliteration, assonance, rhyme and half-rhyme, adjectives and their modifiers, kennings of various kinds, the several ways of interweaving sentences, puns and other wordplay, verb tenses, and contractions. We learn what Snorri considers the best technique: "Here there are two pairs of full rhyme in each line. This is considered to be the most beautiful and choicest, if it is composed well." We learn what he dislikes: "Allegory is held to be well composed if the idea that is taken up is maintained throughout the stanza. But if a sword is called a worm, and then a fish or a wand or is varied in some other way, this is . . . considered a defect."

We learn the names of the verse forms. *Dróttkvætt* is the most formal and flexible; the name means "king's meter." Snorri illustrates forty-eight varieties of it. Some of the more colorful are "fox turns" and "shivering." In a fox-turns stanza, "words are chosen to be placed next to each other that have most dissimilar meanings," like *fire* and *water, sea* and *land*. The shivering verse form was invented by a poet huddled on a rock in the sea after a shipwreck, Snorri says. He was "badly off for clothes and the weather was cold." Placing the alliterative words closer to each other than usual gives the effect of chattering teeth.

In the second section of the "Tally of Verse Forms," which is addressed to Earl Skuli, Snorri ups the ante by adding more mythological kennings. Skuli had a better background in Norse lore than the king did. One anecdote in *King Hakon's Saga* shows Skuli appreciated Snorri's vast knowledge. A one-eyed chieftain named Gaut had wormed his way into King Hakon's confidence, to Skuli's detriment. Skuli joked to Snorri, "Isn't Gaut one of the names of Odin?" "That's true, my lord," Snorri replied. Said Skuli, "Make up a poem about that and show how much alike they are." What Snorri recited—impromptu?—means this: "The sole creator of sorceries offered Hring and Hilditonn battle; Gaut encouraged them to hold that contest. For too long the battle-smith caused strife between the princes, but well might the leader of the army reject his judgment." (The "sole creator of sorceries" and "battle-smith" refer to Odin. Hring and Hilditonn are two ancient princes. The leader of the army is Earl Skuli. Gaut is both Skuli's competitor and Odin.) As Snorri's nephew Olaf White-Poet glossed the poem in his grammatical treatise, "Here is a figurative likeness between Odin and a certain malicious man."

In the third section of the "Tally of Verse Forms," Snorri illustrates "the lesser meters"—less difficult only in comparison to the king's meter, for they still have many rules. The easiest are the old story meter, the song form, and the incantation meter, with which Snorri ends his poem, his meaning now quite clear. "Poetry has been composed about the ruler. . . . This will last forever unless mankind perishes or the worlds end," he claims in one verse. In the next he adds the hook—"What man is going to hear praise thus spoken of one slow to give gold and treasures?"—a not-so-subtle reminder that a praise poem required a gift in return. Snorri goes on to summarize: "Close account have I given of poetic form so that ten tens are told. A man must not be called unworthy of renown if he is able to compose in all verse forms." Finally, he concludes, "I sought honor, I sought meeting with a king, I sought a splendid earl when I cut cold current with keel. . . . May king and earl enjoy age and halls of wealth. This is the end of the poem. May earth, stone-supported, first sink into the sea before the rulers' praise cease."

No poet had ever written such a complicated skaldic poem. With it Snorri was handing the young king his qualifications: There was no better candidate for king's skald. Snorri was a poet "worthy of renown."

If the "Tally of Verse Forms" was the whole of the *Edda,* no one would think much about Snorri Sturluson today. It's a flamboyant display that frankly is no fun to read. Translated, the music of the language gone, the verses fall flat. Without the rest of the *Edda* there are no keys to the riddles—and that was true for King Hakon, too. To the young king, Snorri's kennings were gibberish. Snorri realized this. He did not send the "Tally of Verse Forms" to the king. Instead, he began writing a new section, called "Skaldskaparmal" ("Language of Poetry"), in which he explained all the kennings in the "Tally of Verse Forms" (except a few obvious ones like "waves of honey" for mead).

It took him a long time. Snorri may still have been working on it when he was killed in 1241. One of the six manuscripts in which this part of the *Edda* appears is so disorganized and sketchy it might be a copy of Snorri's notes or a rough draft left on loose sheets of parchment and compiled by someone who didn't know exactly what Snorri had in mind. Even the longest version we have is structurally flawed. Partly it's a dialogue. Partly it's a glossary, a thesaurus, and a Bartlett's *Quotations:* Snorri quotes sixty-four poets, from the ninth century to the thirteenth. And partly it's a collection of myths in Snorri's own lively and ironic prose. As he explains, "These things have now to be told to young poets who desire to learn the language of poetry and to furnish themselves with a wide vocabulary using traditional terms." If such tales were "consigned to oblivion," Snorri continues, no one would understand "what is expressed obscurely" in old poems. A whole literature would be lost, a whole way of speaking—as if Americans today forgot what it meant to be caught between Scylla and Charybdis, to seek the Holy Grail, for the Force to be with you, or to wait for Superman.

It's here in the "Language of Poetry" that Snorri tells how Odin in eagle form stole the mead of poetry. Here he tells of the race between Odin's eight-legged Sleipnir and the giant's long-striding Gullfaxi, and Thor's duel with the whetstone-wielding giant Hrungnir. And here Snorri tells the most famous of Norse legends—famous thanks to Richard Wagner's grand cycle of operas, *The Ring of the Nibelungs*: the story of Sigurd the Dragon-Slayer.

Many stories in this section of the *Edda* feature Loki the Trickster. There's the story of Idunn's apples: Loki, caught by a giant eagle who was dragging him mercilessly through treetops and bouncing him, bruising him, on stony ground, bargained away the goddess Idunn and her golden apples, source of the gods' immortal youth. The gods began to grow old and gray. Forced to confess, Loki was ordered to retrieve Idunn. He borrowed Freyja's falcon cloak and flew to Giantland. Learning the giant was out fishing, Loki turned Idunn into a nut "and held her in his claws and flew as fast as he could" toward Asgard. When the giant got home and found his prize missing, he transformed into giant eagle shape and flew after Loki, "and he caused a storm-wind by his flying." The gods stacked a great pile of wood in the yard of Asgard. As soon as Loki the falcon was safely over the wall, they torched the stack. The giant eagle's feathers caught fire. The giant fell to earth, and Thor killed him. It was to make amends for this killing that the giant's daughter Skadi was permitted to marry one of the gods (whom she picked out by his feet). She also demanded, as part of the settlement, that they make her laugh; she considered it quite impossible. "Then Loki did as follows: He tied a cord round the beard of a certain nanny-goat and the other end round his testicles, and they drew each other back and forth and both squealed loudly. Then Loki let himself drop in Skadi's lap, and she laughed."

Another time Loki, out of mischief, cut off the goddess Sif's long, golden hair. Her husband, the mighty Thor, was not amused. "He caught Loki and was going to break every one of his bones until he swore that he would get black-elves to make Sif a head of hair out of gold that would grow like any other hair." Loki went to the land of the dwarfs. Soon he and the dwarf gold-smith returned to Asgard with Sif's new head of hair. They also brought five other treasures. To get them Loki had wagered his head. The gods agreed he had lost the bet. Thor grabbed hold of Loki and held him still so the dwarf could cut off his head. But Loki was a bit of a lawyer. Presaging Shakespeare's Shylock by several hundred years, he told the dwarf that "the head was his but not the neck."

One of the dwarf-made treasures that Loki brought the gods was Freyr's magic ship, "which had a fair wind as soon as its sail was hoisted" and "could be folded up like a cloth and put in one's pocket." Another was Odin's spear, which "never stopped in its thrust." Loki also gave Odin the gold ring that, every ninth night, spawned eight rings like itself. The dwarfs made a boar with bristles of gold that could run across sea and sky faster than a horse; this became Freyr's mount. Thor got his wife's hair as well as the sixth treasure Loki brought from Dwarfland: the hammer of might.

There's a problem here. Thor has already used his hammer in the "Language of Poetry." The sequence of information makes no sense. And Snorri knew it. At some point while working on this section of the *Edda,* he put it aside and started over. He then wrote what would obtain for him (not the king) undying fame.

"Gylfaginning" ("Tricking of Gylfi") outlines the whole history of the Viking gods, from the creation of the world in fire and ice to its de-struction at Ragnarok. It too is presented in the form of a dialogue. Gylfi, a king of ancient Sweden, goes to Asgard in disguise and there challenges Odin—presented here in the tripartite form of High, Just-as-High, and Third—to a

wisdom contest. Gylfi's questions allow Snorri, through Odin's mouth, to relate his wondrous stories.

Such as the story of Odin's lost eye: At the center of creation sits the great ash tree, Yggdrasil. It has three long roots. One reaches up to the Well of Weird, which is guarded by the three Norns—Urdur, Verdandi, and Skuld (Past, Present, and Future)—"who shape men's lives." Every morning the gods hold court beside the well. To get there they ride their horses up over the rainbow, which acts as a bridge between worlds—except for the mighty Thor, who always walks.

The water of the Well of Weird is suspiciously like the water of Iceland's hot springs. The Norns pour water over the ash tree each day to preserve it from rot, and the twigs, Snorri writes, "go as white as the membrane called the skin that lies round the inside of an eggshell." Such a shiny, white, many-layered patina can be seen on the lips of hot springs.

The second root of the ash tree reaches down to the underworld and ends in the well named Hvergelmir, sometimes translated as "the abyss." A great dragon gnaws on that root—when he is not tormenting the dead. Hvergelmir also has Icelandic overtones: The early settlers applied the first part of the name, *hver* (cauldron), to the strange phenomenon of bubbling hot springs.

The third root of the ash tree is sunk into nothingness, into Ginnungagap, the magical gap that existed before the nine worlds were made. In Ginnungagap lies the Well of Wisdom. It is guarded by the giant Mimir, who is "full of wisdom because he drinks from the spring out of the horn Gjoll. All-Father came there and asked for a single drink from the spring," Snorri writes, "but he did not get it until he had given one of his eyes as a pledge. As it says in the 'Song of the Sibyl':

I know for certain Odin
Where you concealed your eye,
In the famous
Spring of Mimir;
Mead he drinks
Every morning
From the pledge of the Father-of-the-slain.
Do you know any more or not?"

Snorri is not disturbed that the source he quotes somewhat contradicts him or that he later contradicts himself. He says Mimir drinks well water from a horn named Gjoll—later he describes Gjoll not as a drinking horn but as the trumpet the god Heimdal blows to announce the last battle of Ragnarok. The poet of the "Song of the Sibyl" says Mimir drinks mead out of Odin's eye itself.

Other inconsistencies creep into Snorri's mythology. Describing Alfheim, the land of the elves, he says, "There live the folk called light-elves, but dark-elves live down in the ground, and they are unlike them in appearance, and even more unlike them in nature. Light-elves are fairer than the sun to look at, but dark elves are blacker than pitch." Earlier he had told us that the intelligent beings who "live in the earth and in rocks" are called dwarfs, and he gave a long list of their names, including the ones J. R. R. Tolkien made famous in *The Hobbit*. But in telling the story of Sif's hair, Snorri said the trickster Loki "swore that he would get black-elves to make Sif a head of hair out of gold. . . . After this Loki went to some dwarfs called Ivaldi's sons, and they made the head of hair." Tolkien, among other readers, puzzled his head mightily over whether Snorri was describing three races (light-elves, dark- or black-elves, and dwarfs) or just two.

If Snorri left the question of elves and dwarfs vexed, he tidied up the Valkyries nicely. They are lesser goddesses, Snorri says, "whose function it is to wait in Valhalla, serve drink, and look after the tableware and drinking vessels." They are serving wenches for the dead heroes who make up Odin's army—but not powerless serving wenches, as they get to choose their masters. "Odin sends them to every battle. They allot death to men and govern victory." In his *Edda* he doesn't describe them. In *Heimskringla*, though, he quotes a long poem by the tenth-century poet Eyvind Skald-Spoiler (his nickname might mean "Plagiarist") in which Valkyries lean on their spear shafts, are "high-hearted, on horseback," "war-helmeted and with shields"—the classic picture of the Wagnerian battle maiden. Clearly Snorri preferred this romantic, almost courtly, depiction of the ladies of fate. Old poems that Snorri does not quote frame the Valkyries not as maidens but as monsters. They are troll women of gigantic size who ride wolves and pour troughs of blood over a battlefield. They row a boat through the sky, trailing a rain of blood. They weave men's fates on a loom where severed heads are the loom weights, intestines are warp and weft, and the tool called a weaving sword is indeed a sword.

Snorri gives an abbreviated version of the famous tale of Thor's fishing trip. Still smarting from the insults of Utgard-Loki, Thor sneaked into Giantland determined to get revenge. He went disguised as a young boy. (Why such a disguise was effective against giants, Snorri doesn't say; perhaps he was thinking of his audience, the boy-king Hakon.) A giant named Hymir gave Thor a place to sleep one night, and when Hymir set off to go fishing the next morning, Thor asked to come along.

"A little boy like you," Hymir said, "won't be much help. Besides, you'll get cold if I stay out long."

Thor insisted until Hymir gave in. Then Thor asked what they had for bait. "Get your own," the giant answered.

The god tore off the head of Hymir's ox and carried it down to the sea, where Hymir had already launched the boat. Thor got in and started rowing. "Hymir thought there was some impetus from his rowing," Snorri writes. They reached the spot where Hymir usually fished, but Thor insisted on rowing farther and farther, until Hymir began to get nervous. It was dangerous to enter the realm of the Midgard Serpent. Finally, Thor shipped his oars. He baited a big hook with the ox head and threw his line over.

> The Midgard Serpent stretched its mouth round the ox head and the hook stuck into the roof of the serpent's mouth. And when the serpent felt this, it jerked away so hard that both Thor's fists banged down on the gunwale. Then Thor got angry and summoned up his strength, pushed down so hard that he forced both feet through the boat and braced them against the sea-bed, and then hauled the serpent up to the gunwale. And one can claim that a person does not know what a horrible sight is who did not get to see how Thor fixed his eyes on the serpent, and the serpent stared back up at him spitting poison.

The giant Hymir panicked. As Thor raised his hammer to kill the monster, the giant cut Thor's line. The serpent sank into the sea. Thor threw his hammer after it (like a boomerang, Thor's weapon always returns to his hand), "and they say that he struck off its head by the sea-bed," Snorri writes. "But I think in fact the contrary is correct to report to you that the Midgard Serpent lives still and lies in the encircling sea." Thor then hit Hymir, knocking him out of the boat, and waded to shore.

The story of Thor and the Midgard Serpent is alluded to in four skaldic poems written before Iceland and Norway became Christian, between 995 and 1000, so we can be reasonably sure it existed in the pagan past. None of these poems tells much of the story. What they do relate is hidden behind kennings that are nearly impenetrable. One says, "The ugly ring of the side-oared ship's road stared up spitefully at Hrungnir's skull-splitter." And, "Breeze-sender who cut the thin string of gulls' More for Thor did not want to lift the twisted bay-menacer." The "ugly ring" of the sea and the "twisted bay-menacer" are kennings for the Midgard Serpent, but only someone who already knew the story would recognize them. None of the poems is clear about whether the serpent lived or died, and none contains the memorable foot-through-the-boat motif.

Carvings of a human figure in a boat with one foot (not both, as Snorri has it) busting through the bottom and (in one case) something monstrous on the line appear on two runestones in Sweden and Denmark. The stones are undatable but probably pre-Christian. The pictures might refer to this story—hard to say. Runestones are notoriously difficult to interpret. One image has simultaneously been described as Heimdall with his horn, Odin on his high throne, and Saint Olaf on Jacob's Ladder. All that's indisputable about these two stones is that each shows a figure in a boat, or two figures, fishing. On one stone the figure does seem to carry a hammer. A third stone often interpreted as Thor fishing is the tenth-century Gosforth stone in England; it has no foot busting through and no monster. According to some experts, it might instead show Christ calming the Sea of Galilee.

A verse in the *Poetic Edda* also tells of Thor's fishing trip. Again, it is undatable. Some of the thirty-four Eddic verses seem by their archaic language to be very old. These are thought to have been written in Norway, before the founding of Iceland in 870. But the "Song of the Sibyl," which Snorri quotes repeatedly when describing the beginning and end of the world, seems to have been written in Iceland just before the year 1000. Its volcanic landscape is very Icelandic. Several images in the poem have Christian overtones, while its structure and overall approach seem taken from a Latin tradition of sibyls' songs. In one manuscript the last line is a clear reference to Christ: "Then the mighty one will come to divine judgment, powerful, from above, who will rule over all." Reconstructing the pagan Norse religion based on the "Song of the Sibyl" is like reconstructing Christianity based on *Jesus Christ Superstar*.

A runestone from Altuna, Sweden, thought to depict Thor catching the Midgard Serpent. Note Thor's foot protruding through the bottom of the boat. Photo by akg-images.

The oldest manuscript containing the "Song of the Sibyl," as well as "Hymir's Lay," about Thor's fishing trip, is called the *Codex Regius* (King's Book). This manuscript dates to 1270—after Snorri's death but roughly when his nephew Saga-Sturla was writing about Snorri's life and times. The *Codex Regius* is a copy of something older but probably not much older. Scholars believe it is owing to Snorri's influence that the poems of the *Poetic Edda* were set down in writing at all. One fanciful notion is that Snorri sent out teams of poetry collectors on "field trips in the manner of the nineteenth-century folklore collectors." Another theory is that some of the Eddic poems are not ancient examples of pagan verse at all but thirteenth-century imitations, again inspired by—or even written by—Snorri.

"Hymir's Lay" is one of these. Its tale of Thor's fishing trip is longer than Snorri's, and the character of the giant is changed. Thor is not disguised. He is not alone but accompanied by the one-handed god Tyr and the servant boy, Thjalfi. Their purpose in visiting Giantland is to obtain a cauldron big enough to brew ale for all the gods. To win the cauldron Thor must engage in trials of strength, one of which is a fishing contest. When the giant Hymir catches two whales at once, Thor catches the Midgard Serpent to outdo him. There's no tense eyeball-to-eyeball moment in this poem. Nor is Hymir terrified. He doesn't cut the line. When Thor whacks the serpent with his hammer, he doesn't kill it: The worm just roars and sinks into the sea. Thor and the giant row back home, and Thor carries the two whales up to Hymir's hall, but still the giant will not admit he is beaten until Thor breaks his wine goblet, smashing it against the giant's own hard head. Thor picks up the cauldron. It is so heavy his feet break through the wooden floor of the hall (as they did not through the boat). Then Hymir reneges and comes after Thor with a horde of monsters. The mighty Thor wields his hammer mercilessly and kills them all.

Which tale of Thor's fishing trip is the true one, the pagan myth? Probably neither. Several versions of this story and other myths circulated in Snorri's lifetime; some were mere hints in kennings, others well-developed verse or oral tales. Snorri took what he liked and retold them, making things up when need be.

Explaining the beginning of all things, for instance, he tinkered with the role of Ymir, the primordial giant. The idea that his flesh was earth, his blood sea, his bones rocks, his hair trees, his skull the sky, and his thoughts clouds is suspiciously like the cosmology in popular philosophical treatises of the twelfth and thirteenth centuries. These were based on Plato's *Timaeus,* which conceived of the world as a gigantic human body, alive, with a soul. (The detail of Ymir's giant cow does not come from Plato.)

In the story of Sleipnir, the eight-legged horse, Snorri skipped over the crucial fact that the gods broke the mighty oaths they had sworn to the giant builder. In the "Song of the Sybil" that oath-breaking heralds the destruction of the universe. Snorri was more interested in Loki's hilarious predicament as a broodmare and the birth of Odin's splendid horse.

The story of how Skadi picked her bridegroom for his beautiful feet—and how Loki made her laugh—is known only to Snorri. The binding of the wolf

Fenrir and Tyr's loss of a hand is mostly Snorri's invention, as is his tale of how the gods got their dwarf-made treasures (Sif's gold hair, Odin's ring and spear, Freyr's boar and pocket ship, Thor's hammer). Snorri goes into great detail describing Asgard, the gods' home, little of which is supported by any other source.

His tale of the mead of poetry contains a serious misconstrual of an ancient ceremony known from Celtic sources. To consecrate a king, a sacred maiden sleeps with the chosen man, then serves him a ritual drink. Snorri turns it into a comic seduction scene: one night of blissful sex for the lonely giant girl in exchange for one sip of the mead of poetry.

Snorri didn't tell all the myths he liked in the *Edda*. He records one at length in *Heimskringla* but only alludes to it in the "Tricking of Gylfi," as if certain his readers would recognize it. He leaves some stories out that we can't imagine he would overlook—such as the one told in the obscenely funny Eddic poem "Thrym's Lay," in which Thor, to reclaim his stolen ham-mer, pretends to be the goddess Freyja, dressed up in a bridal gown. (It's possible Snorri didn't overlook "Thrym's Lay" but wrote the poem himself as a parody.)

Some of Snorri's myths explain the kennings found in skaldic poems—poems that he alone preserved by including them in his *Edda*. But other myths seem to have nothing to do with kennings. His long comic story of Thor's visit to Utgard-Loki is known from no poem. Fully one-sixth of the "Tricking of Gylfi," it may be entirely Snorri's creation. A poet does refer to Thor hiding in a giant's glove, but it's a different giant. Another mentions Thor's struggle with the knot of a giant's food sack. A kenning for old age refers to Thor's wrestling match with Elli—but it appears in *Egil's Saga*, where Snorri may be quoting himself. Otherwise, the journey and the contests are unknown.

The brilliant character of the giant Utgard-Loki, with his wry attitude to-ward that little fellow Thor who "must be bigger than he looks," may be a stand-in for Snorri himself. They share the same humorous tolerance of the gods. There is little sense throughout the *Edda* that these were gods to be feared or worshipped, especially not the childish, naive, blustering, weak-witted, and fal-lible Thor who is so easily deluded by Utgard-Loki's wizardry of words. What god in his right mind would wrestle with a crone named Old Age? Or expect his servant boy to outrun Thought? It's a story with a moral meant to prick the conscience of a king: *See how foolish you would look,* Snorri is saying to young

King Hakon, *if you didn't understand that words can have more than one mean-ing or that names can be taken literally?*

Another myth Snorri seems to have made up is the poignant death of Baldur the Beautiful. Reading it as a short story, critics have called it Snorri's "greatest achievement as a storyteller" and "the most Virgilian thing in Snorri. The proportions could hardly be bettered." Snorri demonstrates an "unforced control of every element which can contribute to a known and planned-for effect." He shows the same feeling for comic relief as Shakespeare, though not everyone appreciated it: A nineteeth-century scholar slammed "The Death of Baldur" as an absurdity, a grotesque, a burlesque. His colleague in the 1920s castigated Snorri for his "irresponsible treatment" of tradition and questioned his "editorial practice." Snorri, he sniffed, made myths into novellas. That's probably why we remember them.

The god Baldur, Odin's second son, "is best and all praise him," Snorri writes. Baldur is fair and white as a daisy, "and so bright that light shines from him." He is the wisest of the gods, the most eloquent, and the most merciful, "but it is one of his characteristics that none of his decisions can be fulfilled." His palace is called Breidablik (Broad Gleaming): "This is in heaven," Snorri says. Baldur is like the sun in the sky.

One night Baldur began to have bad dreams. Hearing of this, his mother, Frigg, exacted a promise from everything on earth not to hurt him: "Fire and water, iron and all kinds of metal, stones, the earth, trees, diseases, the animals, the birds, poison, snakes," all agreed to leave Baldur alone. After that the gods entertained themselves by using Baldur for target practice. They would "shoot at him or strike at him or throw stones at him. But whatever they did he was unharmed, and they all thought this was a great glory," Snorri writes.

All except Loki the Trickster. He was jealous. He put on a disguise and wormed up to Frigg. "Have all things sworn oaths not to harm Baldur?"

"There grows a shoot of a tree to the west of Valhalla," Frigg replied. "It is called mistletoe. It seemed young to me to demand the oath from."

Loki made a dart of mistletoe and sought out the blind god Hod. "Why are you not shooting at Baldur?"

"Because I cannot see where Baldur is," Hod replied testily.

"I will direct you," Loki offered. He gave Hod the dart. Hod tossed it, and Baldur died. Writes Snorri, "This was the unluckiest deed ever done among gods and men."

Mistletoe? Snorri apparently had no idea what mistletoe was. It does not grow in Iceland, and it is rare in Norway. It is not a tree but a parasitic vine found in the tops of oaks. The Golden Bough of folklore, it was gathered in some cultures at the summer solstice; picking it caused the days to shorten. Originally, it seems, the death of Baldur was a drama of the agricultural year. Snorri did not see it that way. In his mythology time is not cyclical. Baldur does not die off and come back each year like summer. Instead Baldur's death causes Ragnarok, in which the old gods are killed and the old earth destroyed in a fiery cataclysm. The Baldur who rules the reborn earth afterward is not the daisy-white god of summer but a Christ figure. In the "Song of the Sibyl" mistletoe is also Baldur's bane. Snorri didn't make that part up. But the plant's attraction for him (and the "Sibyl" poet) was not any special mythic meaning. What Snorri liked was its name: *Mistilsteinn.* Other Icelandic words ending in *-teinn* referred to swords. And *Mist?* It's the name of a Valkyrie. A plant named Valkyrie's Sword must be deadly.

The "Song of the Sibyl" doesn't say Frigg forced an oath out of everything else on earth. The poem doesn't say Loki wheedled the secret from her or guided blind Hod's hand. No one but Snorri says what happened next: Weeping, Frigg begged someone to ride to Hel and offer the goddess of death a ransom to give Baldur back. Hermod—a god in no other story—volunteered. He took Odin's horse, eight-legged Sleipnir, and set off.

Meanwhile the gods held Baldur's funeral, a strangely comic set piece with many details exclusive to Snorri. They carried his body in procession to the sea, Freyr in his chariot drawn by the golden boar, Freyja in hers, drawn by giant cats. They built Baldur's pyre on his warship, but when they tried to launch it, they could not: Their grief had sapped their strength, and they had to send to Giantland for help. "A great company of frost giants and mountain giants" arrived, including a giantess "riding a wolf and using vipers as reins." Odin called four of his berserks to see to her mount, but "they were unable to hold it without knocking it down," Snorri says. The giantess launched the ship "with the first touch, so that flame flew from the rollers and all lands quaked," performing with a fingertip what all the gods were powerless to accomplish. That made Thor angry. He never liked a giant to one-up him. "He grasped his hammer and was about to smash her head until all the gods begged for grace for her."

Nanna, Baldur's loving wife, then collapsed and died of grief; she was placed on the funeral pyre on the ship beside her husband. (No other source mentions Nanna's death.) The gods led Baldur's horse to the pyre and slaughtered it.

Odin placed his magic ring on Baldur's breast. Then Thor consecrated the pyre with his hammer and it was set alight. Returning to his place, he stumbled on a dwarf. "Thor kicked at him with his foot," Snorri writes, "and thrust him into the fire and he was burned."

The scene shifts back to Hermod's ride to Hel. Snorri was inspired here by the apocryphal story of Christ's Harrowing of Hell, as told in the Gospel of Nicodemus, which was popular in thirteenth-century Iceland. Christ, in the Icelandic translation, rode a great white horse into hell. Hermod rode the eight-legged Sleipnir, also white. He rode for nine nights, through valleys dark and deep, until he reached the river dividing the world from the underworld. He rode onto a bridge covered with glowing gold. The maiden guarding the bridge stopped him. Five battalions of dead warriors had just crossed, but Hermod made more noise. "Why are you riding here on the road to Hel?" she asked. (For Snorri, Hel is both a person and the place she inhabits.)

He was chasing Baldur, Hermod replied. "Have you seen him?"

"Yes, he crossed the bridge. Downwards and northwards lies the road to Hel."

Hermod rode on until he reached Hel's gates. "Then he dismounted from the horse and tightened its girth"—a nice detail showing Snorri really did know horses—"mounted and spurred it on." Sleipnir leaped the gate. Hermod rode up to Hel's great hall, where he found Baldur sitting in the seat of honor. Hermod stayed the night. In the morning he described the great weeping in Asgard and asked Hel if Baldur could ride home with him. (Baldur's horse, burned on the pyre, was safe in Hel's stables.)

Hel is not a monster in Snorri's tale but a queen. She gave it some thought. Was Baldur really so beloved? she wondered. She would put it to the test. "If all things in the world, alive or dead, weep for him," she decreed, "then he shall go back." If anything refuses to weep, he stays in Hel.

The gods "sent all over the world messengers to request that Baldur be wept out of Hel. And all did this, the people and animals and the earth and the stones and trees and every metal, just as you will have seen that these things weep when they come out of frost and into heat," Snorri writes. (He liked to include these little just-so stories.) Everything wept, that is, except a certain ugly giantess. She said her name was Thokk (Thanks) and spoke this verse:

Thokk will weep
Dry tears
At Baldur's embarkation;
The old fellow's son
Was no use to me
Alive or dead,
Let Hel hold what she has.

"It is presumed," Snorri added, "that this was Loki" in disguise. No source is known for this verse; it's likely Snorri's own. Nor does anyone else make Loki the Trickster so clearly responsible for taking Baldur the Beautiful from the world.

With Baldur's death chaos is unleashed. The gods have lost their luck, the end of the world is nigh: Ragnarok, the doom, or twilight, of the gods (scholars disagree on the origin of the word, and so on its meaning). Snorri took the structure of the story of Ragnarok from the "Song of the Sibyl," but he skewed things. In Snorri's account the gods are not grand warriors. Instead they are self-defeated, their every action reeking of futility. By the time Heimdal blows his horn and Odin puts on his golden helmet, the world has been overrun by evil. The gods know they are doomed. Yet they march bravely into battle anyway, Thor shoulder to shoulder with Odin, facing the serpent and the wolf with bitter courage.

Throughout the "Tricking of Gylfi" Snorri gives the myths a subtle Christian coloring, bringing out the correspondences between Norse paganism and Christian teaching. Ragnarok is the gods' doomsday, when the nine worlds are destroyed by fire. But what happens "after heaven and earth and all the world is burned and all the gods and . . . all mankind are dead?" asks King Gylfi, who has been urging the three forms of Odin—High, Just-as-High, and Third—to tell him all these tales. "You said previously that everyone shall live in some world or other forever and ever."

Third replies, "There will then be many mansions" in which mankind will live after Ragnarok. The highest heaven is the Christian-sounding Gimli (Heavenly Abode). Previously Third had told us that Gimli was where All-Father (another name for Odin) lived, the god who made "heaven and earth" and ruled "all things great and small." "But his greatest work is that he made man and gave him a soul that shall live and never perish though the body decay to dust or burn to ashes. And all men who are righteous shall live and dwell with him."

Gimli is not the only heaven. In a place called Never Cold is a feast hall with "plenty of good drink for those that take pleasure in it." (Snorri can't imagine eternity without ale.) There are also several hells: One is "a large and unpleasant hall, and its doors face north. It is also woven out of snakes' bodies like a wattled house, and the snakes' heads all face inside the house and spit poison." There for all eternity will live oath breakers and murderers.

Nor is the end of the world truly the end. "The earth will shoot up out of the sea and will then be green and fair." A new sun will pop into the sky. The gods who are left will reassemble: Two of Odin's sons survived Ragnarok, as did two of Thor's, while Baldur and his killer, the blind god Hod, are released from Hel after the battle. "They will all sit down together and talk and discuss their mysteries"—Snorri can't think of a pleasanter way to pass the time—"and speak of the things that happened in former times," especially of the Midgard Serpent and the wolf Fenrir, those evil monsters who are now dead. "Then they will find in the grass the golden playing pieces" and set up a game of chess. Two humans will also have survived Ragnarok; from them the earth will be repopulated.

It was a tricky thing Snorri was trying to do. Officially, the church labeled Odin—as well as Loki and his monstrous brood—evil. The pagan gods were devils who deliberately tried to lead Christians astray. The myths Snorri saw as so central to skaldic verse were delusions of Satan, not simple entertainments.

Such was the moral of the story of King Olaf Tryggvason's meeting with Odin, as told by Odd Snorrason, the Benedictine monk from Thingeyri monastery in northern Iceland. Odd the Monk was Snorri's source for the passage in *Heimskringla* in which the one-eyed stranger sat by the king's bedside telling stories, "and the king found much pleasure in his talk." Snorri ends his account with the king acknowledging "that this had probably not been any human but Odin, the god heathen men had long worshipped," and insisting that Odin "was not going to succeed in deceiving" Olaf and his men. Odd the Monk's version is much more explicit. The king's guest was

the Fiend, the enemy of all mankind, who changed himself into the form of the wicked Odin, in whom heathen men have for a long time past put their trust,

holding him as their god. He shows by his visit here that he can no longer endure the torment of his burning envy, as he sees the company of his followers fall
away. . . . Wherefore he seeks to catch us in the net of his evil cunning, a net laid
with his crafty tricks. For, by hindering and delaying us from taking rest at the
proper time for sleep, he supposed that we, weighted down by drowsiness, would
disarrange or even neglect the appointed time for divine service.

After which the king promptly goes to church.

Snorri could snip such moralizing out of *Heimskringla* without anyone
making a fuss. The book was about kings, after all. But the *Edda* was not. It
featured those same amusing fables that, King Olaf said, "prevented our sleep
at the proper time" and made us late for church. How could Snorri make such
lore appealing to a Christian king like young Hakon? How could he get it past
the bishops who were Hakon's keepers?

Snorri took two tacks. First, the "Tricking of Gylfi" uses the same narrative device as Chaucer would choose more than a hundred years later to tell
his *Canterbury Tales*: a frame narrative. Chaucer's frame is a group of pilgrims
going to Canterbury to visit the shrine of Saint Thomas Becket; on the way
they tell each other stories, each in a distinctive voice different from Chaucer
the narrator's own. It's a flexible technique that gives authors wide latitude.
They can distance themselves from what their characters say. They can call their
characters fools—or fiends—and still tell their stories.

Snorri's frame is the visit of King Gylfi to the court of Asgard, where he is
tricked by High, Just-as-High, and Third, while he tries to trick them. Snorri
the narrator is not the one answering King Gylfi's questions. Snorri—a good
Christian—would not tell amusing fables of wicked devils. No, the storytellers
are High, Just-as-High, and Third. And who are they? Snorri is vague. They
are "the Aesir-people" who live in a place called Asgard, which is somewhere
not far from Sweden. King Gylfi goes to see them because he is amazed that
they "had the ability to make everything go in accordance with their will. He
wondered whether this could be as a result of their own nature, or whether the
divine powers they worshipped could be responsible." Gylfi does not think the
Aesir people themselves are divine—or at least he's not sure.

Gylfi disguises himself as an old man. He assumes a false name, Gangleri
(Weary of Walking)—which itself is one of Odin's many names. This Gangleri
is not what he seems.

The Aesir saw him coming, Snorri writes, and "prepared deceptive appearances for him."

The grand hall of Valhalla with its roof covered with golden shields is an illusion—or a delusion—as are the three kings sitting there. Because "the High One" is a name for Odin, and Valhalla is Odin's hall, we assume the three are faces of Odin. But Snorri never says so. He says only that High (the lowest of the three) welcomed Gangleri and offered him food and drink. Gangleri "said that he wished first to find out if there was any learned person in there. High said he would not get out unscathed unless he was more learned"—and so the wisdom contest commences. Within the frame of that contest, Snorri can say anything he wants. It's just a game of *Jeopardy!* or *Trivial Pursuit.*

When the contest is over, and Gangleri has exhausted the three kings' store of wisdom, he hears a great crash, and Valhalla disappears. "He found he was standing out on open ground, could see no hall and no castle." Like Thor's visit to Utgard-Loki, it was indeed all a delusion. What had King Gylfi learned? Just a bunch of amusing fables. "He came back to his kingdom," Snorri writes, "and told of the events he had seen and heard about. And from his account these stories passed from one person to another."

Having written his virtuosic praise poem, explained the language of poetry, and filled in the mythological gaps he felt a young poet (or patron of poets) should know, Snorri compiled his book in reverse order: "Tricking of Gylfi," "Language of Poetry," then "Tally of Verse Forms." It wasn't enough. He still couldn't be sure his Christian-educated target would take it the right way, so Snorri wrote a boring prologue to make himself perfectly clear. (It is so boring that scholars used to think someone else had written it.)

"Almighty God created heaven and earth and all things in them," he began, in totally orthodox fashion. But, he continued, men "forgot the name of God and in most parts of the world there was no one to be found who knew anything about his creator." As thinking creatures, people "pondered and were amazed."

After a bit more prehistory and an interlude of geography, Snorri arrives at Troy—which he re-creates with an Icelandic twist. King Priam of Troy, unbeknown to Homer or Virgil, had a grandson called Tror: "We call him Thor." He was "as beautiful to look at when he came among other people as when ivory is inlaid in oak." Thor "explored all quarters of the world and defeated unaided all berserks and giants and one of the greatest dragons." He married golden-haired Sif.

Fifteen generations later a man named Odin was born. He was "an outstanding person for wisdom and all kinds of accomplishments." He set off from Troy with a great following. "They seemed more like gods than men." They conquered Saxland (in Germany), France, Denmark, Sweden, and Norway. To all these countries came peace and prosperity. The men from Asia (as Snorri derives the name Aesir) were taken to be gods.

Why did Snorri place Thor and Odin in Troy? It wasn't his idea. Every European country in the Middle Ages wanted to be founded by a Trojan, thanks to the popularity of Virgil's *Aeneid,* in which Aeneus escapes the Trojan War to found Italy. In the late 1100s, Geoffrey of Monmouth told how Brutus of Troy founded Britain. By the early 1200s, the first Icelandic historian, Ari the Learned, had linked the Aesir to Asia, and the *Skjoldunga Saga,* which may have been written by Snorri's foster brother Bishop Pall, traced the history of Denmark to Troy. Snorri was merely following suit.

His prologue mingles two medieval Christian approaches to the problem of pagan religions. One, the theory of natural religion, argued that pagan religions are imperfect perceptions of the basic truths of Christianity. The wise men of Snorri's prologue were reaching for God but sadly had no teachers. The old religion was a rational, if misguided, groping for truth. The second approach was based on the writings of the Greek philosopher Euhemerus from the fourth century B.C. He argued that the old gods were just exceptional human beings who, as the stories about them grew in the telling, were taken to be divine. Myths, in his view, are just embroidered history. No reason a Christian king like Hakon couldn't enjoy a little ancient history.

But King Hakon may never have read Snorri's *Edda.* We have no record that Snorri sent his masterpiece to Norway—or even that he finished it before he died. As an attempt to secure Snorri a place at Hakon's court, the *Edda,* and the skaldic poetry it tried to revive, was a failure. Once clerics like Odd the Monk were available to write effusive king's sagas in Latin—readable in any court in Europe—why would a king of Norway need a skald? And once a king needed a lengthy treatise, no matter how amusing, just to appreciate the art, skaldic poetry was dead. Unlike Egil Skalla-Grimsson, when Snorri provoked the anger of a king, he could not count on a poem to ransom his head.

Five

INDEPENDENT PEOPLE

Age of axes, age of swords . . . age of winds, age of wolves, until the world
is ruined.

—Snorri, *Edda*

The old gods knew they would die. They knew the monsters
would defeat them—and that Loki the Trickster, once Odin's best friend
and blood brother, would fight on the monsters' side. They knew the signs of
Ragnarok, the signs of their own coming doom.

"Brothers will kill each other out of greed. No one will show mercy to father or son in killing or breaking the taboos of kinship," Snorri writes.

Then comes the Fimbul Winter, mighty and mysterious, with hard frosts
and keen winds and snow drifting in all directions. This winter will last for
three years, with no summers in between. The sun and moon will be eaten by
wolves. The stars will disappear. The earth will shake, mountains will crumble,
oceans overflow.

All fetters and bonds will break. The wolf Fenrir will come ravaging, his
mouth so wide his snout scrapes the sky, while his lower jaw drags in the dirt.
Flames will burn from his nose and eyes. The Midgard Serpent will thrash its
way to land, spitting poison. The sky will split, and Surt will ride through the
gap, wielding his flaming sword, fire giants and troll wives surging behind him.
They will break the rainbow bridge by their passing. On the battle plain they
will join forces with the frost ogres and all of Hel's people, led by the traitor
Loki.

The ash tree Yggdrasil will shake to its roots.

Then the god Heimdall will blow his great horn. The gods will meet in council. Odin, with bitter courage, will don his golden helmet and his fine coat of mail, pick up his spear, and arrange their battle array: He will face the wolf Fenrir and be swallowed whole. Thor will fight the Midgard Serpent and slay it—but be felled in turn by its poisonous breath. Freyr will duel with Surt but lose for lack of his good sword, the one he bargained away to bed a giantess, and Surt will fling fire over the earth and burn the world to cinders.

It would ultimately be reborn, a new green earth rising from the sea. But without Odin, the one-eyed wizard-king, and his companions, nothing would be the same.

On the quay at Bergen in the autumn of 1220, Baron Snorri had bragged to King Hakon and Earl Skuli that there were no greater men in Iceland than his brothers, Thord and Sighvat Sturluson, and his foster brother Saemund of Oddi. Snorri claimed they "would follow his advice entirely" when he returned home. He had been overconfident. Rather than trot in his tracks, his brothers and Saemund did their best to stymie Snorri's plans, whether those were to place Iceland under the king's rule or just to adjudicate the case of the Bergen merchants versus the men of Oddi.

While building was progressing at Reykholt in the year 1221, Snorri lived at Stafholt, where the valley widened out, its lush flat pastures contoured by lava outcrops and enclosed by the lazy bends of the North River and the ox-bows of the Hvita. Dominating the horizon to the north was a steep-sided cone in the strange grayish color that in a horse is called blue dun. Steam rising from the voluminous hot spring at Deildar-Tunga was clear against the sky to the east. Away to the west sat fortress-like Borg, with its harbor on the narrow fjord that opened to the sea.

At Stafholt, Snorri's brother Sighvat sought him out concerning the men of Oddi. Bjorn, who had dragged the Norwegian out of the church, had just been killed in a fight with his kinsman Loft. Snorri's gleeful poem about it—*Bjorn's been stroked / by a sharp caress—/ grand touch was that*—was going around, and Loft was sure to count on Snorri's aid when Bjorn's avengers got organized. Sighvat did not want Snorri to help Loft. He was adamant about it. Whether Sighvat threatened Snorri or bought him off we don't know, only that Snorri agreed to remain neutral. As Saga-Sturla wrote in *Sturlunga Saga* many years later, when Sighvat returned home, "his friends asked how things had gone between him and Snorri. Sighvat said that when they met, Snorri had an axe raised over his shoulder, so sharp that it looked as if it could slice anything at all; ' . . . then I took a whetstone out of my pouch, and I rubbed it along the edge; and after that the axe was so much blunted that before we parted it shone upon me.'"

Snorri also quarreled with his brother Thord, after their mother died late in 1221 at the age of seventy-three. Except for a woodland that brother Sighvat claimed (his farm was closest; he got there first), the wealth she left behind was in jewels and gold and clothes and other valuable things she'd brought with her when she moved to Reykholt three years before. Snorri claimed them. He'd never received his inheritance from his father, after all; she'd spent it. His brother Thord was miffed. Hadn't their mother promised her money to her grandson, his little Saga-Sturla, then age seven? Thord stopped speaking to his brother for three years. Not until 1224 did Snorri patch things up between them, inviting Thord to a magnificent feast. "He said that he wanted them to put aside all their differences" and that they "should never part on a question of property." He had an ulterior motive. Snorri then asked Thord to join him in wresting control of their father's chieftaincy from Sighvat and his son.

Bishop Gudmund the Good also did his part to split up the three Sturlung brothers. While Snorri was in Norway, Gudmund tried to establish a school at Holar, as the archbishop of Trondheim had suggested. Gudmund's enemies burst into Holar, kidnapped him, and held him all winter in secret, intending to send him back to Norway in the spring. Just before the ship sailed, Gudmund's friends discovered his prison and freed him. The bishop resumed his wandering. When Snorri returned from Norway in 1220, he found Gudmund in the South at Oddi. The next year Snorri's brother Thord saw Gudmund reinstated to his see at Holar. Once again hundreds of hungry beggars flocked to the generous bishop. The nearby farmers began to stew—when the bishop's stores ran out, those beggars would cause trouble. Sighvat's twenty-four-year-old son, Tumi, played on their fears. He was angry at his father, who refused to set him up with an estate, and decided to take over Holar as his inheritance. With a nod from the locals, he drove the bishop and his flock away and settled in.

The bishop fled to some islands, where—as the farmers foresaw—he soon ran out of supplies. One winter night, when "the weather was thick and dark," Saga-Sturla writes, "thirty men . . . broke out from the islands; they were all rather rash men." They sailed to Holar in two ships and took Tumi by surprise, "for Tumi's men had said that the wind would keep watch for them." The bishop had sent them to steal food. They were a bit overzealous. They set fire to the buildings. When Tumi and his men ran out of the blaze, begging for quarter, the bishop's men caught them. They killed Tumi and two others; two more had a leg cut off.

Sighvat's revenge for his son was brutal. Just after Easter he gathered three hundred warriors and sailed to Grimsey, the island where Bishop Gudmund was hiding. The bishop had with him seventy armed men, thirty women and servants, and several priests. Sighvat led one party of warriors, his son Sturla Battle-Strong another. They killed twelve of the bishop's men outright and maimed others, gelding two priests. Gudmund, captured, prayed that God would avenge them—and apparently he did: One of Sighvat's ships sank on the return trip and thirty men drowned. Despite his brother Thord's vehement objections, Sighvat forced Bishop Gudmund to sail to Norway that summer. The bishop remained abroad for several years.

Saemund of Oddi, Snorri's foster brother, also did not follow Snorri's lead. In the feud between Saemund's two kinsmen, Bjorn and Loft, Saemund stayed scrupulously neutral—and was lampooned for it. Loft, backed by no chieftain and facing outlawry for killing Bjorn, was in hiding when this ditty went around:

> Loft is in the islands
> Gnawing puffin bones.
> Saemund in the highlands
> Eats berries there alone.

If Saemund had once hoped to fill the shoes of his father, Jon Loftsson, as uncrowned king of Iceland, his chances ended here. He was a laughingstock.

But Snorri—also forced to stay neutral—unexpectedly came out ahead. With Bjorn dead, Loft exiled abroad, and Saemund shamed, the dispute between the men of Oddi and the Bergen merchants died out, its questions unresolved: Had the merchants of Bergen conspired to drown Saemund's son Pall? Had Saemund been within his rights to demand compensation, when the merchants came to Iceland to trade? Had the merchants, on the other hand, been justified in killing Saemund's brother Orm to avenge what they saw as theft and extortion? Or in setting a trade embargo on Iceland when Orm's son-in-law, Bjorn, dragged a Norwegian out of a church and killed him? On the quay at Bergen in 1220, Snorri had promised King Hakon and Earl Skuli that he would convince the Icelanders to "ask King Hakon to intercede for them," allowing the king to settle the dispute. Even though Snorri, having "made no headway with his countrymen . . . did not press the issue," as Saga-Sturla writes in *King Hakon's Saga*, "nonetheless the merchants enjoyed peaceful conditions at this time in Iceland." Snorri knew to leave well enough alone. Trade between Norway and Iceland resumed. The king even sent over his falconers, who spent the years 1223 to 1225 catching silver gyrfalcons to send to England. Snorri's son, Jon Trout, whom he had sent to Norway in 1221 "as a hostage to the earl, until things should work out as had been stipulated," according to *Sturlunga Saga*, was sent home in 1224. Snorri's vow to the king and the earl of Norway was fulfilled.

Or was it? The events of these years could be interpreted in another way. For in addition to writing the *Edda* and parts of *Heimskringla*—which in some ways is a manual of kingship—Snorri spent the 1220s creating marriage alliances with Iceland's up-and-coming chieftains, weaving himself a new web of power that did not depend on his recalcitrant brothers or the feckless men of Oddi. To bring the land under the king, he first had to bring it under himself: Only from the strong footing of uncrowned king of Iceland could he easily step up to being earl.

In 1221 he resumed his post of lawspeaker; he would keep it until 1231. He advertised his willingness to settle disputes, as Jon Loftsson had. The settlements generally, though not always, worked in his favor. When Saemund died of sickness in the winter of 1222, for example, Snorri was asked by Saemund's brood—all illegitimate—to distribute his wealth fairly. Early the next year he rode south with a large retinue. They spent the night at the farm of Keldur on the way to Oddi, where Saemund's young daughter Solveig and her mother lived. Solveig was the girl with whom, Saga-Sturla reports, Snorri "found it altogether delightful" to talk. The implication is that the fat and gouty forty-five-year-old schemer had fallen head over heels for this snip of a girl. Next morning the two rode together to Oddi. On the road they met another young woman, Solveig's cousin Hallveig. The funny little tale Saga-Sturla tells about this rendezvous has sparked years of speculation. Who was Saga-Sturla's source? The writer was only eight years old when the incident occurred. Did he hear the story from Solveig in her later years? If so, why did Solveig make fun of her cousin? Was it she who had fallen in love with Snorri, with his clever tales of gods and kings? Was she jealous of Hallveig?

Hallveig Ormsdottir was the wealthiest woman in Iceland, having inherited from her father, her uncle, and her husband. But she was accompanied by only one man. Worse, she was dressed quite unfashionably, in a blue woolen cape "with the flaps sewn together over her head." She "wore it as a sort of hat." According to Saga-Sturla, "Snorri thought her appearance somewhat ludicrous and smiled at it." It's more likely that Solveig criticized her cousin's dress, while Snorri thought it ludicrous for the wealthiest woman in Iceland to have no entourage.

Did they meet by chance? Probably not. Hallveig was the illegitimate daughter of Snorri's foster brother Orm Jonsson, who had been murdered by the Norwegian merchants. She was the widow of Bjorn, whom Loft's henchman had killed with Snorri's encouragement. She had two small sons. She blamed Snorri for her bereavement and looked to him to make amends. Hearing he was in the district, she rushed out in her everyday clothes, with just one bodyguard, to accost him. But if they spoke, their words were not remembered. His enigmatic smile at her appearance is all we hear about Snorri's first meeting with the woman he would later make his partner in life—they never married—for fourteen years and at whose death he was paralyzed by grief.

Snorri rode on to Oddi, where he divided Saemund's estate to everyone's satisfaction, though he seems to have favored Solveig. Not only did she receive as much as her six brothers, following her father's wishes, but she was allowed to choose first. Saga-Sturla does not mention Saemund's other three daughters. He implies that Snorri had plans for Solveig, perhaps to marry her himself, perhaps to wed her to his son and heir, Jon Trout. In addition to her newfound riches and her conversational skills, Solveig had attractive bloodlines: She was descended, through Jon Loftsson, from King Magnus Bare-Legs of Norway. To have royal blood—or at least to be linked to it through marriage—was required for an earl, not to mention a king, according to thirteenth-century thinking.

But Snorri's plans for Solveig, if any, were thwarted by his brother Sighvat. Sighvat's wife was niece to Thorvald of Haukadale, the leading chieftain in the South of Iceland now that Saemund of Oddi was dead. Thorvald was the brother of Bishop Magnus of Skalholt. More to the point, he was the father of Bjorn, at whose death Snorri had gloated in verse (*grand touch was that*), and

therefore guardian of Bjorn's rich widow, Hallveig. Hallveig's cousin Solveig
also turned to Thorvald of Haukadale for support, entrusting to him her newly
won inheritance. Learning of this through his wife's gossip channels, Snorri's
brother Sighvat raced south and negotiated a match between Solveig and his
son Sturla Battle-Strong. Thorvald held the wedding feast at Haukadale just
after Easter in 1223. Snorri was not invited. Writes Saga-Sturla, "Snorri was
displeased when he learned of Sturla's marriage, and people thought that he
had had something else in mind."

Snorri predictably got back at his brother in the law courts. A feud had
embroiled the men of the West Fjords, in Iceland's Northwest. Both Snorri's
brothers, Thord and Sighvat, were involved, as were four of their nephews, the
sons of their half-sisters. Snorri and Thord supported their nephews, while
Sighvat—and particularly his son Sturla Battle-Strong—had made a pact with
their enemy, another Thorvald, the chieftain of Vatnsfjord. At the Althing in
June 1223 Snorri outlawed Thorvald and stripped him of his chieftaincy.

Sighvat rode to Stafholt, this time with a humbler attitude than when he'd
boasted of taking a whetstone to Snorri's imaginary axe. He had three goals, he
said: for Snorri to gain prestige, for Thorvald of Vatnsfjord to be cleared of all
charges, and for Sturla "to acquire such honor as he demanded." Snorri seemed
amenable. They made a deal, and Sighvat went home. Thorvald's outlawry was
lifted and his chieftaincy restored.

Young Sturla's honor, on the other hand, got short shrift: Snorri had no
intention of keeping that promise. Throughout the winter Snorri worked to
destroy Thorvald's friendship with Sturla Battle-Strong. Multiple messages
passed between them until, by spring, "Thorvald thought he understood that
Snorri would grant him very great honor if he undertook whatever Snorri
might ask of him, no matter against whom." They clinched their new understanding with a wedding: At Stafholt, in the autumn of 1224, Thorvald married
Snorri's illegitimate daughter Thordis, then eighteen.

Snorri was never suffused with fatherly feelings when marrying off his
daughters. He thought only of strategy, never of romance. In this case it would
have been far nicer of him to wed the girl to one of Thorvald's sons, who were
in their teens. But Thorvald of Vatnsfjord controlled the West Fjords. He had
been the unchallenged leader there since 1213, when he murdered the uni-
versally admired chieftain, physician, and scholar Hrafn Sveinbjarnarsson by
burning his house down around his ears. As Snorri once said to his nephews,

they "would never be able to get justice . . . while Thorvald was alive; he said that Thorvald oppressed everyone there in the west." To the casual reader of *Sturlunga Saga,* Thorvald is most memorable from the time those nephews, inspired by Snorri's words, tried to kill him. When they attacked his house, Thorvald was fast asleep, nestled between his two mistresses. Two of his men died defending him before he awoke. He slipped on a woman's dress and ran out of the bedroom. It was pitch dark. The man guarding the door thought he was a girl and let him go. He ran until he reached the next farm, leaving his men—and his mistresses, one of whom was wounded in the fracas—to fend for themselves.

Snorri had yet one more pawn in the game, his illegitimate sixteen-year-old daughter, Ingibjorg. The daughter of Gudrun, who was lovelier than a swan, Ingibjorg seems at first to have been luckier than her sister: She was not given to an old man. Ingibjorg was key to Snorri's deal with the other Thorvald, the chieftain of Haukadale. To undermine the southerner's friendship with Sturla Battle-Strong, Snorri promised to wed Ingibjorg to Thorvald's fifteen-year-old son, Gissur. Snorri also made a match for himself: Thorvald agreed to persuade his ward, rich Hallveig Ormsdottir, to "become Snorri's partner and live in his household." Though it was not officially a marriage (Snorri was still legally married to Herdis of Borg), Hallveig and Snorri marked their relationship by donating a set of bells to ring the hours at the Reykholt church, as recorded in its inventory. Finally, the two chieftains pledged to found a monastery on the island of Videy. Thorvald of Haukadale would resign his chieftaincy, enter the cloister there, and turn his power over to his son—Snorri's new son-in-law.

Like a chess master preparing his moves several turns ahead, Snorri had bound to himself nearly all Iceland. As measures of a chieftain's power, wealth counted, and lands, along with the number of chieftaincies he held. But most important were his alliances with other chieftains, through blood, fosterage, or marriage. Snorri's blood relatives were split between supporting him and preferring Sturla Battle-Strong. Snorri no longer had any ties with his foster family at Oddi. But his marriage alliances were impressive. When Snorri married Herdis, who still ruled Borg, he had gained control of the West of Iceland. Through their daughter Hallbera, married off before he went to Norway, he controlled the Southwest. His daughter Thordis gave him the Northwest, his daughter Ingibjorg the South. And he still had two unmarried sons: his legitimate heir, Jon Trout, and the illegitimate Oraekja.

The queen from a chess set carved during Snorri's lifetime. According to the most recent theory, the chessmen were made at Skalholt in Iceland. They were discovered on the Scottish Isle of Lewis in 1831 and now reside in the British Museum, London. Photo by akg-images.

True, his daughter Hallbera showed a little too much spunk at about this time—she left her much older husband, Arni the Quarrelsome, when he and Jon Trout returned from Norway in 1224—but Snorri took it in stride. He was not a cruel father, only a self-centered one. He did not force Hallbera to stay in the marriage, even though Arni was "a great friend" of the king of Norway's. Instead Snorri took her side. We don't know if she argued that Arni "was unable to give her satisfaction," as in the famous divorce scene from *Njal's Saga*, but Snorri did name Arni as the guilty party (they had no children). He won for Hallbera a full half of the couple's wealth, including Arni's main estate and half of his chieftaincy. Three years later Snorri made another political match for his only legitimate daughter, giving twenty-six-year-old Hallbera to eighteen-year-old Kolbein the Young. Nephew of the Kolbein who had battled Gudmund the Good, Kolbein the Young was the ambitious heir to a rich chieftaincy in the North—and so in direct competition with Snorri's nephew, Sturla Battle-Strong.

To all appearances Snorri had chosen these alliances well. His sons-in-law were wealthy and well connected. The two youngest, Kolbein and Gissur, would prove to be exceptional leaders. Counting his partner Hallveig Ormsdottir's vast property and her former husband's chieftaincy (which Snorri held in trust for her two young sons), Snorri now had influence over three-quarters of the country. It seemed a good plan for a man who aspired to be uncrowned king— or earl—of Iceland.

Not everyone agreed.

Snorri's brother Thord—who was something of a seer, at least in his son's telling—went out of his way to warn Snorri against moving Hallveig into his household. Thord feared, Saga-Sturla writes, that "it might lead to Snorri's losing his life"; his prophecy would prove true.

Snorri was also warned about his sons-in-law. One evening in the summer of 1228 Snorri was lounging in his hot tub at Reyholt in the company of some friends or guests, and "the talk was about chieftains." As Saga-Sturla writes, "Men said that there was no chieftain like Snorri and that no one else could compete with him, on account of his many kinsmen. Snorri agreed that his kinsmen were not unimportant. Sturla Bardarson, who had been standing guard at the bath, led Snorri to the house, and shot this half-verse over his shoulder so that Snorri heard it:

> You have similar in-laws
> As had aforetime—
> Injustice always proves
> Ill—the clever king of Hleidr."

Sturla Bardarson, the peg-legged poet, deacon, and Snorri's nephew by his much older half-sister, certainly was not fond of Snorri's son-in-law Thorvald of Vatnsfjord: Thorvald's men had cut off his leg in 1213. How the poet reached his conclusions, however apt, about the younger two, Gissur of Haukadale and Kolbein the Young, is not known. Deacon Sturla was Snorri's trusted bodyguard, as well as one of the clerics who wrote out Snorri's books and discussed poetry with him. Perhaps on this night he held Snorri's velvet robe and silk slippers while his aristocratic boss luxuriated in his warm bath beneath the walls of Reykholt. Like a courtier accompanying a king, Deacon Sturla led Snorri to the house, through the hidden door, along the stone-lined tunnel, up the spiral stair into Snorri's private studio. And, just in case Snorri took all that pomp and ceremony too seriously, he gave Snorri a piece of his mind. His "not unimportant" kinsmen were as treacherous as those of the legendary king of Hleidr, Hrolf Kraki, whom Snorri had—perhaps just that week—written about.

In his *Edda,* Snorri mentioned King Hrolf to explain why poets called gold "Kraki's seed." Hrolf's mother had remarried; her new husband was King Adils of Uppsala, who was at war with the king of Norway, Snorri wrote. When the king called for his new stepson's aid, promising to reward him well, Hrolf sent his twelve berserks, who fought a great battle on the ice, killed the king of Norway, and routed his army. But when it came time for Adils to pay up, he reneged. Hrolf Kraki marched into his mother's hall, but King Adils had the fires heaped so high the men's clothes were singed. The king taunted his stepson, saying, "Is it true that Hrolf Kraki and his berserks flee neither fire nor iron?"

Hrolf threw his shield on the fire and leaped over it. "He flees not fires who leaps over them."

His berserks did the same. Then they shoved King Adils's men into the blaze.

Hrolf Kraki's mother handed him a gold arm-ring and a drinking horn filled with gold bits. She bade him ride for his life. He and his men leaped onto horses, but King Adils and his warriors were close behind. Then Hrolf Kraki shook the horn, strewing gold across the road like a farmer sowing grain: That is why gold is called Kraki's seed. The Swedish warriors leaped from their saddles to pick it up, but King Adils rode on at a furious pace. Hrolf threw down the gold arm-ring, and King Adils checked his pace enough to pick it up with the point of his spear, at which Hrolf Kraki jeered, "Now I have made him who is greatest among the Swedes grovel like a pig."

Stepfathers who refuse to pay their stepsons what they promised and who try to kill their kinsmen by burning them to death. Stepsons who murder their stepfathers' men. Kinsmen who jeer at and insult each other and argue to the death about gold. Being compared to Hrolf Kraki was not a compliment.

"There was no chieftain like Snorri" in 1228 "on account of his many kinsmen." No one could compete with him—except those kinsmen, and they did.
Though Snorri was richer than anyone in Iceland, honor and power were not
to be bought. Of Snorri's four sons-in-law, three would take part in his murder
in 1241, along with one of his stepsons. The son-in-law who didn't was by then
already dead.

Snorri's fiercest rival for the title of uncrowned king (or earl) was his
nephew Sturla Battle-Strong, the eldest of Sighvat's six living sons. Snorri's
daughters' marriages were all aimed at neutralizing the charismatic Sturla, and
Snorri did not stop there.

Despite Snorri's objections, his brother had given their father's chieftaincy to his son Sturla upon his marriage in 1223. Snorri complained to their
brother Thord, who as the eldest of the three Sturlusons had the most right to
be chieftain of Hvamm. But peaceful Thord did not see the problem. His only
legitimate son, Bodvar, Thord told Snorri, had a "perfectly adequate" chieftaincy coming to him. His other sons were young and illegitimate. He "was
not even certain that they deserved" to be chieftains. Snorri, with control of
all or part of eight chieftaincies, could certainly find one to give to his only
legitimate son, Jon Trout, Thord implied. Snorri's illegitimate son, Oraekja,
might not deserve one.

To Snorri, Thord was living in the past. The days of one-man, one-
chieftaincy were over. No single chieftaincy was "perfectly adequate." His plan
to bring the country under the king of Norway (or at least under himself)
called for Snorri to control as many chieftaincies as possible—in his own name,
through his sons-in-law, or through his sons.

But Snorri could play with Thord's idea that chieftaincies go only to
those who deserve them. After much lobbying he convinced Thord that Sturla
Battle-Strong did not deserve his grandfather's chieftaincy. (Sturla's attack on
Gudmund the Good in 1222 may have played a role in this decision, since pi-
ous Thord greatly admired the bishop.) In 1227 Thord, as head of the family,
formally claimed the chieftaincy. As arranged, he gave Jon Trout two-thirds
(Snorri immediately took it over), keeping one part for his own son, Bodvar.
Afterward "there was great hostility between Sturla and his kinsmen," Saga-
Sturla writes.

As a youth Saga-Sturla idolized his older cousin and namesake. Sturla Battle-Strong was everything Snorri Sturluson was not: a true Viking. He first appears in *Sturlunga Saga* in his grandmother Gudny's dream. Sighvat's wife was overdue with her second child, and Gudny, concerned, kept sending for news. One night she dreamed a man came to Hvamm and announced that the baby had been born and was named Vigsterk (Battle-Strong). Gudny woke to the news that her grandson had indeed been born in the night but was named Sturla after his grandfather.

Sturla Battle-Strong next appears at age eighteen. His father had moved away from the West of Iceland (to be farther from his two brothers) and settled in the North Quarter at a farm called Grund. One of the new neighbors had a famous sword, Byrnie-Biter, that had come from Constantinople. Sturla Battle-Strong wanted the sword, but the farmer refused to sell it. One day Sturla and two men rode to the farm. He sneaked into the farmer's private room and took Byrnie-Biter, but before he could unsheath the sword to look at it, a priest raised a hue and cry. The farmer and the rest of his household "came streaming out, women and men; everyone meant to hang on to the sword, and the throng of people shoved Sturla back outdoors. The sword was twisted from his grasp." Sturla had his battle-axe with him. He swung it up over his shoulder, and the hammer end struck the farmer in the head. He fell senseless "and lay a long while as if dead." Sturla rode home. When his father asked him the news, "Sturla said it was nothing to speak of," but his companions tattled. Sighvat scolded his son severely, even threatening to send him away. But that night he called Sturla privately to him: "This matter doesn't seem as bad to me as I am pretending," he said, "but I have to raise a big outcry." Sighvat was in fact proud of his son—like Egil Skalla-Grimsson's mother, when that budding six-year-old berserk axed a bigger boy. Sturla "had the makings of a real Viking."

Sighvat gave Sturla an estate to manage, Saudafell in the Dales, and by 1221 the twenty-two-year-old warrior was riding south at the head of the Dalesmen to support Thorvald of Haukadale in his attempt to catch and outlaw Loft. People said that "no company had been better behaved than that which Sturla had. He showed himself well intentioned and manly in this affair and gained great respect there in the south." On this trip Sturla first set eyes on his future wife, Solveig, the daughter of Saemund of Oddi, though Sturla "spoke little or nothing to her." It's tempting to blame the hatred between Snorri and his nephew on beautiful Solveig, with whom both men fell in love at first sight, but much more was at stake.

Sturla's reputation was further enhanced by the attack on Grimsey Island in 1222 to avenge his brother Tumi's death at the hands of Bishop Gudmund's men. Sturla leaped from his boat and singled out a man named Aron. As they dueled Sturla wounded Aron badly in the face, but then he slipped on some seaweed; Aron would have killed him if another man had not thrust a shield in the way. Sturla rallied his men "and an assault was made on Aron in which so many spears struck at him that he scarcely could fall." Sturla left him on the beach for dead, but Aron was healed and escaped to Norway. In commemorating the battle the cowardly poet Gudmund Oddson overlooked the fact that Sturla had ganged up on Aron:

> *Sturla the mighty—*
> *The raven ravages the dead;*
> *Christ alone rules glory—*
> *Has avenged Tumi now.*
> *The fortune-blessed Sturla,*
> *Seafaring chastiser,*
> *Has wholly repaid*
> *Robbers and truce-breakers.*

A year later Snorri concluded that "Sturla the Mighty" was getting a little too mighty and determined to take their family's hereditary chieftaincy away from him. By the summer of 1228 Snorri had succeeded. Just after that evening in the hot tub at Reykholt when "the talk was about chieftains," Snorri rode to the Dales to exact an oath of loyalty from the farmers there.

He traveled with three hundred men, including his son-in-law Thorvald of Vatnsfjord. Snorri's brother Thord joined them with 150 more men. As they rode north, one of Snorri's companions related a dream he'd had to Snorri's young nephew, Saga-Sturla, now fourteen and part of the war party. "He dreamed that he seemed to be riding with a troop into the Dales," Saga-Sturla wrote many years later. "He seemed to see coming to meet the troop a large, broad-faced woman, and he thought he could make out an evil smell from her." The Valkyrie gave an ominous warning:

Now must axe-edge
Sharpen our mood.
This we two know.
Do you know more?

Sturla Battle-Strong, warned of their coming by his uncle Thord, left the district but sent out spies. One confronted Thorvald of Vatnsfjord: Would Sturla be safe if he came home? Quipped Thorvald, "I hardly expect he will be able to stay long in his bath." That remark would soon have its echo.

Snorri's men fanned out through the Dales, summoning the farmers to a central location. There they all took the oath, vowing to support Snorri at the Althing or whenever he might call upon them. Snorri's forces then split up.

Thorvald of Vatnsfjord headed home to the West Fjords. Before he left, Snorri's brother Thord, in his role of seer, took him aside. Thord warned Thorvald to beware of the sons of Hrafn, the chieftain Thorvald had burned to death in his house fifteen years earlier. Thorvald on that occasion had spared Hrafn's young sons. The boys were now grown. They had never accepted the settlement that Thorvald—with Thord's help—had made with their family (part of which required Thorvald to go to Rome, where he had been absolved of his crime by the pope himself).

Thorvald shrugged off Thord's warning. "Nothing so trifling will govern my fate."

He was wrong. The feud was no longer just between him and Hrafn's sons; it was part of the much larger struggle for control of all Iceland.

Hrafn's sons had become friends with Sturla Battle-Strong at about the same time as Thorvald had spurned Sturla's friendship in favor of the marriage pact with Snorri. Hrafn's sons had even given Sturla their right to a chieftaincy in the West Fjords.

Sturla's spies tracked Thorvald's movements. When Thorvald sent his son and a good part of his men off on an errand—to arrange a horse fight for the next Sunday—Sturla got word to Hrafn's sons.

Thorvald traveled blithely on. He stopped to visit a friend at a farm called Gillastad. A woman next door was startled when a stranger burst into her kitchen and took a flaming brand from her cooking fire. "What do you want that for?" she asked.

"To warm Thorvald's bath," the man answered.

Nursing the flame, Hrafn's sons rode on to Gillastad and set fires in several places. Skeggi, the farmer, went out at dawn and found his cattle crowded close to the house. He called his farmhands—then noticed men among the cows. He ran inside. "We're under attack," he told Thorvald, "but there aren't many of them." Thorvald said more would likely show up. "The wall of the privy isn't solid," Skeggi said. "We can easily knock through and sneak out there." Thorvald shook his head. They'd be watching that wall, too.

The house began to blaze up. Thorvald went to the kitchen, where the flames were worst. "He threw himself over the fire and stretched out his hands before him like a cross; later men found him there." A woman, perhaps one of his mistresses, was dead beside him. Hrafn's sons let everyone else escape the fire. Thordis, Snorri's daughter, was apparently overcome by smoke. Men went in after her and dragged her out through a hole they knocked in a wall. Thordis and Thorvald's one-year-old son, Einar (Snorri's only legitimate grandchild), is not mentioned as having been with them on this journey.

Hrafn's sons rode straight to Sturla Battle-Strong. He sent them on to his father, Sighvat, who welcomed them warmly, according to *Sturlunga Saga*. At the same time Sturla sent a messenger to Snorri to announce the killing and ask for a truce. "Snorri was to grant it in his own name, in that of his son and of his brother Thord, as well as in the name of the men of Vatnsfjord." Snorri deputized the priest Styrmir the Wise to make the truce, but Sturla "thought that was not safe and would not grant such a truce."

Snorri sent his son Jon Trout north to fetch his half-sister Thordis and her child, but she refused to return to her father's house. Leaving the estate at Vatnsfjord in the care of Thorvald's sons (the oldest of whom was about eighteen), Thordis moved to a farm Thorvald had owned farther west—farther out of her father's orbit. There she followed in the footsteps of her strong-minded grandmothers. She did not remarry but entertained a lover or two.

Sturla Battle-Strong, meanwhile, offered compensation to Thorvald's sons for the killing. They refused it. As autumn darkened into winter, messages flew between Vatnsfjord and Reykholt. In mid-January, Thorvald's sons made their move. They gathered fifty men and announced they were going south to see Snorri. One night they altered course. They broke into a farmstead, tied everyone up, took several flaming brands, and rode straight to Sturla's farm of

Saudafell. "The troop was so enthusiastic," writes Saga-Sturla, "that every man kept urging on the next. None held back." They made a great deal of noise. Most of them, after all, were teenaged boys.

Sturla wasn't home—he had been warned—and inside were mostly women. Writes Saga-Sturla: "At that time the homestead of Saudafell was splendid: the hall was hung throughout with tapestries and equipped with shields in front of the tapestries, while the byrnies hung in front of the women's quarters. Solveig, the mistress of the house, had had a child shortly before, and she had then risen from her bed and lay in the main room. Her daughter Thurid, and her mother Valgerd, with many other people, were also there."

The war party broke into the house "with blows and curses and fell upon everything that was in front of them." They tore through the bedrooms, piercing the mattresses with swords. The priest tried to protect himself with a pillow "while they were jabbing and stabbing at him." The poet saved himself by hiding in the rafters. Writes Saga-Sturla, "It was piteous to hear the women and the wounded men."

Thorvald's sons ransacked the house, calling for Sturla's head. They shook their bloody weapons at Solveig, threatening to carry her off with them. Convinced, finally, that Sturla was not at home, they turned to plundering, smashing open chests and seizing their contents. They took two axes and two gold-inlaid spears. They took the shields, tying them together in packs. They stole all the horses they could catch. A quick-thinking servant woman saved Solveig's jewelry box. When a man demanded it, she shamed him into leaving it behind by pretending it was filled with a medicinal salve. The old woman "whose breasts were hewn off, would have suffered enough even if she were able to get the salve in the chest," she said.

When word reached Sturla, he was in his bath. He asked immediately if Solveig had been harmed. Hearing she was safe, he said nothing more. He rode home to find fifteen wounded; three soon died, including the old woman who had been so gruesomely maimed. "Blood ran through the whole house, all the drink had been poured out, and everything that the enemy could lay hand on was destroyed."

News of the raid on Saudafell sped around the country, provoking comments in verse. Sturla's poet, Gudmund Oddson, started the contest with his ditty about hiding in the rafters, trembling in fear.

Snorri replied; his verse was sneering. Turning Gudmund's idioms on end, he implied that Sturla deserved what he got. Snorri mocked Sturla as his

father's tool and praised Thorvald's sons for remembering their murdered father, though Snorri suggested they hadn't gone far enough with this little farmhouse brawl. Overconfident of his own popularity, Snorri made no effort to
distance himself from the raid.

Another Reykholt poet responded to Snorri. Gudmund Galtason's loyalty was torn: He had been friends with Hrafn, whom Thorvald had burned
to death in 1213 and whose sons had reopened the feud by burning Thorvald.
Gudmund agreed with Snorri's accusations against Sturla but warned that the
raid was serious, not to be dismissed as a brawl.

Both poems were artful and complex as only skaldic verse can be. When
they were recited at Saudafell, Sturla's poet dropped his clowning. In an equally
refined verse he twisted Snorri's and Gudmund's phrasing to argue that
Thorvald's sons had indeed remembered their father in the raid: Thorvald was
just as brutal, plundering his neighbors, ruling the West Fjords by terror, picking on unarmed women and servants. And who put the boys up to it? "The
men of the district talk suspiciously of Snorri."

Sturlunga Saga records six more verses. One came from the chieftain who
dominated the East Quarter, the only part of Iceland where Snorri had no toe-
hold. Another came from Arni the Quarrelsome, Snorri's former son-in-law,
in the Southwest. A third was ascribed to Sturla himself. The final three were
composed by two farmers in the Dales. "Everyone judged Snorri harshly," Saga-
Sturla writes, "if he had been party to the raid."

The poems don't give Snorri that *if*. They judge Snorri quite harshly, not
only for trying to kill his own nephew but for sending boys to do his dirty
work. Four verses focus on Ysja, the old woman whose breasts were cut off in
the melee. What warriors these Thorvaldssons are! They avenged their father
by torturing a helpless beggarwoman. The poems would be comic if the details
weren't so distressing.

Two verses are by the same man and show how public opinion changed as
the full story came out. In the first verse he praises the boys for the boldness of
their deed and crows that Sturla fled rather than face them. Then, apparently,
he heard Snorri's poem and learned of his involvement. He wrote:

> *Men murdered old Ysja—*
> *Ill work to spill peace—*
> *Although they'd have failed*
> *Had they not followed Snorri.*

That warrior powerful
Who has clearly avenged
His kinsmen—in ditties!
There's your honor, Snorri!

The other Dalesman concurred, concluding the cycle with this poem:

Snorri has avenged his Thorvald,
His poetry is his power.
Fiery play around the head
Of his daughter's husband, dead;
Still to stern warriors
Such verse spells fear,
As fire flames its gold revenge
Among our mightiest men.

These verses reminded everyone that it was Snorri's obligation to avenge his son-in-law Thorvald of Vatnsfjord. Instead Snorri pushed the risk off onto those boys, and what happened? They killed an old woman and made everything worse, while Snorri sat safe at home making up ditties. *His poetry is his power*—meaning he has nothing else. Poems were no replacement for action. If Thorvald's sons had killed Sturla Battle-Strong, they would have removed Snorri's fiercest rival. Instead their bungled attack made Sturla stronger. And Snorri was to blame.

Just as a poem had marked the end of Saemund of Oddi's brief reign as the uncrowned king of Iceland—*Loft is in the islands / Gnawing puffin bones. / Saemund in the highlands / Eats berries there alone*—so these poems about the Saudafell raid, soon on the lips of every Icelander, marked the end of Snorri's: *There's your honor, Snorri!*

Sturla gathered men. "The talk was that the men were to attack Snorri; this idea was presented to the men in the hall, but they all fell silent at the suggestion." Several refused outright. "Thus the idea came to nothing." But it would come up again.

Snorri rode to the Althing of 1229 with seven hundred men. Sighvat and Sturla Battle-Strong also had a large force of men from the North, as well as the backing of the men of the East, while those of the South remained neutral. Snorri stayed in his booth, Valhalla, throughout the assembly. He was sick with a bout of the recurring skin disease erysipelas, which turned his cheeks the color and texture of orange peel, so his son Jon Trout spoke for him at court. It did not go well. Sturla Battle-Strong regained one-third of Hvamm-Sturla's chieftaincy. No settlement was reached in regard to the murder of Thorvald of Vatnsfjord or the raid on Sturla's house at Saudafell.

Jon Trout chose this difficult time to ask his father to put up a bride-price so he could marry. At twenty-six he was ready to step away from his father's shadow, and his requests were reasonable. He had his eye on Helga, Solveig's younger sister, a daughter of Saemund of Oddi, and he wanted to offer Stafholt as his bride-price and take over the management of the church estate with his wife. Snorri balked. He said Jon should stay at Borg and manage his mother's property. Jon walked out in a huff. He booked passage on a ship to Norway. Hearing this, Snorri immediately reversed his decision. He offered Jon Stafholt. He promised to pursue the match with Helga. But Jon was stubborn. It was too late, he said. His mind was made up. He sailed as soon as the Althing ended. He would never return.

Snorri's refusal to give his grown son an inheritance has long been cited as an example of his critical flaw: greed. He was good at amassing wealth. He was incapable of sharing it, even with his sons. A more generous reading sees in this incident Snorri's business sense. He had earned his riches by being a skillful manager, sometimes, as in the case of Reykholt, bringing back to prosperity an estate its previous owner had run into the ground. Snorri's answer to Jon was not simply no but that Jon should take over Borg, which was itself a fine estate. Stafholt, Snorri may have reasoned, was in good hands. But Borg, with its extremely diverse holdings, needed a watchful eye. Until now he had left it to Herdis, his estranged wife, but he thought their son Jon could do a better job. For a schemer and planner like Snorri, it may have been simply a business decision. But everyone, then and now, saw it as greed.

At the same Althing, Kolbein the Young abandoned Snorri's daughter Hallbera, for reasons no one knows, though it may have been because of her poor health. She was visiting in her father's booth when Kolbein simply rode away from the assembly. He "paid her no attention." She went home to Reykholt, but her father sent her north to Kolbein. "She stayed there a short time but did not come into Kolbein's bed," says *Sturlunga Saga*. "After that she returned to Borg where she remained with her mother."

In November, Sturla Battle-Strong attacked Vatnsfjord. Finding the brothers not at home, he did no damage. Instead he followed the progress of the boys' escape boat and, when the winds forced it ashore, captured them. He enhanced his reputation by accepting self-judgment—and his wealth by assessing Thorvald's sons a fine worth ninety cows. The boys paid it in the form of a ship, rights to driftage on several beaches, and some silver and gold. It seemed their feud was ended.

A year passed. In 1230 Snorri did not even bother to go to the Althing, sending Styrmir the Wise to act as lawspeaker on his behalf. "The great hostility" between Snorri and his nephew "began to diminish somewhat," Saga-Sturla writes. Then he adds his famous comment, like a great thankful sigh, halfway through his part of *Sturlunga Saga*: "Things now began to go better between Snorri and Sturla; Sturla spent some considerable time at Reykholt and gave much thought to having copies made of the saga books which Snorri was writing." It is all Saga-Sturla ever says about Snorri's writing. And it is the last peaceful scene he grants us in his long, violent book. Scholars used to reading the "saga books" like those Snorri wrote, *Heimskringla* and *Egil's Saga*, or the later masterpieces like *Njal's Saga* or *Laxdaela Saga*, are shocked by the darkness of *Sturlunga Saga*. One Icelandic historian at the turn of the twentieth century said of the Age of the Sturlungs: "Men were more grim, treacherous, deceitful, savage, and revengeful. Fair play was not known and men became half trolls. . . . Any respect for good morals was abandoned. . . . It became customary to break faith even with those nearest and dearest to one. Dignity and fair dealing were at a discount. Those who continue to obey the dictates of duty are fools." It was the axe age, the age of swords and wind and wolves. The age when brother fought brother and father betrayed son.

The next year, 1231, Snorri entertained Bishop Gudmund the Good in his booth at the Althing. With the bishop was a priest said to be a good physician, and Snorri sent him to Borg, where his daughter Hallbera was lying ill. She had not been well since her young husband abandoned her two years before. The doctor said he would prepare a bath "which would cure her if she could endure it. She was eager to be cured and wanted to risk the bath." She soaked the required time. She stepped out of the tub. A robe was wrapped around her, "then pains struck her in the chest, and shortly afterwards she died." Hearing of her death, Kolbein the Young immediately rode south and married Helga, Saemund's daughter, the young woman Jon Trout had his eye on.

It was too late for Jon Trout to complain. Word came to Snorri hard on the heels of his daughter's death: His son and heir had been killed in Norway in a drunken brawl. The bearer of the bad news was his daughter Ingibjorg's husband, young Gissur of Haukadale. When Jon Trout had first arrived in Norway, he stayed with Earl Skuli, who received him well, Snorri learned. The next spring Jon went to Bergen and met King Hakon. He asked the king's leave to return to Iceland, but the king refused. Jon had by then used up all his money. He found a room at the bishop's palace but had to share it with several other Icelanders, including Gissur.

One night, Gissur said, he and Jon came home from a royal feast in the wee hours. They were very drunk. "It was pitch-dark in their loft and their beds were not ready," as Saga-Sturla reports the tale. Jon scolded the servants. Another Icelander, a poet called Olaf the Black, defended them. "Jon seized a piece of firewood and struck at Olaf." Gissur caught hold of Jon and held him—was Gissur trying to break up the fight, as he claimed? Or, as he was later accused, was he Olaf's accomplice in the murder? For Olaf had an axe. He struck Jon in the head, then fled from the room. Gissur said that when he realized Jon had been wounded, he ran to catch Olaf but couldn't find him.

Gissur returned to Jon and bound up his wound. "It did not seem to be a great wound," Gissur told Snorri. "Jon made little of it and was on his feet." He "took no care of himself. He went to the baths, and drank at home in the course of the day." That evening he was stricken with pain. He lay down and died.

Not everyone believed Gissur's tale. Rumors flourished. Gissur went to his father-in-law again and swore Snorri a solemn oath that "he had in no way plotted with Olaf against Jon's life, and indeed had tried in every way he could to separate them. Snorri let it be seen that he understood very well what Gissur was saying."

Gissur's wife, Ingibjorg, could not be consoled. Their marriage had never been happy, Saga-Sturla writes, though he blames Ingibjorg for that, saying Gissur "loved her very deeply." She bore a son and named him Jon after her lost half brother, but the infant soon died. "After that they were in as much disharmony as before." Snorri and Gissur's father "tried every way of bringing them to peace with one another." Each gave the young couple money to make their household more comfortable, "but it was as if they had done nothing." Ingibjorg left her husband and returned home to Reykholt. The last of the advantageous marriages Snorri had arranged had failed. His carefully woven web of alliances fell to shreds, his hopes and schemes destroyed.

It may have been now that Snorri wrote *Egil's Saga*, particularly its poignant final third, when the aging berserk loses his beloved sons and finds he must make do with the less-than-satisfactory heir left to him. Egil's moving poem, "Lament for My Sons," must have come often to Snorri's lips in the dark days of 1231.

It had already been a terrible summer. A volcano had erupted out at sea off the southwestern tip of Iceland. It belched out ash day after day. A dirty gray pall, inches deep, had covered the fields and farmhouses of western Iceland— because of the wind direction, the rest of Iceland may have been spared, but Snorri's Borgarfjord was hard hit. People and their animals suffered. The ash blew about in the wind, blinding them, stinging them with needles of glass. They could hardly breathe. Some days at noon the sky was so dark it seemed like a deep winter's night. The ash buried the grass, stunting its growth; hay would be hard to come by in Borgarfjord that winter. Ash from some Icelandic eruptions is laden with toxic fluorine. If such was the case for this one, the grazing animals soon lost their teeth. Their bones became deformed and they died. And when the flocks died in summer, famine was not far off.

During a volcanic eruption five years earlier, in 1226, Snorri lost a hundred cows that he had kept pastured close to Stafholt. A hundred cows was a fortune— a large farm might have only fifty cows; a family could make do with five. Yet Snorri had shrugged off that loss. At Christmas that year he held a long-remembered feast in his new Norwegian-style hall at Reykholt. It was "a Yule-drinking according to the Norwegian custom," Saga-Sturla writes, though he doesn't, unfortunately, elaborate. The hall was filled with promising young men. The writer himself attended, as a twelve-year-old, along with his older brother Olaf White-Poet. Snorri's sons Jon Trout and Oraekja were there, as were Klaeng and Orm, the sons of Snorri's partner, Hallveig. The oldest son of Thorvald of Vatnsfjord came. Snorri's poet Sturla Bardarson was in attendance, as was his friend Styrmir the Wise and a man named Bard, identified as "a personal retainer" of the king of Norway. Sturla Battle-Strong and his brothers had not been invited.

After the eruption of 1231, after so many personal losses, Snorri held another Christmas feast. His two legitimate children, Jon Trout and Hallbera, were dead. His daughter Thordis's husband was dead, and she had turned her back on her father. His daughter Ingibjorg had walked away from the good match he had made her. But he still had his partner, Hallveig, and her great wealth (though after six years of cohabitation they had no children). He still held eight chieftaincies. And he still had one son, the illegitimate Oraekja, age twenty-six. Snorri Sturluson was not defeated yet.

He invited his brother Thord and his sons to the feast. He invited Sturla Battle-Strong this time as well. The drink was plentiful, the food hearty, the hot tub luxurious. While everyone was relaxed and convivial, he told Sturla Battle-Strong he wanted the sons of Thorvald of Vatnsfjord to come south to meet with him. Snorri had it in mind to marry the boys to Hallveig's sisters, who were then at Reykholt. He wanted the support of Thorvald's sons (as well as Sturla's support) when he sued Kolbein the Young for Hallbera's inheritance. Snorri asked Sturla Battle-Strong to speak the words of the formal truce oath, giving the boys permission to ride through Sturla's lands.

"I will let you arrange this matter of a truce now," Sturla said. "Here is my hand on it, if you like."

Snorri took Sturla's hand and spoke the truce, concluding with the traditional words:

> He shall be branded a truce-breaker who violates this pledge or destroys this peace—to be banished and driven away from God and good men, from heaven and all holy man; he shall be deemed unfit to live among men, and, like a wolf, shall be an outlaw everywhere—wherever Christians go to church or heathens hold sacrifices, wherever fire burns, the earth grows, a speaking child calls his mother and a mother bears a son, wherever people kindle fires, where a ship sails, shields glitter, the sun shines, snow drifts, a Lapp goes on skis, a fir tree grows, where a falcon flies on a long summer's day with a fair breeze blowing under both wings, where the heavens turn, where lands are lived in, where the wind washes water down to the sea, where men sow seed—in all those places the truce-breaker shall be barred from churches and Christians, from heathens, from houses and holes, from every place except Hell alone. Now we shall all agree and be at peace with one another and be of good will, whether we meet on a mountain or on a beach, whether on a ship or on skis, on earth or on ice, at sea or on horseback— just as when one meets his friend at the ford or his brother on the road; we shall be in concord as a son should be with his father and a father with his son, in all their exchanges . . . . To this may God and all good men be my witnesses, and also those who hear my words and are now present.

Afterwards, Thord took his brother aside. "It did not seem to me that our kinsman Sturla had quite the expression I might have wished, while you were speaking the truce formula."

Snorri shrugged off his brother's misgivings. "Sturla will keep the truce properly," he said. He was wrong.

A little before Lent, Snorri sent Oraekja north to meet Thorvald's sons and escort them to Reykholt. Oraekja waited at the meeting spot for several days, but the boys did not come, so he rode home. Soon after, the boys rode into the Dales, and Sturla Battle-Strong ambushed them. They mentioned the truce. They offered him money. They vowed to sail abroad and never come back. On Sturla's orders his men surrounded the boys and stoned them until they were battered and exhausted, denying them even a fair fight—and a hero's death. They executed the two oldest boys—ages twenty-one and eighteen—by cutting off their heads. The others they let go.

As they rode home, Sturla chatted with his poet. "They talked about how Snorri would like this slaying." They wondered "whether he would compose verses about it."

The news, when it reached Reykholt, made Snorri furious, but he felt his hands were tied. "He didn't want to lose Sturla's support at the Althing in the summer in his case against Kolbein the Young." When Sturla offered to pay compensation for the killings, Snorri accepted it.

At the Althing, Snorri and his kinsmen ganged up on Kolbein, who was only twenty-three. Snorri gained half of Kolbein's chieftaincies. Kolbein pledged to support him at the assemblies. To top it off, Kolbein would marry his sister Arnbjorg to Snorri's son Oraekja, to whom Snorri would then turn over a church estate in the North called Melstad, a chieftaincy, and the value of two hundred cows. They shook hands on it.

But come autumn Snorri did not attend Oraekja's wedding. He gave no excuses. He had made no arrangements concerning the estate at Melstad, so Oraekja brought his bride home to Deildar-Tunga, where he had been living with his half-sister and her husband. In the spring he asked his father for Stafholt instead of Melstad.

Snorri refused. Instead, Oraekja should take over the Vatnsfjord chieftaincy until his sister Thordis's five-year-old son by Thorvald was grown, he decided.

Oraekja did not go to Norway like his brother Jon Trout when he was denied Stafholt. Instead he went berserk. If Snorri's actions in the 1230s were devious, Oraekja's were insane.

He went to Vatnsfjord. He gathered up every free man he could and set about robbing and plundering—like a true Viking—throughout his own district.

Then Oraekja raided the lands to the south, along the edges of the fjord, in the district of his uncle Thord.

Oraekja raided the lands of his cousin Sturla Battle-Strong, who in the summer of 1232 had gone abroad in answer to a letter from the archbishop of Trondheim concerning his crimes against Bishop Gudmund the Good. Sturla had left his property in the hands of his friend Odd Alason—who was then the lover of Thordis, Oraekja's half-sister. Oraekja attacked and killed Odd, burning his house down. Thordis, luckily, was not there to suffer through a second house burning.

Then Oraekja rode to the North Quarter, joined forces with Kolbein the Young, and raided in his uncle Sighvat's district.

Sighvat gathered an army and faced them down. Oraekja convinced Kolbein to back off, with difficulty. "Kolbein wanted to draw his sword, but Oraekja came up and held him firmly while many others took part in trying to calm him. But Kolbein was furiously angry." The bishop of Skalholt came to arbitrate, and Oraekja and his men turned toward home. "They behaved ruthlessly throughout the western district, seizing horses and stores whenever they thought they needed them," Saga-Sturla writes. They pillaged Hvamm, the ancestral Sturlung estate, which Oraekja's uncle Thord then owned. "They destroyed hay and other provisions . . . and killed a nine-year-old ox." Perhaps it was part of their settlement with Sighvat, for at the same time Kolbein and one of Sighvat's sons rode south with two hundred men and raided the estates that Snorri's partner, Hallveig, owned there.

As if he didn't quite understand what was going on, Snorri called for Oraekja to ride south with him to defend those southern estates against Kolbein's depredations. Oraekja was more than happy to comply. But before his troop joined Snorri's, they learned that Kolbein had ridden back north. Annoyed at missing a fight, Oraekja began pillaging along the peninsula to the west—in his cousin Bodvar's territory. Oraekja even wrecked his cousin Olaf White-Poet's house: "All the hay was strewn about and spoiled, the summer fodder eaten up, and the buildings destroyed."

Back in his own district, "Oraekja went around all the West Fjords extorting property from people. . . . Oraekja also drove many other men from their homesteads." He was totally out of control.

This was not the style of governance Snorri approved of, but he seems not to have done anything about it. At the suggestion of his uncle Sighvat,

Oraekja even attacked Snorri's own territory in 1233, riding against Reykholt with eighty men. Snorri was then in the Southwest at his estate of Bessastad. Forewarned, he took ship to Stafholt and rode quickly to Reykholt, gathering two hundred men as he came. He reached Reykholt before his son. His men "were dispersed throughout the stronghold in several buildings. Oraekja's men went all around the stronghold but could not attack." Oraekja agreed to negotiations. It was a trick. "It happened that those who were inside the stronghold noticed nothing until all Oraekja's men had got into the house"; they had "gone up the covered way from the hot spring." Luckily for Snorri, by that time he had acquiesced to his son's demands. He had agreed that Oraekja should take over the rich church estate of Stafholt. The impressive wall around Reykholt was useless against someone who knew the secret way in through the bathhouse door.

It would take the return of Sturla Battle-Strong to Iceland in 1235 to put an end to Oraekja's Viking raids. Ended too would be any possibility that Snorri could rule Iceland as the Norwegian king's earl. In fact Snorri's whole attitude toward the idea would subtly change.

Sturla Battle-Strong had found Norway on the brink of civil war between King Hakon and Skuli, his father-in-law and former regent, now not an earl but a duke. Sturla met with the archbishop and was urged to go on pilgrimage as penance for his crimes against the church. He rode to Rome, where he received absolution for the misdeeds of his father as well as for his own sins. Sturla's penance had a carnival atmosphere. He was led barefoot through the streets of Rome—we can imagine his long blond hair loose over his shoulders, his massive chest and manly thighs bared. At the doors of each cathedral he was whipped. "People stood near and marveled," Saga-Sturla reports, "striking their breasts and bewailing that such a fine man was so grievously treated. No one, woman or man, could keep from tears."

Sturla Battle-Strong returned to Norway and spent the winter with King Hakon—now a vigorous thirty to Sturla's thirty-five—"and the king and Sturla often talked together," says *Sturlunga Saga*. What did they talk about? Independent Iceland becoming a colony of Norway, according to *King Hakon's Saga*. Saga-Sturla elaborates: "The king asked how hard it would be to impose monarchy on the land, and he said that there would be more peace if one [ruler] were in charge. Sturla responded positively and said that it would not be difficult if the person who undertook it was tough and resourceful. The king asked if he would undertake it."

Perhaps when he stood on the quay in Bergen in 1220, Snorri thought he had agreed to "persuade the Icelanders to give themselves into the protection of the Norwegian rulers" only in the matter of the lawsuit between the men of Oddi versus the Bergen merchants. Or perhaps, as time went by and Snorri "made no headway with his countrymen," as Saga-Sturla writes, but "nonetheless the merchants enjoyed peaceful conditions," Snorri convinced himself that such was the case.

His own writings show that he had conflicting feelings about kingship. From his earliest childhood he had admired kings and wanted to meet them, certainly. He was proud of the royal blood of his foster father, Jon Loftsson. The whole point of Snorri's *Edda* was to praise and educate—and influence— a young king. Creating *Heimskringla,* Snorri dropped from his sources all the witty tales of Icelanders outwitting the kings. In *Heimskringla* the kings are center stage. There are good kings and bad kings, kings who are builders and kings who are adventurers, but overall there is an assessment of what it means to be a king. For Snorri the job of king is fivefold: A king promotes prosperity. He upholds the law. He resolves disputes and keeps the peace. He protects the land against outside attack. He is a leader. As uncrowned king of Iceland, Snorri tried to accomplish all five tasks. As the Norwegian king's earl, he would have had to renounce the fourth.

A famous passage in his *Saga of Saint Olaf* shows how difficult this was for Snorri to contemplate. The episode appears in no other source. It may have come from oral tradition. It may have come from Snorri's own soul. Regardless, the wording is his—and the passion. In 1024 King Olaf of Norway sent a messenger to the Icelandic Althing. He "bade me say that he will be your king if you will be his subjects, and both be friends and help one another in all things." The Icelanders applauded. They all wanted to be friends with the king. To seal the bargain, the messenger said, the king would like the Icelanders to give him the island of Grimsey. Several men murmured that the friendship of a king was worth at least one rocky little island. Then a man named Einar stood up:

> If you wish to have my opinion, then I would say that it were best for the people
> of our country not to subject themselves here to pay tribute to King Olaf. . . . We
> would impose that bondage not only on ourselves but both on ourselves and our

sons and all our people who live in this land; and that bondage this land would never be free or rid of. And though this king be a good one, as I believe he is, yet it is likely to be the case, as always hitherto, that when there is a change in the succession there will be some kings who are good and some who are bad. But if our countrymen would preserve their freedom, such as they have had ever since they settled here, then it would be best not to let the king get any hold here, whether it be a piece of land or our promises to pay fixed taxes.

If you want the friendship of a king, he continued, send him hawks or horses or tents or sails. "That would be a good investment if it is repaid by friendship." But an island, no matter how small, could become a base for warships, a foothold for invasion, and then, Einar implied, where would we be? Einar's oratory swayed the Althing. Grimsey remained Icelandic, and Iceland remained free.

How would it be to live under a king? Snorri imagined that at the beginning of *Egil's Saga*. The king who first united Norway, Harald Fair-Hair, had conquered the Uplands and Trondheim, bringing their petty kings under him, and was fighting his way through the district of North More. A Viking from that region, Solvi Splitter, called for aid from the king of South More: "We may be in trouble now, but it won't be long before the same happens to you. Take my word for it, Harald will be turning up here at any moment, just as soon as he's got all the people of North More and Romsdale where he wants them and made slaves of them." Solvi Splitter called the king's plans "tyranny and injustice."

In the next chapter Snorri is even more explicit. Once he'd conquered a region, the narrator of *Egil's Saga* explains, the king "kept a sharp eye on the landed men and rich farmers." They had three choices: They could swear him loyalty. They could leave the country. Or "they could resign themselves to the most savage terms, perhaps even death." Harald took over farms and estates. He claimed even the sea and the lakes. Everyone owed him taxes. "Many a man went on the run from this tyranny," Snorri adds. "And that's when Iceland was discovered." Could the man who wrote these words have ever seriously intended to hand his country over to the king of Norway? Had he ever looked forward to paying taxes?

On the quay at Bergen in 1220, perhaps Snorri simply heard what he wanted to hear. He was a skillful lawyer. He could help the young king win this one case and pacify the Bergen merchants. No need for Earl Skuli to send warships. Snorri would take care of everything.

But King Hakon's conversation with Sturla Battle-Strong in 1234 makes it clear that Snorri had been deluding himself. Hakon wanted to rule Iceland in 1220 and he wanted to rule it now. When Sturla Battle-Strong returned to Iceland late in 1235, the game changed. Unlike Snorri, Sturla was indeed "tough and resourceful." Like King Harald Fair-Hair, he gave his countrymen three choices: swear loyalty, leave the country, or "resign themselves to the most savage terms."

Even before Sturla returned, it's clear that Snorri had lost his nerve. One day in the spring of 1235, Snorri rode with six men to meet his brother Thord halfway between their two farms. Snorri had no reason to mistrust Thord, the peaceable and pious one of the three Sturlusons. Through all the many pages of *Sturlunga Saga*—written by his son, to be sure—Thord double-crosses no one. Yet when Snorri and his few companions forded the river on their way to the meeting place, "they saw a great company of men under the ridge. They turned their horses about at once and rode swiftly back south." Thord sent men racing after them. They caught up to Snorri and explained. It was not an ambush. It was a holy day, didn't Snorri know? Thord's friends were gathering for a feast. "It was a long time before Snorri would ride back," says *Sturlunga Saga*. There was indeed a feast. The mead flowed. The brothers pledged undying friendship. Thord's son Saga-Sturla was sent home with Snorri—as a hostage, though *Sturlunga Saga* does not say it in so many words. Snorri was still nervous.

He had good cause.

On Palm Sunday 1236, Sturla Battle-Strong and his father Sighvat rode into Borgarfjord at the head of an army twelve hundred strong. Having heard a rumor of their coming, Snorri and his partner, Hallveig, had fled after first transferring ownership of Reykholt to his—and Sighvat's—brother Thord. Saga-Sturla, later recording these events in *Sturlunga Saga,* gives his uncle little excuse for fleeing, saying only that "Snorri was not ready for this move against his brother in the holy days of that season." Nowhere else is Snorri portrayed as being so religious. To emphasize his piety here seems just a sly way for Sturla to once again call his uncle a coward.

Thord, on the other hand, is consistently portrayed as a pious man. He rode to meet Sighvat's army, his son writes, and said, "God will punish you for attacking your own brother on a holy day."

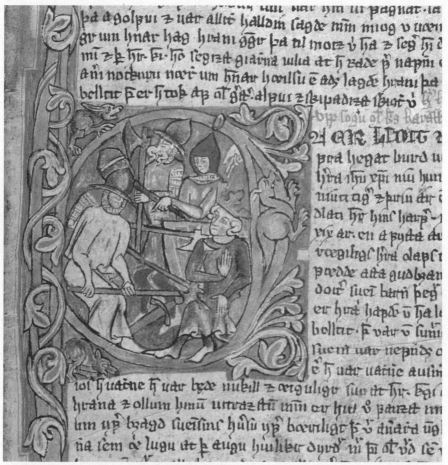

The killing of King Olaf, from the fourteenth-century manuscript Flateyjarbók, GKS 1005 fol. As Snorri wrote in his Saga of Saint Olaf, "when there is a change in the succession there will be some kings who are good and some who are bad." To preserve Iceland's freedom, "it would be best not to let the king get any hold here." Copyright © The Árni Magnússon Institute, Reykjavík. Photo by Jóhanna Ólafsdóttir.

Sighvat smiled. "You are angry, kinsman, and one should never mark an angry man's speech."

Sturla Battle-Strong took over Reykholt and Stafholt. He soon controlled all of Borgarfjord. He sent word to his cousin Oraekja, who had been amassing ships and men in the West Fjords to come to Snorri's aid, and offered him a deal. "Oraekja was to go south at once with Sturla and remove all his forces from the West Fjords. He was to make his residence at Stafholt, while Sturla was to have

Reykholt and hold Snorri's property peacefully for Oraekja." They would meet again in midsummer, when Sturla's father, Sighvat, would announce the peace settlement that would apply to all.

Oraekja was too stupid to see through Sturla's fine words. He disbanded his troops. He settled in at Stafholt. When the promised midsummer meeting did not occur, he shrugged. When Sturla asked him to ride to Reykholt, he did. There Sturla stripped Oraekja of his weapons, parted him from his friends, and put him back on his horse. Sturla forced Oraekja to ride east toward the glacier, well into the wilderness, away from any farm, to the dark lava tunnel called Surt's Cave. They dismounted and clambered over the rough boulders that half-blocked the entrance. They walked far into the black tunnel, some-times over smooth sand, sometimes climbing again over boulders. The only sounds were their own footsteps, their own breathing; the only light was the dim twinkle ahead from a hole in the cave's roof.

They reached the cavern beneath the hole: The stronghold, it was called. Sturla told one of his henchmen to cut a piece off a spear shaft and shape the wood into a hook. Sturla said he should carve out Oraekja's eyes with it.

Shocked, Sturla's man delayed. "He could not make out how to use the instrument," *Sturlunga Saga* reports.

Sturla handed him a knife.

Oraekja called on Saint Thorlak for aid.

Sturla's henchman "stabbed the point of the knife, as far as the wrap-pings, into his eyes. When this was done Sturla bade him think of Arnbjorg"—Oraekja's wife, sister of the chieftain Kolbein the Young—"and gelded him, removing one testicle."

Then Sturla rode away, leaving behind a single guard.

Word soon got out. Oraekja's cousin Saga-Sturla organized a rescue party, including Oraekja's loyal wife, Arnbjorg. When they reached Surt's Cave, Oraekja was gone. His guard had taken pity on him. Saga-Sturla and Arnbjorg caught up with him at the cathedral of Skalholt, where he had taken refuge. His eyes healed—thanks to the miraculous Saint Thorlak. Saga-Sturla does not mention Oraekja's lost testicle, but neither did he have any children. Late in 1236 Oraekja boarded a ship for Norway.

The men of Borgarfjord were a little cooler toward Sturla Battle-Strong after Oraekja's torture. Snorri, who had been hiding in the East of the country, as far from Reykholt as he could get, began sending messages to his old friends. He moved back toward the West, staying for a time with his former son-in-law Gissur at Haukadale, now the leading chieftain in the South. Sturla, spying on his uncle's movements, also made overtures of friendship to Gissur. Then he called up more men.

The tension grew.

Snorri had given Borg to his nephew Olaf White-Poet a few years before. During Lent, Olaf rode to Skalholt. He had written a poem about Saint Thorlak, he said, and wanted to deliver it to the bishop. "But he really wanted to meet Snorri," his brother Saga-Sturla writes. They met at Gissur's estate. Snorri told Olaf to have everything ready at Easter, when he would return to Borgarfjord. A spy brought word of Snorri's plans to Sturla Battle-Strong.

In the meantime March 1237 brought the death of the divisive bishop, Gudmund the Good. But Snorri's brother Thord, the peacemaker, also took ill and died soon afterward.

A man in the West had a dream. He saw two armies come together. A Valkyrie rode at the head of one, "large and evil-looking, in her hand a cloth which hung down in tatters and dripped blood." She whipped the cloth about, "and when the ragged ends touched a man's neck she jerked off his head."

Snorri came from the South at Easter. He was joined by four hundred men. Sturla Battle-Strong, he learned, had seven hundred at Reykholt. "Snorri wanted to ride forward at once during the night and bring matters to a head with them; he said that it might be their foes would not be ready or would not have got together yet, if they attacked them quickly."

Snorri's cousin, the chieftain Thorleif of Gard, son of Snorri's mother's brother, disagreed. They had too big an army to sneak up on anyone. He preferred a fixed battle.

Snorri demurred. He would not take the chance of falling into Sturla Battle-Strong's hands, to be blinded and gelded like Oraekja.

Thorleif would not budge, so Snorri turned away. With one other man he rode back to the South. If he had once thought it ludicrous for his partner, Hallveig, the richest widow in Iceland, to ride through the peaceful countryside with only one companion, how much more ludicrous was it for Snorri Sturluson, once the richest and most powerful chieftain in Iceland, the chieftain to whom no others could compare, to be sneaking away from a battlefield at night, with only one bodyguard?

Saga-Sturla, writing this passage in *Sturlunga Saga,* brands his uncle a coward for leaving his kinsmen in the lurch on the battlefield. Most readers have agreed. But Snorri was never a fight-to-the-last-man Viking. That conceit, in his opinion, was fine in books but foolish in real life. If he could not be sure of winning, he chose not to fight.

Sturla Battle-Strong rode from Reykholt on April 28, 1237, with five hundred men. Finding his army more evenly matched with that of Thorleif of Gard than expected, Sturla opened negotiations. They failed: Sturla would accept only self-judgment. Thorleif retreated to his farm of Baer. Sturla attacked. In the melee that became known as the Battle of Baer, twenty-nine of Thorleif's men died—Saga-Sturla names each one. Many more were wounded, including Thorleif himself, who fled into the church, his men following. The church was small. "Not half of those who wanted to could get in, and all the fallen lay dead before the church doors. But Sturla's men assaulted them, thrusting at and striking every man they could."

Thorleif granted Sturla Battle-Strong self-judgment. Thorleif agreed to go abroad, taking with him Olaf White-Poet and several other of Sturla's kinsmen. The next summer, when they rode to the harbor at Eyr on Iceland's southern coast, Snorri was waiting there for them. His second trip to Norway would occur under very different circumstances from his first. Instead of the uncrowned king of Iceland, seeking to increase his honor and riches, he was simply Snorri Sturluson the storyteller, fleeing for his life.

Six

THE RING

In this book I have written the old sagas. . . . And although we know not the truth of these, we know, however, of occasions when wise old men have reckoned such things to be true.

—Snorri, *Heimskringla*

Why is gold called "Otter's ransom"? One day, Snorri writes, Odin and Loki went wandering. They came to a waterfall where an otter crouched, a salmon in its mouth. Loki threw a stone and killed the otter.

"Two at one blow!" he crowed, fetching both otter and salmon.

The gods wandered on. At a farmhouse they begged shelter for the night. The farmer was gracious until he saw the dead otter. His mood blackened: Otter was his son. He called his other sons, Fafnir and Regin. "Bind them," he commanded.

Fafnir and Regin trussed the two gods up. To ransom their lives Odin and Loki agreed to fill the otter's skin with gold and then cover it entirely with more gold.

Loki was loosed. He traveled to the world of the black elves. He caught a dwarf named Andvari and demanded his gold. Andvari carried it all from his cave—it was a substantial haul—all but one small gold ring that he tried to hide.

Loki noticed. "Hand it over."

"Do not take this ring," the dwarf pleaded. With it alone he could recoup his losses.

Loki took the ring.

The dwarf cursed it: The ring would bring doom upon whoever possessed it.

Loki the Trickster grinned. He'd pass the word.

He carried the gold to Otter's father. Odin stuffed the otter's skin. He covered it with gold. But still one whisker was showing. Sadly, Odin took the small gold ring, the cursed ring, from his pocket and covered the whisker.

Odin and Loki went on their way, free. That is why gold is called Otter's ransom.

But it's not the end of the story, a story that would be retold as the Icelandic *Volsunga Saga,* later as the German *Nibelungenlied,* much later in Wagner's *The Ring of the Nibelungs,* and, by way of Andrew Lang's *Red Fairy Book,* would become J. R. R. Tolkien's favorite childhood tale, with its eerie evocation of "the Nameless North." Reading it, said Tolkien, "I desired dragons with a profound desire. Of course, I in my timid body did not wish to have them in the neighborhood. But the world that contained even the imagination of Fafnir was richer and more beautiful, at whatever cost of peril."

Snorri continues: Otter's brothers, Fafnir and Regin, demanded a share of the gold. When their father refused, they murdered him. Then Fafnir turned on Regin: "Go, before I kill you too." Regin fled. Fafnir carried the gold up onto the glittering heath. He swelled and grew scaly. A fire lit in his belly. He lay on his hoard, prince of dragons now, and brooded.

Regin became the swordsmith of a king. He took in a boy named Sigurd, one of the Volsungs. He told him about the dragon and the gold. He made Sigurd a sword. Sigurd climbed to the heath. He dug a trench in the dragon's path and lay in it. As the monster crawled down to the water at dawn, it slithered over the trench. Sigurd thrust his sword up into his belly.

Regin, who had been watching from a safe distance, drank the dragon's blood and lay down to sleep, ordering Sigurd to roast the dragon's heart while he napped. But Sigurd burned his finger. When he put it in his mouth to soothe it, suddenly he understood the twittering of the birds. Regin, the birds said, meant to murder him to avenge his brother and get the gold.

So Sigurd killed Regin, his own foster father. Then he led his horse to the dragon's lair and took away all the gold. He rode until he came upon a castle on a crag, in which a beautiful woman lay sleeping. She wore a helmet and a coat of mail. She was the Valkryie Brynhild. He woke her.

Sigurd killing the dragon, carved on the door panels of medieval Hylestad stave church. Now in the Historisk Museum, Oslo. Photo © akg-images.

Then he rode on until he came to the realm of the Niflungs. He fell in love and married the king's daughter, Gudrun. Her brother, Gunnar, was obsessed with Brynhild. The brothers-in-law rode back to her castle on the crag.

Their way was blocked by a wall of flickering flame. Gunnar's horse would not jump it. Sigurd's horse was not afraid—but would allow no one but Sigurd to ride him. So Sigurd took on Gunnar's shape. He leaped the wall of fire. He wooed and wed Brynhild, but in bed he lay his sword between them. In the morning they traded rings. Sigurd gave her the ring of power, the cursed ring that Loki had taken from the dwarf Andvari. And so begins the famous love triangle, the tragedy that would destroy everyone involved.

Snorri was fifty-nine when he arrived in Norway for the second time. He was fat and gouty. Probably he was bald, his beard gone gray. He may have suffered from a recurrence of erysipelas, which turned his cheeks orange. He may have had books under his arm—books that would do more to immortalize the Norwegian kings than anything before or since. But he did not cut a striking figure. He was no longer the uncrowned king of Iceland, no longer recognized by his peers as its leading chieftain. He had little chance of convincing King Hakon to back him instead of his nephew Sturla Battle-Strong. He may not even have tried.

Snorri spent the winter of 1237 in Trondheim with Petur, son of Duke Skuli. The king and the duke, on good terms for once, were both in the South. Snorri didn't see either of them until spring, when Duke Skuli returned to Trondheim, leaving his wife to tend to their daughter, Queen Margret, who had just given birth to King Hakon's son and heir; this child, Magnus, would become king of Norway—and Iceland—in 1264.

Duke Skuli greeted Snorri as an old friend. They spent the summer scheming and storytelling and sharing poetry—one night over ale Snorri compared Skuli's enemy of the moment, one-eyed Gaut, to Odin. Then, in late autumn news arrived from Iceland: Sturla Battle-Strong had overstepped.

He had double-crossed Gissur of Haukadale and had taken him hostage. Gissur's friends rallied to his cause. His jailers—men Sturla thought dependable—released him. Kolbein the Young backed Gissur, and early one morning Gissur's army from the South joined Kolbein's army in the North, having ridden the hard highland road between the glaciers. Sturla knew of their pact. He gathered men to him, but on August 21 Gissur caught Sturla unprepared at a farm called Orlygsstad. Sturla was still in bed when the war cry went up.

Men grabbed for their clothes and weapons. They couldn't catch their horses. Their shields were all tied in bundles—no time to untie them, the battle had begun. Sturla's father, Sighvat, came rushing onto the battlefield swinging his axe. He was struck down, and Kolbein speared him as he lay. Sighvat's men tried to protect him—one threw a shield over him, another even lay on top of him—to no avail. Snorri's brother was hacked to death there on the ground. Sighvat was sixty-eight. The enemy stripped his corpse of all but his underwear.

Sturla himself was pressed back into a sheep pen. His only weapon was the ancient spear Grasida, "inlaid, but not very strong." It had once belonged to the saga hero Gisli the Outlaw, and Sturla carried it for the aura it lent him. But fame and romance did not make up for poor-quality steel. "The spear bent and several times he had to straighten it out under his foot," Saga-Sturla writes; he was there.

Weak from loss of blood, Sturla Battle-Strong fell. Gissur ran up. He tore off Sturla's helmet. He took a broadaxe from one of his men and struck his fallen enemy "mightily on the head from the left, behind the eye, a deep but narrow wound. The men who were near said that Gissur leapt into the air with both feet when he struck Sturla, so that they saw the sky between his feet and the earth." Gissur took Sturla's purse full of money, the ring off his finger, and his ancient, flimsy spear.

Sturla's men fled into the church. Gissur called them by name. Saga-Sturla was granted quarter. So were a few others. But Sturla's two brothers were not. They hid in the church as long as they could but finally asked to visit the outhouse. They did not want to foul the holy sanctuary. Gissur gave them permission. When they exited the outhouse, he seized them. They were executed. A third brother had died on the battlefield. A fourth, the youngest, escaped into the mountains. The last son of Sighvat Sturluson was safe in Norway.

Snorri sent him a poem: *Like swine swept by wolves . . . are we.* "He thought the death of his brother Sighvat a very great loss," says *Sturlunga Saga*. Then Snorri asked Duke Skuli to help him return to Iceland. He sensed a power vacuum—an opportunity.

As soon as winter thawed to spring, Snorri made ready. He was aboard ship, waiting for a wind, when a royal messenger arrived with a letter from the king. Hakon forbade any Icelanders to sail home that summer. "Snorri and his men read the letter, and Snorri then replied, 'I am going.'"

For a landed man, a baron, to defy the king's explicit order was, Snorri knew, an act of treason. He no longer hoped for honor or riches from King Hakon. At their farewell feast he and Skuli had come to an agreement. Four men witnessed it, including Snorri's nephew Olaf White-Poet, his son Oraekja, and his cousin Thorleif of Gard. The fourth man was Arnfinn, the duke's marshall. No one is quite sure what the agreement was. "Arnfinn's story was that the duke gave Snorri the title of earl," Saga-Sturla says. Earl was a step up from baron. But Sturla never met Arnfinn, who died in 1241. Saga-Sturla cites another source. In the annals of the monastery at Videy in 1242, Snorri's friend Styrmir the Wise marked the anniversary of Snorri's death, naming him *Snorri fólgsnarjarl.* The title could mean "Secret Earl." Or it could mean earl of Folgsn, a large royal estate near Trondheim.

Was Snorri secretly the earl of Iceland? Did he truly sell out his country's independence this time? Was he planning to collect taxes in Duke Skuli's name? To force his countrymen to follow Duke Skuli's laws and accept his judgment in their disputes? Or did Snorri simply accept lands and riches in Norway from his friend? Whatever the title means, Saga-Sturla adds, "None of the Icelanders there thought that [it was] true." They did not believe Snorri was earl of anything—not of Iceland, not even of a little fiefdom in Norway. Because to be earl *of anything* was to be a traitor to King Hakon. Only a king could make an earl, whether of Iceland or of Folgsn.

Soon after Snorri left Norway, defying King Hakon's orders and having made some pact with Duke Skuli, the duke declared himself King Skuli, the rightful ruler of Norway. King Skuli's reign lasted a year. In May 1240 Hakon's troops caught Skuli unaware in Trondheim. Skuli fled to the woods and took refuge in a monastery. His enemies set fire to it. Skuli came out, holding a buckler before his face. "Don't strike me in the face," he said. "It's not the custom to do that to noblemen."

In Iceland, Snorri kept quiet about his earldom. He made no mention of Skuli—duke or king. After landing in the Westman Islands in the summer of 1239, he met his beloved Hallveig at one of her estates in the South, and the two rode home to Reykholt. Snorri took up his pen again. He may have finished *Egil's Saga* in these years, with its unflattering portrayal of kings. He may have worked on *Heimskringla*, which establishes a model for Norwegian-Icelandic relations, or on the difficult middle section of the *Edda* that captures the essence of Icelandic culture. Scribbled at the end of the Reykholt church inventory is the comment that at about this time Snorri gave the scriptorium six calfskins to be made into parchment, perhaps to make copies of his own books. His daughter Ingibjorg donated another twelve calfskins.

Though no longer lawspeaker, Snorri picked up his role as negotiator, weaving a new web of power using the few kinsmen he had left. For his cousin Thorleif of Gard he arbitrated a settlement for the Battle of Baer. When Solveig, widow of Sturla Battle-Strong, went to Norway, she gave her estate at Saudafell to Snorri; he turned it over to Saga-Sturla. Snorri placed Oraekja at Stafholt (though "Snorri was much displeased with the expenses which he incurred for his followers"). Snorri did his best for Sighvat's youngest son, Tumi, who alone had escaped the slaughter at Orlygsstad, marrying him to one of Hallveig's sisters. Snorri held the wedding feast at Reykholt, then accompanied Tumi to the Althing to negotiate with Gissur of Haukadale and Kolbein the Young: Snorri's former sons-in-law were now the leading chieftains in Iceland. Snorri brought a hundred men. It wasn't enough. He and Tumi spent the assembly hiding in the church, "while Kolbein's men rode at frenzied speed around the plain below in a violent manner." Gissur was willing to talk, but without Kolbein they could reach no settlement.

It was a setback, but by now Snorri was used to them. Word had come of Duke Skuli's death late in 1240: Snorri had mourned his friend and tempered his ambitions. His agreement with the duke—earl of something—had thankfully not gotten out. Or so Snorri thought. In secret Gissur of Haukadale had become King Hakon's new favorite among Iceland's chieftains. Gissur held a damning letter from the king that named Snorri a traitor. The king may not have accused Snorri of colluding with the false king Skuli. He did not have to. Everyone knew Snorri was a traitor—if a minor one. On the quay at Bergen, when Snorri accepted the title of baron, he had sworn King Hakon his allegiance. Yet he publicly defied the king's written command and sailed from Norway in the spring of 1239. The king ordered Gissur to capture Snorri and send him back to Norway—or to kill him. Gissur bided his time.

Then in June 1241 came a shock from which Snorri could not recover. His beloved Hallveig died of sickness. "This seemed to Snorri a very great loss," writes Saga-Sturla, "and so it was for him." He was paralyzed with grief, all at sea, careless of his own safety, as if his world had ended. Dividing Hallveig's inheritance with her sons, Klaeng and Orm—who had lived with him since they were boys—Snorri bungled it. They asked for half of Snorri and Hallveig's joint property, as if the couple had been married. Snorri quibbled. He'd share everything to the east of Thingvellir, the lands Hallveig had brought into their partnership, but no part of anything in the West. Was it greed, as Saga-Sturla implies, or good business sense to refuse to divvy up the church estates of Stafholt and Reykholt? Was it greed or just careful accounting to point out he'd bought Bessastad with his own money? He gave Hallveig's sons half of his money and valuables—even half of his precious books—but managed only to make enemies of them. Klaeng and Orm rode to Gissur to complain.

It was the excuse Gissur had been waiting for. "It was unfortunate that they had not been able to make a just division with Snorri," he said, adding that "in this matter he would be willing to lend them his support." Gissur sent word to Kolbein the Young. The two met secretly in the far highlands, in the black sand wasteland between the glaciers. Gissur showed Kolbein the king's damning letter. They drew in Arni the Quarrelsome, who had also once been Snorri's son-in-law. Arni was King Hakon's man; he had carried the letter from Norway, though he had not known its contents. They told Hallveig's sons—Orm refused to have anything to do with the plan and rode off, but Klaeng joined them.

Someone tried to alert Snorri. Late in September he asked Oraekja and Saga-Sturla to meet him at Saudafell, where Tumi, Sighvat's son, then lived. "Snorri was very cheerful," Saga-Sturla reports. They sat around drinking beer and discussed the problem of Hallveig's sons. Snorri showed them an anonymous letter he had received. "It was a kind of coded message and they were unable to read it but it seemed to them to be some sort of warning." Snorri folded it back up. It seemed he just didn't care anymore. They would never see him again.

Snorri rode home to Reykholt. He posted no guard on his elaborate wall. He may even have left the drawbridge down or the hidden door to the hot tub unbarred.

Gissur had spies watching the estate. Late at night on September 22, he rode up with seventy men. Kolbein's army of four hundred blocked the pass to the north. Klaeng and Arni the Quarrelsome barred the way west.

Gissur's men walked into Reykholt unopposed. They broke into the building where Snorri slept. He leaped out of bed in his nightshirt and ran next door into the fine Norwegian-style loft house he had built at the height of his power twenty years before. He was heading, perhaps, for his writing studio and the secret spiral stair that led from it to the tunnel and the hot tub and escape—

It is cold in Iceland in late September. The birch leaves are bright gold, the berry shrubs crimson. The songbirds have all flown. Swans flock in the marshlands, sounding their haunting note. Night falls quickly and lingers long; the wind has the bite of ice. When the rain lets up, the northern lights wash the sky with streams of emerald and turquoise and sometimes blood. An old fat man in his nightshirt, barefoot, would not get far in the cold and dark of a late September night.

In the loft house Snorri met Arnbjorn, one of the priests of Reykholt. "They decided that Snorri should go into the cellar," Saga-Sturla writes. This cellar did not connect with the tunnel, as near as archaeologists can tell. It might have been simply a storeroom above ground for beer, ale, and wine. Snorri hid there, alone in the dark, weaponless, shivering, while Gissur's seventy men loudly searched every room in every house.

"Gissur found Arnbjorn the priest and asked where Snorri was. He said he didn't know." The priest was a poor liar. Gissur did not believe him. He said slyly that "they couldn't very well come to an agreement with him if they couldn't find him." The priest thought Snorri might be found if he were promised quarter.

Did he inadvertently look toward the door—or the trapdoor—to the cellar as he said this? For at his words "they discovered where Snorri was."

Gissur gave no promises. He sent five men—thugs all—into the cellar.

The captain gestured to one of his mates. "Strike him down," he said.

"Don't strike," said Snorri.

"Strike."

"Don't strike!"

The man struck. So did another.

Twenty-one years later, in 1262, the chieftains at the Althing swore oaths of loyalty to King Hakon of Norway, agreeing to pay his taxes and accept his laws. Iceland lost its independence. Gissur of Haukadale was named earl.

Oraekja and Saga-Sturla had tried to avenge Snorri's death. They retook Reykholt and executed Klaeng. They marched on Gissur and pinned him in Skalholt Cathedral. Called to parley, they were double-crossed and captured. Oraekja was exiled to Norway, where he died in 1245. Saga-Sturla, some years later, was offered peace if his thirteen-year-old daughter wed Gissur's sixteen-year-old son. Their treaty might have lasted, but others of Gissur's enemies intervened. The day after the wedding they set fire to Gissur's house. The bride was rescued from the blaze. Her young husband, Gissur's two other boys, and his wife burned to death. One of Gissur's henchmen rushed out but was recognized: "None here now remembers Snorri Sturluson, if *you* get quarter," said his killer. Gissur saved himself by hiding in the kitchen, submerged in a barrel of whey, as the burning house collapsed about him. His revenge was awful. He hunted down and killed the burners. Saga-Sturla was shipped off to Norway.

Old King Hakon was then fighting in Scotland. His son, King Magnus, greeted Saga-Sturla coldly, only grudgingly allowing him to travel with the court. One day, while they waited for a wind, the sailors asked him to tell a story. Saga-Sturla held them rapt for hours. The queen, curious, commanded him to tell the same story to her and the king. It was the saga of Hulda the Trollwoman (which unfortunately no longer exists). The king and queen were enchanted. When Sturla finished the tale, he recited poems he had composed in honor of King Magnus and his father. "I believe you are even more eloquent than the pope," said the king. He commissioned Sturla to write a saga about his father, King Hakon, and, Sturla implies, sat there at his shoulder telling him what to say.

Saga-Sturla was sent home to Iceland in 1271 with a new law code and the title of king's lawman (replacing Iceland's elected lawspeaker). He lived in peace for the rest of his life, writing *Sturlunga Saga,* telling the story of Snorri Sturluson and Iceland's loss of independence "in ice-cold words." He might also have copied—and so preserved—his uncle Snorri's works before he died in 1284. Or that task may have fallen to his brother, Olaf White-Poet, who was in Denmark studying the runes when Snorri was slain. Olaf came home in the mid-1240s and established his school at Stafholt, dying there in 1259.

The oldest extant saga manuscript, a copy of *Egil's Saga* from the mid-1200s, might have been set down on parchment by Saga-Sturla or Olaf. By 1330 at least three copies of *Heimskringla* were in circulation and three of Snorri's *Edda.* The *Codex Upsaliensis* (Book of Uppsala) is thought by some readers to be closest to Snorri's intention (others think it a tasteless condensation). It begins, in red letters, "This Book is called Edda. Snorri Sturluson has put it together according to the manner herein set forth. First there is [told] of the Aesir and Ymir. Next is Skaldskaparmal and the names of many things. Last is Hattatal, which Snorri made on King Hakon and Duke Skuli." The manuscript also contains the "Tally of Court Poets," a genealogy of the Sturlungs down to Saga-Sturla, and a list of lawspeakers that ends with Snorri in 1231. To make the *Edda* more useful, the scribe added a handy table to "Hattatal" that links the names of each verse form to the first line of the matching stanza. In a second manuscript, the *Codex Regius* (King's Book), the scribe numbered the verse forms and added a list of technical terms.

But if Snorri's *Edda* was studied, as these additions show, it was not loved. Poems from the 1300s cite it in derogatory ways. A verse on Gudmund the Good "will be considered very rigid by the headmasters of the Eddic art," its author, an abbot, writes. He cares not. He eschews those "esoteric rules" and particularly dislikes kennings, "for kennings increase no man's strength but darken joy." The author of a hymn to the Virgin Mary abjures kennings in favor of "plain words . . . familiar words, given with joy." He argues, "It is most important that the true sense be rightly understood, though the rule of the Edda, quite unclear, might sometimes have been disregarded. Whoever chooses to compose elaborate poetry chooses to present in the poem so many obscure old expressions that may scarcely be counted: I declare this hinders understanding."

A hundred years after Snorri's death, the songs of the skalds—and the myths needed to read them—were cast aside. Few Icelanders missed them. By then the church had wiped out the last traces of the Viking gods, renaming Tuesday, Wednesday, Thursday, and Friday as Third Day, Midweek Day, Fifth Day, and Fast Day. No longer was there a weekly reminder of Tyr's lost hand, Odin's ravens, Thor's hammer, or Freyja's golden tears. Snorri's "Tricking of Gylfi," so carefully crafted to make the old myths palatable to Christian readers—and keep the old poems alive—had failed.

His rules on meter, rhyme, and alliteration lived on in the long epic ballads called *rímur* (rhymes) that came into fashion. More than a thousand sets of rimur were written from 1350 through the 1800s. Visiting Iceland in 1871, an English poet heard a rhyme being chanted to a tuneless melody by a drunk straddling a low grass roof. It is a "ballad in four-line stanzas with a burden at each stanza's end," he explains, "and every stanza ends with a queer long note, which with our friend on the roof is a dismal bellow." Yet even the rimur poets cited Snorri's *Edda* only to dismiss it: "There is no pleasure in speaking in riddles, according to the dark rules of Edda." "Poets would do better not to be everlastingly fumbling over the Edda." "No help of Edda have I got, she is thought hard to master, and she has never got into my brains!" Nor did any of these poets, happily trashing Snorri's masterpiece, mention his name. Snorri Sturluson was forgotten.

Outside Iceland matters were worse. Iceland was no longer the land of poets, as it had been in the thirteenth century when Saxo Grammaticus, writing his Latin *History of the Danes*, called Icelanders his best sources: "The diligence of the men of Iceland must not be shrouded in silence; since the barrenness of their native soil offers no means of self-indulgence, they . . . devote all their time to improving our knowledge of others' deeds, compensating for poverty by their intelligence. They regard it a real pleasure to discover and commemorate the achievements of every nation; in their judgment it is as elevating to discourse on the prowess of others as to display their own."

An English poet of the fifteenth century took a different view: "Of Iceland to write is little need / Save of stockfish."

A hundred years later the European view had not changed. Iceland, wrote Thomas Nashe in 1594, is "one of the chief kingdoms of the night," wreathed in "sulphureous stinking smoke," containing only "stockfish, whetstones, and cods' heads." As for the Icelanders' "means of self-indulgence," Nashe finds it not poetry but a kind of frozen ale "that they carry in their pockets like glue. . . . When they would drink, they set it on the fire and melt it."

At roughly the same time an Icelandic priest published *A Brief Commentary on Iceland* in Copenhagen; it was translated into English by Richard Hakluyt in 1598. The priest, Arngrim Jonsson, was inspired by "a very deformed impe," as his bishop called a book of "filthy and most slanderous" German rhymes. The Danish king, who since 1363 also ruled Norway and Iceland, had leased the island's harbors to Germans. In exchange for fishing rights the Germans were to send merchant ships to supply Iceland with "sufficient and unspoilt necessities." After a winter in Iceland one of these German merchants published his memoirs in verse.

Replying to this "hoggish rhymer," Arngrim did not mince words. To the German's assertion that Icelanders sell their dogs dear but give away their children, Arngrim replied in part, "What should move such great men, following the despiteful lies and fables of mariners, to defame and stain our nation with so horrible and so shameful a reproach?" To the German's claim that Icelanders sleep ten to a bed, men and women mixed, and wash their hands and faces in urine, Arngrim warned, "I could also gather together many such filthy, unmannerly, and bawdy fashions noted by others even in his own country" of Germany.

Trying to correct a common error in books about Iceland, Arngrim inadvertently announced to the world the existence of medieval Icelandic manuscripts. The idea that Icelanders "celebrate the acts of their ancestors and of their times with songs, and they grave them in rocks," Arngrim wrote, was false.

Icelanders do not set up rune stones, yet "we deny not but that some worthy acts of our forefathers be preserved in the songs and poems of our country-men, as also in prose."

By 1595 Arngrim's bishop was receiving letters from England asking for copies of "the monuments of history which are here thought to be extant." He replied that "we have little to show, besides the history of the kings of Norway," meaning Snorri's *Heimskringla.*

In Denmark and Norway this was wonderful news. The *History of All the Kings of the Goths and Swedes,* published in 1554, traced that country back to Noah's grandson. Among its many accomplishments, Sweden claimed to be the sole home of the Goths who conquered Rome. The Danes and Norwegians scurried to their own archives to find competing histories, and ancient manu-scripts suddenly became valuable. Kings vied with each other to amass the best collections.

Arngrim gathered twenty-six Icelandic manuscripts, including copies of Snorri's *Edda* and *Heimskringla.* He composed a history of the kings of Denmark, based on the (now lost) *Skjoldunga Saga* perhaps written by Snorri's foster brother Pall. Arngrim commissioned an updated *Edda,* in which the "Tricking of Gylfi" was turned into sixty-eight short tales and the "Language of Poetry" into an alphabetized index. Arngrim's most important work was *Crymogaea* (Greek for "Ice Land"). Fatefully, he published it in Germany in 1609; parts came out in English in 1625. Considered "the manifesto of Icelandic patriotism," *Crymogaea* identified Icelandic as the pure Norse tongue, the language of the Vikings. It told the history of Iceland through stories of saga heroes like Egil Skalla-Grimsson (especially how they outwitted kings) and introduced the gods Odin, Thor, and Loki, citing Snorri's *Edda.* Finally, it explained the runic alphabet.

Runes became instantly popular. Linked with magic and the occult, they were thought to be a Viking brand of hieroglyphics. The Danish physician and antiquary Ole Worm printed Egil's "Head Ransom" in runes (it appears that way in no medieval manuscript), as well as several Icelandic poems with Latin translations. Worm began corresponding with Arngrim in 1626. Along with runes they discussed unicorns, whales' teeth, and Ultima Thule (was it Iceland?), as well as more everyday subjects. Writes Arngrim, "That herb by some called . . . tobacco, pray tell me in your next [letter] what effect it has when inhaled through a tube and exhaled by the mouth and nose, as we have seen our sailors do it; also how much is the correct dose, and is it to be taken full or fasting?"

Arngrim sent Ole Worm manuscripts, though they did not always survive the trip. One set of books was "so injured by shipwreck, so wet and dirty, that hardly a letter was decipherable." In another, drier, shipment came one of the three most famous manuscripts of Snorri's *Edda*. Sizable, well preserved, and with an "air of wealth and perfection about the whole book," it is thought to have been made at Thingeyri monastery in Iceland in about 1330. This manuscript is now called *Codex Wormianus* (Worm's Book). At the request of Cardinal Mazarin of France, Worm sent a copy to Paris. In return came a medallion bearing the likeness of the Sun King, Louis XIV, and a watch "of ingenious workmanship enclosed in an exquisite gold box inlaid with amber"— rewards Snorri would have thought fitting for his poetry.

Another manuscript of Snorri's *Edda* came into the hands of the bishop of Skalholt in 1640. It is a little book, dark and grimy. The top lines of many pages have rotted away; the first page is missing. The bishop had a clean copy made and sent both to the king of Denmark, from which the manuscript earned its name, *Codex Regius*. Three years later Bishop Brynjolf acquired another small, grubby manuscript. Its poems reminded him of Snorri's myths, so he named it *Edda* as well and attributed it (on no evidence at all) to Saemund the Wise. The bishop sent it to the king, and it too is called *Codex Regius*.

Snorri's *Edda* was published, with Danish and Latin translations, by Peder Resen in Copenhagen in 1665. Resen did not follow either manuscript but used the popular version divided into sixty-eight tales, to which he added two poems from Saemund's *Edda*. Resen called the *Edda* (meaning both) the ancient moral code of the Vikings, the ethics of the North.

Heimskringla too had been printed by then. A manuscript from Bergen was partly translated in the mid-1500s. Ole Worm commissioned a complete Danish version and published it in 1633 as *Snorri Sturluson's Chronicle of the Norse Kings*. Snorri's name was thus attached to *Heimskringla* for the first time, based (presumably) on this now-lost manuscript.

Fifty years later a young Icelander named Arni Magnusson came to study in Copenhagen; he, more than anyone else, is credited with saving the sagas. Arni had been brought up at Snorri's ancestral estate of Hvamm. In Copenhagen, he first worked as a copyist and translator for Thomas Bartholin, Jr., who in 1689 brought out a seven-hundred-page history of the Danes.

Drawing examples from Snorri's *Heimskringla, Egil's Saga,* and other sagas, Bartholin's *Danish Antiquities Concerning the Reasons for the Pagan Danes' Disdain for Death* made popular the Viking stereotype of the bold, blond, laugh-in-the-face-of-death hero.

Arni became a professor at the University of Copenhagen in 1701, and the next year the king sent him back to Iceland to gather statistics about his country's land and people. His massive *Land Register,* compiled over ten years, describes every farm in Iceland, its size and shape, buildings, people, cows, sheep, horses; the bulk of butter and cloth it owed in tithes; the quality of its turf, peat, hay, and woodlots; its fishing and driftwood rights; and the extent of the property ruined by volcanic ash or sand or rendered useless by quagmires, bogs, erosion, or flooding. Off the record Arni asked every farmer about manuscripts—and poked about in every farmhouse. He collected every scrap. He found two pages from a thirteenth-century manuscript with holes punched in them to make a flour sifter. He found pages used as dress patterns, shoe soles, knee patches, and even the stiffening in a bishop's mitre. He pieced them back into books: One sixty-page manuscript came from eight different farms.

When his collection was packed for shipping to Copenhagen in 1720, it filled fifty-five wooden chests and required thirty packhorses to carry it. In 1728 Copenhagen caught fire. Half the city was incinerated, including the university library. Arni, disbelieving that fate could be so cruel, refused to evacuate his private library until the fire reached the end of his street. He and two other Icelanders had time to rescue only the oldest books. The rest were lost, including, Arni cried, "books that will never and nowhere be found until doomsday."

The *Codex Wormianus* of Snorri's *Edda,* which Arni owned, survived. So did the *Codex Regius,* kept in the king's private archive. (The *Codex Upsaliensis* was safe in Sweden.) Two of the three manuscripts of *Heimskringla* burned. (The third was also in Sweden.) Happily, exact paper copies of these manuscripts had already been made.

By the mid-1700s Snorri's fame was wide—and a little weird. This was the Age of Reason, of John Locke and Isaac Newton. But what captivated readers about this so-called gothic literature was gore.

> *His shaggy throat he opened wide,*
> *While from his jaws, with carnage filled,*

*An old Norse manuscript recycled into the stiffening for a bishop's mitre.
Arni Magnússon's efforts saved many other medieval manuscripts from
being similarly repurposed. Copenhagen, Arnamagnæan Collection,
AM 666 b fol. Used by permission.*

Foam and human gore distilled:
Hoarse he bays with hideous din,
Eyes that glow and fangs that grin.

So we meet the dog of Hel in "The Descent of Odin" by Thomas Gray, better known for his "Elegy Written in a Country Churchyard." Gray's two imitations (as he called them) of Icelandic poems in 1761 started the craze for soothsayers and werewolves and walking dead that led, by century's end, to the chills and horrors of the gothic novel.

Fast in Gray's footsteps was Thomas Percy, bishop of Dromore. Percy, who named among his friends Samuel Johnson and James Boswell, printed *Five Runic Pieces* in 1763: "The ship sailed in a sea of blood. . . . The king dyed his sword in crimson. . . . The wolf mangled the festering wounds. . . . Odin hath seen where the dead bodies lie." Percy's blood-drenched translations (the word he preferred to *imitations*) are not very literal. But alongside the Vikings' contempt of death, Percy did point out their "fondness for poetry," which they called "the gift of Odin" and "the songs of the gods."

Percy got Egil's "Head Ransom" (including the lines just quoted) from Ole Worm. But his understanding of Snorri came from Paul-Henri Mallet, the Swiss tutor to the crown prince of Denmark and later a professor in Copenhagen, who published the "Tricking of Gylfi" (divided into thirty-three legends and without what he termed its ridiculous prologue) in French in 1755. An expanded treatise came out in 1763; it was available in German by 1765 and in English by 1770, translated by Percy himself under the title *Northern Antiquities*.

Mallet drew heavily from the two *Edda*s and *Heimskringla*, amplifying Snorri's works with other sagas and sources such as Tacitus, Saxo Grammaticus, the *Anglo-Saxon Chronicle*, Adam of Bremen, and Saxon law codes. Mallet writes, "It will appear pretty extraordinary to hear a historian of Denmark cite, for his authorities, the writers of Iceland, a country cut off, as it were, from the rest of the world, and lying almost under the northern pole." But Iceland's medieval skalds, he declares, were "famous throughout the north for their songs"—which he describes as grand, sublime, remote, enigmatic, striking, affecting, bold, astonishing, whimsical, unintelligible, abstruse, overstrained, complicated, and obscure. He credits Snorri with compiling these songs into chronicles while decrying his taste for "the marvelous."

Northern Antiquities revealed a world not only savage and sublime but imbued with a passion for liberty. The religion of the Vikings was as "simple and martial as themselves," Percy wrote. Their form of government was "dictated by good sense and liberty," while their "restless unconquered spirit" was "apt to take fire at the very mention of subjection and constraint." Or, as Joseph Sterling wrote, in the preface to his 1782 *Icelandic Odes,* "To them we are indebted for laying the foundation of that liberty which we now enjoy."

For the German philosopher Johann Gottfried Herder, father of nationalism, Mallet's *Northern Antiquities* was "a treasure chest for a new German genius . . . creating poems that would suit us better than the mythology of the Romans." In 1795 Herder broke with his friend Goethe over the *Edda.* Goethe's *Roman Elegies,* Herder said, were trite and immoral. The Norse myths were "more useful to a German poet," because they were closer to the German soul. Mythology, Herder argued, is nothing less than a "history of the fatherland." To be a nation thus meant having a mythology. But what was Germanic mythology? Herder translated the "Tricking of Gylfi" into German to provide one. He also began collecting German folk songs "for love of the nation."

"For love of the nation" was the mantra of the 1800s. In Norway, P. A. Munch relied on *Heimskringla* for his *Norske Folks Historie.* Norwegians claimed Snorri as a "Norwegian writer" (some still do); *Heimskringla* was the bible of Norway's fight for independence. By the end of the century a hundred thousand copies of Snorri's collection of kings' sagas circulated in two Norwegian translations. "It was thanks to Snorri more than to any other single person," wrote one (Icelandic) historian, "that the Norwegians finally regained their national sovereignty." Subject to Denmark from 1380 to 1814, Norway was given to Sweden as war booty after the Napoleonic wars (Denmark had sided with the losing French). Not until 1905 would Norway regain a king of its own.

Patriotic Icelanders also called on Snorri for inspiration. The king of Denmark lit the spark in 1831, when he set up four Danish regional assemblies. German-speaking Holstein had agitated for one since the defeat of Napoleon. Slesvig, half German, half Danish, had the second. The third represented Jutland, while the fourth covered the rest of Denmark as well as Iceland and the Faroe Islands—which was not to the taste of Icelanders still mourning the abolishment of the Althing.

In 1835 four Icelandic students founded a political magazine in Copenhagen. They printed their manifesto in the form of a poem, which "was exactly what was needed in order to unite the Icelandic people," says a modern historian. The only one of their ancestors it evokes is Snorri:

Ah! But up on the lava where the Axe River plummets forever
Into the Almanna Gorge, Althing is vanished and gone.
Snorri's old site is a sheep-pen; the Law Rock is hidden in heather,
Blue with the berries that make boys—and the ravens—a feast.
Oh you children of Iceland, old and young men together!
See how your forefathers' fame faltered—and died from the earth!

Four lines of the poem are engraved on a plaque now standing on the site of Snorri's booth at the Althing, the place he called Valhalla.

The Althing reconvened, with royal permission, in 1845. In 1874 the country received a new constitution and, in 1904, home rule. One of its first demands was that Denmark return the manuscripts Arni Magnusson had collected. The Danes declined.

In 1918 Iceland became a sovereign state in a "personal union" with the Danish king—much like the situation in 1262, when the chieftains swore individual oaths of loyalty to King Hakon. For its coat of arms the new nation turned once again to Snorri. King Harald, Snorri wrote in *Heimskringla*, was angry at the Icelanders, who had composed lampoons about the king. He ordered a "troll-wise man" to test the country's defenses. Disguised as a whale, the wizard swam close to Iceland's eastern shore: "Then came a great dragon down from the dale" and "blew poison at him." The wizard swam along the north coast, "but there came against him a bird so big that its wings neared the fells on both sides of it." The wizard-whale fled west: "Toward him came a great ox that waded out in the sea and began to bellow horribly." Swinging wide, he swam south, "but against him there came a great hill giant who had an iron staff in his hand and bore his head higher than the fells." King Harald was dissuaded from attacking. Iceland's coat of arms bears a dragon, an eagle, an ox, and a giant.

The Icelanders repeated their demands to "bring the manuscripts home." Arni Magnusson's *Land Register* was returned in 1928. Not enough. The Althing passed resolutions in 1930 and 1938, then World War II interrupted the country's literary quest. In April 1940 Germany invaded Denmark; a month later the British occupied Iceland. One result was Iceland's final break with Denmark. The independent Republic of Iceland was established at Thingvellir in 1944; in 1947 the Althing resolved once again to "bring the manuscripts home."

This time Denmark formed a committee. Reporting in 1951, the scholars could not agree which manuscripts (if any) to return. Would these treasures of Old Norse be properly cared for in Iceland? Manuscript institutes named for Arni Magnusson opened in 1955 in Iceland and 1956 in Copenhagen. In 1961 a list of manuscripts was drawn up, and Iceland agreed to give Denmark twenty-five years to deliver them. Ten years later—after being photographed and conserved—the first set steamed into Reykjavik harbor aboard a Danish coast guard cutter. Thousands of Icelanders stood by the docks. Thousands more watched the first live outdoor broadcast of the state television station. Eventually 1,666 manuscripts and more than seven thousand charters (1,350 originals, the rest copies) were returned from Arni Magnusson's collection— slightly more than half of it. Another 141 manuscripts were sent home from the Royal Library. The last arrived in Iceland in 1997.

"People still say: 'We want to see the manuscripts,'" wrote a curator of the collection in 2004. The manuscripts "are at one and the same time the repository of medieval Icelandic culture and its visible symbol," he said. They are Iceland's "main source of pride."

Iceland today is littered with remembrances of Snorri and his works. A main street in the capital is called Snorrabraut (Snorri's Road). Side streets carry names out of his *Edda*: Loki, Thor, Baldur, Freyja, and Mimir, among others. Saga characters are remembered on street signs, too, including Egil, though he is better known for his beer: In 2011 Egil's Gold was judged the best standard lager in the world. A trawler is named *Snorri Sturluson*. A coast guard vessel is *Odinn*. Edda and Heimskringla are publishing houses. A genetics company is Urdur, Verdandi, og Skuld—the three Norns, Past, Present, and Future—who, Snorri wrote, sit by the Well of Weird. Snorri's Reykholt is much the same as in 1241, though nothing medieval but his hot tub remains. Beside an imposing church are a school, hotel, and research library. Up a spiral stair is a writer's studio.

Fear made the British invade Iceland in 1940—fear that the Icelanders were truly as Germanic as the Germans had long claimed. As early as the 1790s,

*A gift from the king of Norway, a statue of Snorri
Sturluson by the Norwegian artist Gustav Vigeland
(1869–1943) was placed at Reykholt in 1947. The image is said to be modeled on Snorri's description of the
Norwegian king Sigurd Sow in his* Saga of Saint Olaf.
*Snorri is now thought to have been fatter and more
fashion-conscious. Photo by the author.*

Herder had called Snorri's *Edda* Germanic. Herder inspired the Brothers
Grimm: German nationalism provides the subtext of *Grimms' Fairy Tales,* for
the study of myths and fairy tales—folklore—presupposes a folk with a common past and values.

In addition to bringing "Rapunzel," "Hansel and Gretel," and "The
Golden Goose" to nurseries across Europe, in 1815 Wilhelm Grimm retold

verses from the *Poetic Edda* in his charming fairy-tale style. His brother, Jacob, cites Snorri's *Edda,* the *Poetic Edda, Heimskringla,* and other sagas in his *German Mythology* of 1835. Jacob Grimm gives Snorri no credit as an author. He quotes him. He allows that Snorri makes conjectures. But when comparing the two *Edda*s to Saxo's Latin *History of the Danes,* Grimm finds the Icelandic texts "a purer authority for the Norse religion"—no matter that Snorri and Saxo were writing at roughly the same time. "As for demanding proofs of the *genuineness* of Norse mythology, we have really got past that now," Grimm asserts. He finds the myth of Baldur "one of the most ingenious and beautiful in the Edda," noting it has been "handed down in a later form with variations: and there is no better example of fluctuations in a god-myth." By the "later form" he means Saxo's, written between 1185 and 1223. The pure version is Snorri's, written between 1220 and 1241. Grimm does not find his conclusion illogical; he sees no teller behind Snorri's tale. He chops the *Edda*s and the sagas into themes: worship, temples, priests. A chapter each on Odin, Thor, and other major gods. One on goddesses (lumping in a lot of non-Norse deities). Wise women. Heroes. Giants. Creation. He cites words in Gothic, Greek, and Sanskrit. Using scientific principles, he chases word forms from language to language, creating a text that today is mind boggling. Lofty and erudite, it has none of Snorri's wit. It is philology.

Originally, philology meant love of words. An Englishman redefined it to mean the scientific study of written languages in 1786 when he argued that Sanskrit, Greek, and Latin had "some common source which, perhaps, no longer exists." (We now call that source Indo-European.) In 1814 a Danish philologist worked out how Icelandic, Danish, Norwegian, and Swedish related to Slavic, Celtic, Finnish, Greek, and Latin. By the 1880s an Icelandic philologist would compare the "field of Northern scholarship" before the new science as "a vast plain, filled with dry bones, and up and down there walked a company of men, doing their best to set these bones in order, skull by skull, thigh by thigh, with no hope or thought of the breath that was to shake this plain with the awakening of the immortal dead." Philology provided that breath of life.

At some cost. Many philologists, like Jacob Grimm, were German nationalists. Take the Icelandic sources out of *German Mythology* and all that's left is an empty shell. Thomas Carlyle, who focused on Snorri's works in his 1840 series of lectures *On Heroes, Hero-Worship, and the Heroic in History,* spoke of "Scandinavian paganism" as "the creed of our fathers; the men whose blood still runs in our veins, whom doubtless we still resemble in so many ways." But his term *Scandinavian* (which even the philologists could not define) did not stick.

James Steven Stallybrass quotes Carlyle in his 1880 English translation of Grimm, then adds, "What Mr. Carlyle says of the Scandinavian will of course apply to all Teutonic tradition, so far as it can be recovered; and it was the task of Grimm in his *Deutsche Mythologie* to supplement the Scandinavian mythology (of which, thanks to the Icelanders, we happen to know most) with all that can be gleaned from other sources, High-Dutch and Low-Dutch, and build it up into a whole. And indeed to prove that it *was* one connected whole; for, strange as it seems to us, forty years ago it was still considered necessary to prove it."

What does Grimm mean by *Deutsch?* Not only the German-speaking parts of Europe, but also Scandinavia, Iceland, the Netherlands, and the parts of France and Russia that were settled by Vikings—even England, Stallybrass concludes, "for the English are simply a branch of the Low German race which happened to cross the sea." If one nation has one mythology, then the nation of Grimm's *Mythology* spans all northern Europe.

Philology doesn't sell like fairy tales. It took an artist, Richard Wagner, to make the Norse myths popular—and fully German. Grimm's *German Mythology* was one of ten books Wagner said inspired his grand opera cycle, *The Ring of the Nibelungs.* Fourth on the list was the *Edda* (like most people at the time, he didn't discriminate between Snorri's *Edda* and the *Poetic Edda,* since the translations jumbled both works together). Number ten was Snorri's *Heimskringla.* Wagner made his list in 1856, just after completing *Das Rheingold* and *Die Walküre;* he wouldn't finish *Siegfried* until 1871 and *Götterdämmerung* until 1874. The first full performance of the cycle was in 1876.

It was twenty-five years in the making. The idea of an opera based on Siegfried—or Sigurd—the Dragon-Slayer and the accursed gold ring of the dwarfs came to Wagner in 1851. A German translation of the *Poetic Edda* and some tales from Snorri's *Edda,* Wagner wrote, "drew me irresistibly to the Nordic sources of these myths," the most expansive of which was the Icelandic *Volsunga Saga.* Wagner had, three years before, written a ten-page story called "Siegfried's Death" based on a medieval German poem. But it wasn't enough for an opera. "Now for the first time, also, did I recognise the possibility of making him the hero of a drama; a possibility that had not occurred to me while I only knew him from the medieval *Nibelungenlied.*"

This *Song of the Nibelungs* was written at about the same time as Snorri's *Edda*. Some of the same characters appear: Sigurd the Dragon-Slayer, Brynhild, Gudrun. But half of the *Song* takes place after their deaths; it has no counterpart in Wagner's *Ring*. And much that Wagner loved exists only in Icelandic: the dragon, the ring, the Valkyries, the sibyl; the characters of Odin, Thor, Loki, Freyr, Freyja, and Frigg; the giants, the dwarfs, Idunn's apples, the rainbow bridge, the magical helmet, Valhalla, the Twilight of the Gods. Eighty percent of Wagner's motifs are Icelandic. Five percent are German. Most of the remaining 15 percent are shared, though some—like the Rhine Maidens—are Wagner's own invention, for he was nothing if not creative. Like Snorri he took bits and pieces of myth and made of them something magical.

Unlike Snorri's art, Wagner's had political effects. *The Ring* became the German national epic. With its bold, blond heroes it reinforced the mind-set that produced Nazism. Wagner was Hitler's favorite composer. "I recognize in Wagner my only predecessor," said the Führer. "I regard him as a supreme prophetic figure." "If I listen to Wagner, it seems to me as if I hear rhythms of the primeval world," a world of doom and disaster.

Nazis were not stirred by Wagner's music alone. They liked his politics. In 1850, just before discovering Snorri, Wagner wrote the essay "Judaism in Music." "If we hear a Jew speak, we are unconsciously offended," Wagner wrote, "by the entire lack of purely-human expression in his discourse." We hear only a "creaking, squeaking, buzzing snuffle." Critics have heard echoes of these thoughts in the music Wagner wrote for the dwarf Alberich, "the abhorrent Jewish counterpart of Wotan," as one says.

Wagner's anti-Semitic views were widely shared, and Snorri, unfortunately, was bundled with them. Racist and anti-Semitic societies at the turn of the twentieth century took Norse names; one was even called the Edda Society.

Between 1911 and 1930 a German publisher brought out twenty-four volumes of translations from Icelandic. An introduction spoke of the special "life force" of the German people that led them to perform heroic deeds—and not only in the Saga Age. Viking blood created the British Empire, according to this scholar; Viking blood made Napoleon great. And Vikings were, of course, German. Vest pocket–sized editions of excerpts from the *Edda*s helped prepare German fighters to face death heroically in World War I.

In 1936 the Swiss psychiatrist Carl Jung claimed that Odin's spirit lurked in the collective unconscious of the Germanic people. Odin "is a fundamental characteristic of the German soul, an irrational, psychic factor, which acts like a cyclone on the high pressure of civilization and blows it away." When the Germans' inner Odin awoke, they became Nazis. In 1945, 127,000 copies of a popular edition of the *Edda*s were printed. The last eleven thousand were labeled "Special Edition for the Hitler Youth." Snorri's tale of Ragnarok, the final heroic battle before the rise of a new world order, was taken as a metaphor for the Third Reich.

Snorri's works—in fact all Icelandic literature—were so identified with Nazism that studying them became suspect in England and America. Even today there is a chilling connection of Snorri with neo-Nazi groups, as well as with anti-Christian neopagan cults (often quite racist themselves) and the blood-and-death–themed rock music known as Viking metal.

J. R. R. Tolkien held a grudge against Hitler, a "burning private grudge," Tolkien wrote in 1941, for "ruining, perverting, misapplying, and making forever accursed, that noble northern spirit, a supreme contribution to Europe, which I have ever loved, and tried to present in its true light. Nowhere, incidentally, was it nobler than in England."

Ever since 1770 when Thomas Percy spoke of the Vikings' "good sense and liberty," Englishmen had taken pride in their "northern spirit." Expeditions to Iceland became popular, beginning in 1772 with one led by Sir Joseph Banks, who found it "a country rougher and more rugged than imagination can easily conceive." Its people "smelt so fishy and rank that it was disagreeable to come near them," yet they were honest, obliging, and faithful, with "an inexpressible attachment for their native country." Their chief amusement was "to recount to one another the history of former times."

Nineteenth-century English travelers described Iceland as "perfectly barren," with cliffs in "the strangest shapes," "bare, rugged, and gloomy hills" backed by lofty snow-capped mountains "forming a most magnificent scene; but such a one as seemed to forbid the approach of man." There were "hideous precipices," "barren and precipitous rocks," "black and naked rocks of strange fantastic shapes," and "lofty black mountains [that] frowned in bleak majesty." The land presented "a most hideous appearance": a scene that was "exceedingly dismal" and gloomy and "contributed to excite strong feelings of horror." Another traveler found it "inexpressibly desolate . . . the home of ravens and foxes," the wind always "moaning over the landscape. Yet this," he cried, was "the ancient home of Snorri Sturluson!"

Snorri lured many travelers to Iceland. Some were curious about the man himself. Wrote Frederick Metcalfe in 1880:

> Here we have a Macaulay in the thirteenth century, a man to whom all who wish to be good storytellers, to interest the mind and stir the heart, may well apprentice themselves—a man in a remote valley of Iceland, that sunless land of snow and ice, that howling wilderness of lava and cinder heaps, over which night broods so many weary hours of the year. . . . You should see the place, the site of his abode, with the bath of hewn stone, in that valley of bogs and reek, and you would be lost in amazement if you did.

Others were drawn by Snorri's tales, and those by his contemporaries, of Iceland's laws and its ancient outdoor parliament at Thingvellir. Lord Dufferin, writing in 1856, remarked, "At last I have seen the famous Geysirs, of which everyone has heard so much; but I have also seen Thingvellir, of which no one has heard anything. The Geysirs are certainly wonderful marvels of nature, but more wonderful, more marvelous, is Thingvellir; and if the one repay you for crossing the Spanish Sea, it would be worthwhile to go round the world to reach the other."

Approaching those same assembly plains, wrote William Morris in 1871, "My heart beats, so please you, as we near the brow of the pass, and all the infinite wonder, which came upon me when I came up on the deck of the 'Diana' to see Iceland for the first time, comes on me again now, for this is the heart of Iceland." Yet of Iceland in general, he adds, "It is an awful place: set aside the hope that the unseen sea gives you here, and the strange threatening change of the blue spiky mountains beyond the firth, and the rest seems emptiness and nothing else: a piece of turf under your feet, and the sky overhead, that's all; whatever solace your life is to have here must come out of yourself or these old stories, not over hopeful themselves."

The "old stories" were first retold in English by Sir Walter Scott, inspired by the Brothers Grimm. Later Jacob Grimm met George Webbe Dasent, who would become a professor at King's College, London (and assistant editor of the *Times*). Dasent published translations of Snorri's *Edda* in 1842 and *Njal's Saga* in 1861. His two-hundred-page introduction to the saga turned it into "a kind of medieval Icelandic *Middlemarch*" that describes life in the Saga Age in intricate detail, says a modern reader.

Samuel Laing, an antiquarian from the Orkney Islands who translated *Heimskringla* in 1844, placed Snorri on the same shelf as Homer and Herodotus. Snorri's kings and heroes, Laing wrote, are the forefathers of the English nation, not just "of the people, but of the institutions and character of the nation, to an extent not sufficiently considered by our historians."

In 1851 Benjamin Thorpe retold the *Edda*s in book one of *Northern Mythology*, amending the parts of Snorri he considered ludicrous. He filled out the volume with German folklore, while books two and three featured Scandinavian tales of trolls, elves, dwarfs, werewolves, witches, ghosts, water sprites, priests, knights, and fiddlers.

As an Oxford student leafing through Thorpe's book "on a cold May night when the north wind was blowing," William Morris found his attention fixed by one of the tales. He retold it, in gloomy gothic style, for the *Oxford and Cambridge Magazine* in 1856. Soon he was seeking out Icelandic translations as "a good corrective to the maundering side of medievalism." He began learning the language in 1868, meeting three days a week with the Icelandic scholar Eirikr Magnusson. The two would pick a saga and read it aloud side by side, with Magnusson explaining points of grammar. He then made a literal translation, Morris revised it for style, and they published it. They would work together on their Saga Library for twenty-five years.

Meanwhile Morris became a leader of the Arts and Crafts movement, managing a firm that designed stained glass, metalwork, wood carvings, furniture, jewelry, wallpaper, fabrics, tapestries, and carpets. He founded the Kelmscott Press, which produced fine illustrated books. He became a prominent socialist and wrote *The Decorative Arts: Their Relation to Modern Life and Progress*; *Hopes and Fears for Art*; *Art and Socialism*; and *Useful Work versus Useless Toil*.

In the literature of the North, Morris sensed the "air of freedom." From visiting Iceland in 1871 and 1873, he wrote, "I learned one lesson: that the most grinding poverty is a trifling evil compared with the inequality of classes." He loved the "glorious simplicity of the terrible and tragic, but beautiful land, with its well-remembered stories of brave men." Riding a horse through the wastes of Iceland, he said, "gave me that momentary insight into what the whole thing means that blesses us sometimes and is gone again."

The *Times Literary Supplement,* reviewing Morris's translation of *Heimskringla,* remarked, "In the Sagas he found men walking free, not hampered with a complex civilization, but making 'the pomp of emperors ridiculous' by their native courage, their high spirit, their honour, their lively knowledge of real things, such as horses and boats. His political theories were mostly the result of his Icelandic reading; the Sagas were the touchstone that refuted the vanity of modern life. He could not get over the difference between modern England and the open life of the Sagas, where individual men are not lost in averages and statistics."

Morris and Magnusson's *Stories of the Kings of Norway Called The Round World* was hailed as "a magnificent literary work." A poem Morris wrote based on *Laxdaela Saga* elevated Icelandic literature to "Sunday afternoon picnic reading status." Gushed one fan, "We take Morris's poem into the woods with us and read it aloud, greedily, looking to see how much *more* there is in store for us."

Morris produced two versions of the story of Sigurd the Dragon-Slayer. It was, he thought, "the Great Story of the North, which should be to all our race what the Tale of Troy was to the Greeks." But the *Volsunga Saga* he and Magnusson translated, he conceded, was "rather of the monstrous order." His retelling in verse from 1876, *The Story of Sigurd the Volsung and the Fall of the Niblungs,* fills out the characters' thoughts and emotions in a novelistic manner, casting Sigurd as a typical Victorian golden boy. It has been called "the greatest of all his poems." According to Morris's daughter, it was the book he "wished to be remembered by."

He did not get his wish. Morris also wrote a number of romances, as he called them, on Icelandic themes. One, *The Wood Beyond the World,* published in 1894, is considered the first fantasy novel—defined as a novel set in an imaginary medieval world where magic works—making Morris the father of the genre. Another, *The House of the Wolfings* from 1889, was purchased by the young J. R. R. Tolkien in 1914 with his winnings from a college English prize. It was one of the only contemporary novels Tolkien liked (literature for him ended with Chaucer). He also bought Morris's translation of the *Volsunga Saga.*

Tolkien had known the tale of Sigurd the Dragon-Slayer since he was a tot. A child-friendly version appeared in Andrew Lang's *Red Fairy Book,* which was published in 1890, two years before Tolkien was born; reading it had made him desire "dragons with a profound desire." By sixteen, having already learned Latin, Greek, French, German, Anglo-Saxon, Middle English, and a little Welsh, he picked up *Volsunga Saga* in Icelandic and began puzzling it out. He soon was relaying the gory parts to his friends. As a professor of Anglo-Saxon at Oxford in the 1920s and '30s, he wrote his own version of the tale in two alliterative lays; they were not published until 2009.

Tolkien had entered Oxford in 1911 planning to study philology. Under W. A. Craigie, who revised Thorpe's *Northern Mythology,* Tolkien read Snorri's *Edda* (including the ludicrous parts), the *Poetic Edda,* and the sagas. During World War I he fought for eight months on the Somme and returned to England with trench fever in November 1916. He spent much of 1917 in the hospital, where he began writing the fantastical tales that would become *The Silmarillion.* After the war he returned to Oxford, only to learn that philology "is in some quarters treated as though it were one of the things that the late war was fought to end." It was a "German-made" science.

He took a teaching post at Leeds University in 1920 and created a linguistics syllabus that was decidedly pro-Icelandic. He was helped in this effort by E. V. Gordon, who would publish *An Introduction to Old Norse* in 1927. Gordon and Tolkien also formed the Viking Club for their students, mixing beer bashes with saga reading and the composing of rude and silly songs in Old Icelandic and Anglo-Saxon. Philology, Tolkien wrote, "appears to have lost for these students its connotations of terror if not mystery."

When Tolkien replaced Craigie as professor of Anglo-Saxon at Oxford in 1925, he again ran afoul of the antiphilologists. But he was determined to return Icelandic literature to the *English* canon. He suggested substituting Snorri for a few of the many hours devoted to Shakespeare. (Tolkien's dislike of Shakespeare would grow over time. In the 1950s he would wish "a murrain," a disease of sheep's feet, on the bard for having debased the idea of elves with his "damned cobwebs" in *A Midsummer Night's Dream.*) It took Tolkien six years to win over his Oxford colleagues. He did so with a version of the Viking Club, inviting his fellow dons, including C. S. Lewis, to read Icelandic literature aloud with him.

They began with Snorri's *Edda.* Reading it in Icelandic was slow going but addictive, Lewis recalls: "Hammered my way through a couple of pages in about an hour, but I am making some headway. It is an exciting experience." Lewis, who would later write the classic fantasy series *The Chronicles of Narnia,* had also been smitten as a boy by "pure 'Northernness.'" Lewis had devoured William Morris's long poem *The Story of Sigurd the Volsung,* then the rest of Morris's books. Popular versions of Snorri's tales had inspired Lewis to write an adolescent tragedy about the Norse gods, "Loki Bound." Now Lewis and Tolkien spent late nights "discoursing of the gods and giants of Asgard": "Arising from the perplexities of Odin, we had a long and interesting discussion on religion," Lewis writes. They discussed dragons and whether myths were simply lies or, as Tolkien put it, if all creation was "myth-woven and elf-patterned." After hearing Tolkien read *The Hobbit* aloud, Lewis encouraged him to publish it. As Lewis wrote to a childhood friend in 1933, "It is so exactly like what we would both have longed to write (or read) in 1916: so that one feels he is not making it up but merely describing the same world into which all three of us have the entry."

That world was largely Snorri's, though Tolkien never admitted it. When he introduced Snorri's *Edda* to his friends, Tolkien did not call it that. To him it was the *Younger Edda,* as opposed to the purer, poetic, and fully anonymous *Elder Edda.* He did not think of Snorri as an author. But we shouldn't blame Tolkien for not giving credit where it is due: He did not even speak of himself as an author. While working on *The Lord of the Rings,* he wrote, "The thing seems to write itself once I get going, as if the truth comes out then, only imperfectly glimpsed in the preliminary sketch." Of *The Silmarillion,* he said, "The mere stories were the thing. They arose in my mind as 'given' things. . . . always I had the sense of recording what was already 'there,' somewhere: not of 'inventing.'"

Many characters and motifs his readers assumed Tolkien had invented were in fact already there (if muddled or in disguise) in the works of Snorri Sturluson. The wizard Gandalf, Tolkien said, was an "Odinic wanderer," like the old man with a broad-brimmed hat and a staff who wanders the nine worlds in Snorri's tales and sits by King Olaf's bedside, keeping him up late with wondrous stories. All powerful, Gandalf, like Odin, has a quick temper and a wry sense of humor, and he rides the best horse.

Gandalf's name comes from Snorri's list of dwarfs (as do the names of most all Tolkien's dwarfs). But Gandalf is nothing like a dwarf, Tolkien insisted. Nor is he an elf, though the Icelandic *gandálfr* means "elf with a staff." Snorri did not clearly distinguish his light elves, dark elves, black elves, and dwarfs. "Tolkien (like Grimm) was prepared to say that Snorri Sturluson had just got it wrong," notes one modern scholar. "But unlike Grimm he insisted on providing a story to explain *how* Snorri got it wrong." Tolkien's light elves had seen the light of the two sacred trees. His dark elves lived in woodlands, loving stars and twilight. His dwarfs were Snorri's dwarfs, dwelling in the earth or in halls of stone and crafting fabulous weapons and ships and jewelry. The black elves became Tolkien's orcs and goblins, who battle against the dwarfs for control of their great underground halls.

None of Snorri's sources divides elves into light, dark, and black. It sounds suspiciously like the description of Christian angels in the Old Norse *Elucidarius,* which circulated in Snorri's time. Nor did Snorri say much about light elves, except to make them almost gods: "What troubles the gods? What troubles the elves?" he asks, quoting the "Song of the Sibyl" as Ragnarok looms. Tolkien's elves, like Snorri's, are "fairer than the sun to look at," but their characters are more like the Tuatha de Danaan of Irish myth or the Hidden Folk of Icelandic folklore.

In addition to the wizard, dwarfs, and elves, Iceland and Icelandic literature inspired Tolkien's dragon, shape-shifter, warrior women, riders, giant eagles, and trolls, not to mention his wargs, barrow-wights, magic swords, Mount Doom, and the cursed ring of power.

In Tolkien's opinion, medieval literature had far too few real dragons: He counts only three. Of these, his Smaug draws from the dragon of *Beowulf* a little, from Snorri's Midgard Serpent not at all, and most from Fafnir, the dragon slain by Sigurd. What Tolkien liked best about Fafnir was his riddling talk and his vulnerable unarmored spot, both found only in the Icelandic *Volsunga Saga,* which Snorri may have known but did not write.

Beorn, the warrior in *The Hobbit* who turns into a bear, is Norse. Snorri's Odin could change into "a bird or a beast, a fish or a dragon," while Egil's grandfather, Kveld-Ulf, became a wolf at twilight. Berserks (loosely, Bear Shirts) usually take on a bear's frenzy, but a few in the sagas shape-shift into actual bears. Tolkien was thinking of these when he patterned Beorn's hall after an illustration of a Viking feast hall in E. V. Gordon's *Introduction to Old Norse.*

The warrior woman Eowyn in *The Lord of the Rings* is a Snorri-type Valkyrie—her people, the Riders of Rohan, are an overlay of Icelandic saga on Anglo-Saxon lay. The one thing Anglo-Saxon literature is missing, and for which the sagas are notable, is the love of horses.

Tolkien's giant eagles appear in the *Edda* (though they are not the hero's friends). Snorri describes the god Loki bashing at one with a stick. "Then the pole was stuck to the eagle's body and Loki's hands to the other end. The eagle flew at such a height that Loki's feet banged down against the stones and gravel and trees, and his arms he thought were going to be wrenched from his shoulders. He shouted and begged the eagle most earnestly for a truce."

Trolls populate *Heimskringla* as they do *The Hobbit,* and in both books they feast on men (or dwarfs). Snorri has fun retelling the story of an Icelander who barely escapes being eaten: "When they had slept there a short while a great troll woman came to the house, and when she came in she swept quickly about her, took the bones and everything that she thought eatable and thrust them into her mouth. She then grabbed the man nearest her, tore him and slit him in half and cast him on the fire."

Even the landscape of Tolkien's Middle-earth (except for the very English Shire) is Icelandic, though Tolkien never visited Iceland except vicariously through the sagas and *Edda*s or by reading travelers' tales. The hobbit Bilbo Baggins's ride to "the last homely house" of Rivendell, for example, matches one of William Morris's excursions from the 1870s point for point. Both riders are fat, timid, tired, and missing the small comforts of home. Each sets out on a charming pony ride that turns dreary, wet, and miserable. The wind is cold and biting. The landscape is doleful, black, rocky, with "slashes of grass-green and moss-green," Tolkien writes. Chasms open beneath their feet. Bogs and waterfalls abound. The pony stumbles, the baggage (mostly food) is lost, the fire refuses to light. The rider nods off on the last leg and is astonished: There was "no indication of this terrible gorge till one was quite on the edge of it," Morris writes. Narrow, it lay between steep cliffs cut by a deep green river. "We rode down at right angles into the main gorge, with a stream thundering down it; we rode round the very verge of it amidst a cloud of spray from the waterfall." Finally the gorge debouched into a green valley with a handsome farmstead. "A sweet sight it was to us: we rode swiftly down," Morris writes, and soon were happily "out of the wind and rain in the clean parlor, drinking coffee and brandy, and began to feel that we had feet and hands again."

Bilbo Baggins is a far cry from Snorri's laugh-in-the-face-of-death Viking heroes; he is more like Snorri himself: fat, cowardly, clever, a collector of old lore, and overly fond of his food and drink. But Beorn the shape-shifter would be at home in Snorri's books, as would Eowyn the shield maiden and Aragorn the secret king. Gandalf the wizard, treed by wolves, gleefully determines to kill as many as he can before they eat him. The dwarf Thorin

Oakenshield, captured by wood elves, is as sullen and surly as Egil Skalla-Grimsson before the king, outnumbered but not at all cowed. All illustrate the "theory of courage," which Tolkien called "the great contribution of early Northern literature," meaning both Icelandic and Old English literature. It is a "creed of unyielding will": The heroes refuse to give up even when they know the monsters—evil—will win. For that is the big difference between Snorri's Ragnarok and the Christian Doomsday. Odin and the human army of Valhalla do not win. They have no hope of winning. They are doomed and they know it. There's a "shadow of despair" about these heroes, an "intense emotion of regret," as in Tolkien's fantasy. For even if his Middle-earth is saved from the evil forces of Sauron, the elves must leave; magic will dwindle. Still, men and elves, dwarfs, wizards, and hobbits fight and die for the good and the right.

The *Hobbit, The Lord of the Rings,* and *The Silmarillion* are indebted to Snorri in one last way. Tolkien was enchanted by saga style, with its ruthless violence, its tangle of laws and family trees, its emphasis on revealing character, not on developing it. Like Snorri in the *Edda,* Tolkien knew the worth of humor. Peculiar, grim, sly, adolescent, aslant, their wit is balanced by the depth of their lore. Which, playfully, they decline to give away all at once. They leave gaps, forcing the reader's imagination to fill them. Like riddlers who ask, *What did Odin whisper into dead Baldur's ear?* or *What have I got in my pocket?* they cheat. They know the worth of glamour—in its first meaning of enchantment or deceit. By *fantasy* Tolkien meant "a quality of strangeness and wonder" that frees things and people from "the drab blur or triteness of familiarity." It restores "a clear view."

The Hobbit was published in England in 1937. Tolkien, wrote C. S. Lewis in the *Times,* "has the air of inventing nothing. He has studied trolls and dragons at first hand and describes them with that fidelity which is worth oceans of glib 'originality.'" The reviewer for the *New York Times* in 1938 was less familiar with Icelandic literature: "This is one of the most freshly original and delightfully imaginative books for children that have appeared in many a long day."

Tolkien completed *The Lord of the Rings* in 1949. His publisher initially rejected it but relented in 1954. It proved so popular that, between 1954 and 1966, the three hardcover volumes each were reprinted ten to fourteen times. With the US paperback edition in 1965, Middle-earth became a campus cult. One student's mother told the *New York Times* in 1967, "To go to college without Tolkien is like going without sneakers." Said a bookseller at Cody's in Berkeley, "This is more than a campus craze; it's like a drug dream." Three million copies had sold by then. Translations came out in thirty-eight languages, including Icelandic.

Tolkien won the International Fantasy Award in 1954. In 1974, a year after his death, the World Science Fiction Convention created a Gandalf Award. Tolkien was given posthumous Hugo and Locus awards in 1978. He crashed out of the genre ghetto in 1996, when the BBC's *Book Choice* and the British bookstore chain Waterstone's polled readers on "the five books you consider the greatest of the century." Five thousand of the twenty-six thousand votes cast named *The Lord of the Rings*. A poll by the *Daily Telegraph* had the same result, as did those of the Folio Society and the British TV program *Bookworm*. In only one "best book" poll from the 1990s did *The Lord of the Rings* come in second; first was the Bible. To date *The Lord of the Rings* has sold an estimated three hundred million copies, fifty million alone since Peter Jackson's three-part film version debuted. The trailer for the first film, released in April 2000, set an Internet record of 1.7 million downloads in twenty-four hours; more than four hundred fan websites tracked the films' progress. As of 2010, when he began work on a two-part, 3-D version of *The Hobbit*, Jackson's Tolkien franchise had earned $3 billion at the box office and incalculable sums from home video.

Through Tolkien, Snorri Sturluson has inspired dozens of writers. Fantasy and science fiction now account for 10 percent of books published, and few books on the fantasy shelves of modern libraries or bookstores are free of wandering wizards, fair elves and werewolves, Valkyrie-like women, magic swords and talismans, talking dragons and dwarf smiths, heroes who understand the speech of birds, or trolls who turn into stone. An incomplete list of fantasy writers indebted to Snorri includes Douglas Adams, Lloyd Alexander, Poul Anderson, Terry Brooks, David Eddings, Lester del Rey, J. V. Jones, Robert Jordan, Guy Gavriel Kay, Stephen King, Ursula K. LeGuin, George R. R. Martin, Anne McCaffrey, and J. K. Rowling.

Snorri has inspired countless comic books—from Marvel's *Thor* to the Japanese anime *Matantei Loki Ragnarok*—and games, including the wildly popular Dungeons and Dragons, World of Warcraft, and Eve Online.

Three writers in recent years who have revealed their love for Norse mythology are Michael Chabon, A. S. Byatt, and Neil Gaiman. What drew them to the Norse myths—rather than to the Greek or the Celtic—was Snorri's artistry: his humor, his narrative skill, and the way he made the gods human.

Michael Chabon discovered *D'Aulaire's Book of Norse Myths* in third grade. He loved the book's "odd blend of gorgeousness and violence, its wild prodigies and grim humor. . . . Moreover (and to my eight-year-old imagination this more than anything endeared them to me) the Norse gods are *mortal*. Sure, you probably knew that already, but think about it again for a minute or two. *Mortal gods*. Gods whose flaws of character—pride, unfaithfulness, cruelty, deception, seduction—while no worse than those of Jehovah or the Olympians, will one day, *and they know this*, prove their undoing." Plus there was a "bright thread of silliness, of mockery and self-mockery" running through the tales— Snorri's master touch.

A. S. Byatt published *Ragnarok*, her retelling of Snorri's tale, in 2011. Like Chabon, Byatt preferred the Norse gods because they were "peculiarly human," she said. "They are human because they are limited and stupid. They are greedy and enjoy fighting and playing games. They are cruel and enjoy hunting and jokes. They know Ragnarok is coming but are incapable of imagining any way to fend it off, or change the story. They know how to die gallantly, but not how to make a better world."

Asked in an interview if he had a favorite myth, Neil Gaiman, whose *Sandman* comics have a strong Norse component, said, "I keep going back to the Norse ones because most myths are about people who are in some way cooler and more magical and more wonderful than us, and while the Norse gods probably sort of qualify, they're all sort of small-minded evil, conniving bastards, except for Thor and he's thick as two planks." Gaiman remembers having a copy of Roger Lancelyn Green's *Tales of the Norsemen* when he was about seven. "I still remember the sheer thrill of reading about Thor, and going into this weird cave that they couldn't make sense of with five branches—a short one and four longer ones—and coming out in the morning from this place on their way to fight the giants . . . and realizing they'd actually spent the night in this giant's glove, and going, Okay, we're off to fight these guys. Right." It is a tale told only by Snorri.

In 2001 Gaiman published *American Gods*. It won the Hugo and Nebula awards, was the first "One Book One Twitter" title in 2010, and, in 2012, was made into an HBO television series. *American Gods* essentially updates Snorri's *Edda*, for both Gaiman and Snorri ask, what do we lose when the old gods are forgotten?

Snorri's Odin, in Gaiman's book, goes by the name Mr. Wednesday. In this passage he reveals himself—by paraphrasing Snorri: "His right eye glittered and flashed, his left eye was dull. He wore a cloak with a deep monk-like cowl, and his face stared out from the shadows. 'I told you I would tell you my names. This is what they call me. I am Glad-of-War, Grim, Raider, and Third. I am One-Eyed. I am called Highest, and True-Guesser. I am Grimnir, and I am the Hooded One. I am All-Father, and I am Gondir Wand-Bearer. I have as many names as there are winds, as many titles as there are ways to die.'"

Mourned Snorri in his *Edda*, "But these things have now to be *told* to young poets." They have forgotten the names of Odin. The old lore is dwindling and will soon vanish into neverwhere. "But these stories are *not* to be consigned to oblivion," he insisted. And because of the books he wrote, they were not.

"And now," wrote Snorri, in the voice of Odin, "if you have anything more to ask, I can't think how you can manage it, for I've never heard anyone tell more of the story of the world. Make what use of it you can."

Acknowledgments

On the 770th anniversary of Snorri's death, I dabbled my feet in his hot tub at Reykholt and leaned back to look up through the steam at the faint wisps of northern lights playing above. I gave thanks to the generations of writers and scholars who preserved, edited, and translated his books and those of his nephews and peers, or speculated on their lives and times. Through their efforts, Snorri lives on.

Most recently Óskar Guðmundsson published an exhaustively researched biography in Icelandic, *Snorri: Ævisaga Snorra Sturlusonar 1179–1241* (Reykjavík: JPV útgáfa, 2009), that attempted to establish for the first time the exact sequence of events in Snorri's life. I departed from Óskar's chronology only occasionally; I also relied on his guidance when I became hopelessly enmired in Icelandic genealogies.

Other scholars and friends graciously agreed to read parts or all of this book in manuscript. I am indebted to Matthew J. Driscoll of the Arnamagnaean Institute, Copenhagen; Torfi Tulinius of the University of Iceland, Reykjavík; Oren Falk of Cornell University; Peter Travis of Dartmouth College; Sigríður Sigurðardóttir of the Byggðasafn Skagfirðingar at Glaumbær, Iceland; and Paul Acker of Saint Louis University; Christina Romano of Woodside, California; and Ginger McCleskey of El Cerrito, California. I am grateful for their insightful comments and encouragement; all errors in the book are my own.

My research was facilitated by the open access policies of Dartmouth College Library and the National Library of Iceland. Snorrastofa, the cultural center at Reykholt named for Snorri Sturluson, gave me permission to use its library and made me comfortable in its writer's apartment. My friend Þórður Grétarsson and his parents, Grétar Guðbergsson and Guðný Þórðardóttir, looked after me, as they do so well, when my research took me to Reykjavík.

The artist Jeffery Mathison lent this book, as he has all my books, his cartographic talent. For help obtaining other illustrations, I am indebted to Guðmundur Oddur Magnússon of the Iceland Academy of the Arts; Guðrún Sveinbjarnardóttir of the National Museum of Iceland; Jón Torfason and Eiríkur G. Guðmundsson of the National Archives of Iceland; Sigurgeir Steingrímsson of the Árni Magnússon Institute in Iceland; Stella Calvert-Smith of akg-images; Matthew J. Driscoll, once again, of the Arnamagnaean Institute, Copenhagen; archaeology student Catherine Wood; Gísli Pálsson of the University of Iceland; and Linda Wooster of St. Johnsbury Academy's Grace Stuart Urcott Library in St. Johnsbury, Vermont. Thanks to Laura Lancaster and Carla Benton of Palgrave Macmillan for extensive hand-holding during this process.

My enthusiastic editor, Luba Ostashevsky, gave this book the necessary nudge, and my agent, Michelle Tessler, didn't talk me out of it. To both I am grateful.

No stories would ever be told without the support of my husband, Charles Fergus, who understands what Iceland means to me.

Notes

*T*hroughout the text of this book, I have standardized and Anglicized the spelling of Icelandic words and names (even within quotations) in order to minimize the reader's confusion. In these notes, they are given in the authors' original spellings.

Two primary sources provide direct information on Snorri's life, both written by his nephew Sturla Þórðarson (whom I have nicknamed Saga-Sturla) ca. 1264–1284. *Íslendingasaga* (*Saga of the Icelanders*) is part of the long compilation called *Sturlunga Saga*; I have consistently used the translation by Julia McGrew in McGrew and George Thomas, *Sturlunga Saga* (New York: Twayne, 1974), 1:117–447. All references to the *Saga of the Icelanders* in these notes are to this translation. *Hákonarsaga Hákonarsonar* (*King Hakon's Saga*) has not been translated. I used the edition by Guðbrandur Vigfússon in *Icelandic Sagas and Other Historical Documents Relating to the Settlements and Descents of the Northmen on the British Isles*, vol. 2 (London: Her Majesty's Stationery Office, 1887). Translations are my own unless otherwise noted.

The inventory of the church at Reykholt, or *Reykjaholtsmáldagi*, the oldest manuscript in Icelandic, contains information about Reykholt in Snorri's day, some of it possibly in his own hand. All references are to the edition by Guðvarður Már Gunnlaugsson, translated by Margaret Cormack (Reykholt: Reykholtskirkja-Snorrastofa, 2000).

The McGrew and Thomas two-volume translation of *Sturlunga Saga* also includes *Sturlusaga* (*Saga of Hvamm-Sturla*) about Snorri's father (1:57–13), translated by McGrew; *About Sturla Thordarson*, translated by McGrew (2:487–99); and the *Saga of Gudmund Arason the Priest*, about Snorri's kinsman, Bishop Gudmund the Good (2:91–143), translated by Thomas. The *Saga of Thorgils and Haflidi* (2:25–70), the *Saga of Hrafn Sveinbjarnarson* (2:207–26), the *Saga of the Men of Svinafell* (2:323–46), and the *Saga of Thorgils Skardi* (2:347–488), all translated by McGrew, are also cited. References are to these translations unless otherwise noted.

Snorri's *Edda, Egil's Saga,* and *Heimskringla* have been brought out in English translation many times. When citing these texts, I have chosen the translation with which I was most familiar or that seemed most apt, occasionally adapting the wording slightly or combining several translations. The retellings of Snorri's myths at the beginning of each chapter are my own translations, with occasional quotations from the Faulkes or Young translations of the *Edda.*

Sturluson, Snorri. *Edda.* Translated and edited by Anthony Faulkes. 1987. Reprint, Vermont: Charles E. Tuttle, 1995. [Referenced as *Edda* (Faulkes).]

———. (published anonymously). *Egil's Saga.* Translated by Hermann Pálsson and Paul Edwards. New York: Penguin, 1978. [All references in the notes to *Egil's Saga* are to this edition.]

———. *The Heimskringla, or Chronicle of the Kings of Norway.* Translated by Samuel Laing. 1844. Reprint, New York: E. P. Dutton, 1930. [Referenced as *Heimskringla* (Laing).]

———. *Heimskringla: History of the Kings of Norway.* Translated by Lee M. Hollander. 1964. Reprint, Austin: University of Texas Press, American-Scandinavian Foundation, 1964. [Referenced as *Heimskringla* (Hollander).]

———. *Heimskringla, or The Lives of the Norse Kings.* Translated by Erling Monsen. 1932. Reprint, New York: Dover 1990. [Referenced as *Heimskringla* (Monsen).]

———. *The Prose Edda: Tales from Norse Mythology.* Translated by Jean I. Young. 1954. Reprint, Los Angeles: University of California Press, 1964. [Referenced as *Edda* (Young).]

Preface: Gandalf

ix   **"What troubles the gods?"**: adapted from *Edda* (Faulkes), 55.

ix   **Tolkien . . . C. S. Lewis**: T. A. Shippey, *The Road to Middle-Earth* (Boston: Houghton Mifflin, 1983), 61, 220; Humphrey Carpenter, *Tolkien* (Boston: Houghton Mifflin, 1977), 137, 149; and Carpenter, *The Inklings* (Boston: Houghton Mifflin, 1979), 25–31. On Shakespeare see *The Letters of J. R. R. Tolkien,* ed. Humphrey Carpenter (Boston: Houghton Mifflin, 2000), 213; and C. S. Lewis, *Selected Literary Essays,* ed. Walter Hooper (Cambridge, UK: Cambridge University Press, 1969), 88–105.

x   **"The gods seated themselves"**: *Edda* (Young), 41–42.

xi   **Tolkien had read Morris's Journals**: Marjorie Burns, *Perilous Realms* (Toronto: University of Toronto Press, 2005), 81–83.

xi   **The name of the wizard:** Carpenter, *Letters of J. R. R. Tolkien*, 31, 119;
         John D. Rateliff, *The History of the Hobbit* (New York: HarperCollins,
         2007), 1:ix, 15, 30, 168; Burns, *Perilous Realms*, 71, 95–104.

Introduction: The Wizard of the North

1   **"Odin was the cleverest":** *Heimskringla* (Monsen), 4.

1   **a fat man:** Sigurður Nordal, *Snorri Sturluson* (1920; repr., Reykjavík: Hel-
         gafell, 1973), 67.

2   **two boy-kings:** Henry Goddard Leach, *Angevin Britain and Scandinavia*
         (Cambridge, MA: Harvard University Press, 1921), 50–52; and Kevin J.
         Wanner, *Snorri Sturluson and the "Edda"* (Toronto: University of Toronto
         Press, 2008), 82.

2   **landed man, or baron:** Einar Ól. Sveinsson, *Age of the Sturlungs* (Ithaca,
         NY: Cornell University Press, 1953), 38.

3   **certain of his authorship:** Óskar Halldórsson, "Sagnaritun Snorra Sturlu-
         sonar," in *Snorri: átta alda minning* (Reykjavík: Sögufélag, 1979), 113–38;
         Jonna Louis Jensen, "Did Snorri Sturluson write Heimskringla?" in Vladi-
         mir Stariradev, ed., *Snorri Sturluson and the Roots of Nordic Literature*
         (Sofia: University of Sofia, 2004), 96–101; Vésteinn Ólason, "Er Snorri hö-
         fundur *Egils sögu?*" *Skírnir* 142 (1968): 48–67; Torfi Tulinius, *The Matter of
         the North* (Odense: Odense University Press, 2002); and Tulinius, *Skáldið í
         skriftinni* (Reykjavík: Hið íslenska bókmenntafélag, 2004).

3   **what *Edda* . . . means:** Eiríkr Magnússon, "Edda" (1896), repr. *Saga-Book*
         23 (1990–93): 317–38; Anthony Faulkes, "Edda," *Gripla* 2 (1977): 32–39;
         Helga Kress, "What a Woman Speaks," in Elisabeth Møller Jensen, ed., *The
         History of Nordic Women's Literature* (Copenhagen: KVINFO, 1993–1998),
         www.nordicwomensliterature.net/article/what-woman-speaks.

3   **"textbook on mythology":** Sigurður Nordal, introduction to *Edda*
         (Young), 12–13.

3   **cryptic hints:** Thomas A. DuBois, *Nordic Religions in the Viking Age* (Phil-
         adelphia: University of Pennsylvania Press, 1999), 42, 66.

4   **"peculiar grim humor":** H. A. Guerber, *Myths of the Norsemen* (1909;
         repr., New York: Dover Publications, 1992), xiv.

4   **"The Round World" or "The Orb of the Earth":** William Morris and
         Eiríkur Magnússon, trans., *Stories of the Kings of Norway Called The
         Round World* (London: Bernard Quaritch, 1893); and John Lindow, *Norse
         Mythology* (Oxford: Oxford University Press, 2001), 23.

4　**"biography of great men"**: Thomas Carlyle, writing in 1840, quoted by Heather O'Donoghue, *From Asgard to Valhalla* (London: I. B. Tauris, 2007), 155.

5　**dine on candle wax**: O'Donoghue, *From Asgard to Valhalla*, 106.

6　**"wellspring of Western culture"**: Guerber, *Myths of the Norsemen*, back cover of the 1992 reprint.

7　**"bequeathed a mythology"**: Jorge Luis Borges, "Las *kenningar*," in *La historia de la eternidad* (Buenos Aries: Emecé Editores, 1936), translated by Richard Howard and César Rennert in Jorge Luis Borges, *Selected Poems, 1923-1967* (bilingual edition), ed. Norman Thomas di Giovanni (New York: Delacorte, 1972), 163.

7　**"disguised himself"**: *Edda* (Faulkes), 7.

7　**"never at a loss for words"**: *Egil's Saga*, 78–79.

8　**the one-eyed wizard-king**: *Heimskringla* (Monsen), 5, 167.

Chapter One: Odin's Eye

9　**"Wisdom is memory"**: From a metrical list preserved in a manuscript of Snorri's *Edda*, quoted by Judy Quinn, "From Orality to Literacy in Medieval Iceland," in Margaret Clunies Ross, ed., *Old Icelandic Literature and Society* (Cambridge, UK: Cambridge University Press, 2000), 54.

9　**mighty, magical gap**: Adapted from the translation of *Ginnungagap* by Margaret Clunies Ross, *A History of Old Norse Poetry and Poetics* (Cambridge, UK: D. S. Brewer, 2005), 177.

10　**creation of the world**: *Edda* (Faulkes), 9–13.

10　**like the Christian God**: Clunies Ross, *History of Old Norse Poetry*, 181.

10　**favored Thor**: Gunnar Karlsson, *The History of Iceland* (Minneapolis: University of Minnesota Press, 2000), 19; and Martin Arnold, *Thor* (New York: Continuum, 2011), 60.

11　**a good sailing wind**: Annette Lassen, "Oðinn in Old Norse Texts Other Than *The Elder Edda, Snorra Edda*, and *Ynglinga Saga*," *Viking and Medieval Scandinavia* 1 (2005): 91–108.

11　**god of kings**: Thomas A. DuBois, *Nordic Religions in the Viking Age* (Philadelphia: University of Pennsylvania Press, 1999), 58; Karlsson, *History of Iceland*, 19; and Simonetta Battista, "Interpretations of the Roman Pantheon in the Old Norse Hagiographical Sagas," in Margaret Clunies Ross, ed., *Old Norse Myths, Literature, and Society* (Odense: University Press of Southern Denmark, 2003), 177.

11   **"more imaginative efforts"**: Kevin J. Wanner, *Snorri Sturluson and the "Edda"* (Toronto: University of Toronto Press, 2008), 137; Roberta Frank, "Snorri and the Mead of Poetry," in Ursula Dronke et al., eds., *Speculum Norroenum* (Odense: Odense University Press, 1981), 159–69; and *Edda* (Faulkes), 61–64.

12   **Deildar-Tunga**: Guðrún Sveinbjarnardóttir et al., "Land in Landscapes Circum *Landnám*," *Journal of the North Atlantic* 1 (2008): 1–15.

12   **cows or "cow equivalents"**: Árni Daníel Júlíusson, "Manorial Desmesnes in Medieval Iceland," *Viking and Medieval Scandinavia* 6 (2010): 10–12; Jesse Byock, *Viking Age Iceland* (New York: Penguin, 2001), 27; Bruce Gelsinger, *Icelandic Enterprise* (Columbia: University of South Carolina Press, 1981), 36; and Óskar Guðmundsson, *Snorri* (Reykjavík: JPV útgáfa, 2009), 24.

13   **Iceland was an anomaly**: Byock, *Viking Age Iceland*, 66; Orri Vésteinsson, "A Divided Society," *Viking and Medieval Scandinavia* 3 (2007): 117–40; Karlsson, *History of Iceland*, 173–76; and Einar Ól. Sveinsson, *Age of the Sturlungs* (Ithaca, NY: Cornell University Press, 1953), 49.

14   **Stone-Throwing Summer**: *Saga of Gudmund Arason the Priest*, 96. Two sources date Snorri's birth: One says 1178, the other 1179; I have chosen thc carlicr date.

14   **"With laws shall our land be built"**: *Njal's Saga*, trans. Magnus Magnusson and Hermann Pálsson (1960; repr., New York: Penguin, 1976), 159. See also *Laws of Early Iceland*, trans. Andrew Dennis, Peter Foote, and Richard Perkins (1980; repr., Winnipeg: University of Manitoba Press, 2006).

16   **candidate for bishop**: Kirsten Wolf, "Pride and Politics in Late-Twelfth-Century Iceland," in Thomas A. DuBois, ed., *Sanctity in the North* (Toronto: University of Toronto Press, 2008), 244.

16   **"old and honored teacher"**: *Saga of Hvamm-Sturla*, 110.

16   **uncrowned king**: Halldór Hermannsson, *Sæmund Sigfússon and the Oddaverjar* (Ithaca, NY: Cornell University Press, 1932), 10–17.

16   **"the devil is standing by Sturla"**: The lawsuit over Deildar-Tunga is told in the *Saga of Hvamm-Sturla*, 103–13; the case of the stolen cloth, 61–63; the bishop's oath, 72.

20   **"darkness across the south"**: *Annals of Flatey* for the year 1184, trans. Elizabeth Rowe, personal communication, October 12, 2007.

20   **"mountains in this land"**: Oren Falk, "The Vanishing Volcanoes," *Folklore* 118 (April 2007): 5, 7–8.

22   **"glaciers blaze"**: Oren Falk, Ibid.

22   **"what were the gods angry about"**: *Kristnisaga*, ed. B. Kahle (Halle: Verlag von Max Niemeyer, 1905), 39; my translation.

23   **Jon Loftsson's estate**: Sveinsson, *Age of the Sturlungs*, 53, 109; Guðmundsson, *Snorri*, 47; and Hermannsson, *Sæmund Sigfússon*, 23.

23   **Stave Church Homily**: Anonymous, "Icelandic homily for the festival of the dedication of a church," *Ecclesiologist* 4 (February 1848): 216–20.

23   **"take his words more seriously"**: Milton Gatch, "The Achievement of Aelfric and His Colleagues in European Perspective," in Paul E. Szarmach and Bernard Felix Huppé, eds., *The Old English Homily and Its Backgrounds* (Albany: State University of New York Press, 1978), 55.

24   **It came naturally**: *Heimskringla* (Monsen), 328–333, 407–409.

24   **"Magnus was not chosen king"**: *Heimskringla* (Monsen), 794; and Sverrir Jakobsson, "The Peace of God in Iceland in the 12th and 13th Centuries," in Pavel Krafl, ed., *Sacri canones servandi sunt* (Prague: Historicky ustav AV CR, 2008), 205–13.

25   **"He would not give way"**: Mary Charlotte J. Leith, *Stories of the Bishops of Iceland Translated from Biskupa sögur* (London: J. Masters, 1895), 117.

25   **Saemund the Wise**: Njörður P. Njarðvík, *The Demon Whistle* (Reykjavík: Iceland Review, 1995); and Hermannsson, *Sæmund Sigfússon*, 29, 45–48, 51–52.

27   **the monk Gunnlaug**: Guðrún Nordal, *Tools of Literacy* (Toronto: University of Toronto Press, 2001), 312.

27   **Gerbert the Wizard**: Nancy Marie Brown, *The Abacus and the Cross* (New York: Basic Books, 2010), 232–43.

27   **Ari the Learned**: In Icelandic, Sæmund and Ari carry the same nickname; I have used a different standard translation for each to help the reader distinguish them.

27   *Saemund's Edda:* Clunies Ross, *History of Old Norse Poetry*, 7–8; and Lindow, *Norse Mythology*, 12.

27   **Saemund . . . liked to tell magical tales**: Hermannsson, *Sæmund Sigfússon*, 48.

27   **Bishop Jon's schoolhouse**: Ragnheiður Traustadóttir et al., *Hólar í Hjaltadal Excavation Report* (Hólar: Hólarannsóknin, 2002); Hermannsson, *Sæmund Sigfússon*, 29–31; Helga Kress, "What a Woman Speaks," in Elisabeth Møller Jensen, ed., *The History of Nordic Women's Literature* (Copenhagen: KVINFO, 1993–1998), www.nordicwomensliterature.net /article/what-woman-speaks.

28   **120 books**: Hermann Pálsson, *Helgafell* (Reykjavík: Snæfellingaútgáfan, 1967), 59.

28   **Books commonly used to teach Latin:** Brown, *The Abacus and the Cross*, 34–39; and Diana Whaley, "A Useful Past," in Clunies Ross, *Old Icelandic Literature*, 164.

29   **"scarcely be possible for a writer":** Anthony Faulkes, "The Sources of *Skáldskaparmál*," in Alois Wolf, ed., *Snorri Sturluson* (Tübingen: Gunter Narr, 1993), 64–67.

29   **Oddi certainly taught Latin:** Marlene Ciklamini, *Snorri Sturluson* (Boston: Twayne, 1978), 20; and Karlsson, *History of Iceland*, 39.

29   **Bishop Klaeng:** Leith, *Stories of the Bishops of Iceland*, 60–63; Karlsson, *History of Iceland*, 39; and Guðrún Nordal, *Tools of Literacy*, 37.

29   **"respectable men were educated":** *Kristnisaga*, translated by Karlsson in *History of Iceland*, 40.

30   **had to make a choice:** Wanner, *Snorri Sturluson and the "Edda,"* 67.

30   **good at everything:** *Saga of the Icelanders*, 162.

30   **"greet the king grandly," "eager to play chess," master craftsman:** *Sverrir's Saga*, *Orkney Saga*, and *Saga of Hrafn Sveinbjarnarson*, translated by Guðrún Nordal in *Tools of Literacy*, 36, 31, 171.

30   **Iceland's book culture:** Jónas Kristjánsson, *Icelandic Sagas and Manuscripts* (1970; repr., Reykjavík: Iceland Review, 1980); Jónas Kristjánsson, *Icelandic Sagas, Eddas, and Art* (New York: Pierpont Morgan Library, 1982); Halldór Hermannsson, *Icelandic Manuscripts* (Ithaca, NY: Cornell University Press, 1929), 12–13; and Gísli Sigurðsson and Vésteinn Ólason, eds., *The Manuscripts of Iceland* (Reykjavík: Árni Magnússon Institute in Iceland, 2004), 47, 51–52.

31   **book chest:** *Saga of Gudmund Arason the Priest*, 106–8.

31   **sermons:** Ian Kirby, "The Bible and Biblical Interpretation in Medieval Iceland," in Clunies Ross, *Old Icelandic Literature*, 294, 292; and Margaret Cormack, "Sagas of Saints," in Clunies Ross, *Old Icelandic Literature*, 303.

32   **laws on sales of cloth:** Diana Whaley, *Heimskringla* (London: Viking Society for Northern Research, 1991), 39; and Jenny Jochens, *Women in Old Norse Society* (Ithaca, NY: Cornell University Press, 1995), 156.

32   **Easter table:** Kirby, "Bible and Biblical Interpretation," 294.

32   **keeping the calendar:** Guðmundsson, *Snorri*, 148; Sveinsson, *Age of the Sturlungs*, 108n; and Guðbrandur Vigfússon, *Sturlunga Saga* (Oxford: Clarendon Press, 1878), 1:cxl.

32   ***Book of the Icelanders:*** Sverre Bagge, *Society and Politics in Snorri Sturluson's Heimskringla* (Berkeley: University of California Press, 1991), 15; Theodore Andersson, "The King of Iceland," *Speculum* 74 (October 1999): 923–34; Whaley, in Clunies Ross, *Old Icelandic Literature*, 169–70; Gísli

Sigurðsson, *The Medieval Icelandic Saga and Oral Tradition* (Cambridge, MA: Harvard University Press, 2004), 21; Vésteinn Ólason, *Dialogues with the Viking Age* (Reykjavík: Heimskringla, 1998), 44; *Íslendingabók, Kristni Saga*, trans. Siân Grønlie (London: Viking Society for Northern Research, 2006), ix–xiii, 6, 21n, 28; and *Heimskringla* (Monsen), xxxvii.

33   **Knowing genealogies**: Whaley, "Useful Past," 192; and Quinn, "From Orality to Literacy," 46.

33   *Book of Settlements:* Whaley, "Useful Past," 173; and Jens Ulff-Möller, "The Genealogies of West-Icelandic Family Sagas and Their Relation to the Sturlung Family," in Henrik Williams, Agneta Ney, and Fredrik C. Ljungqvist, eds., *Á Austrvega: Saga and East Scandinavia* (Gävle: Gävle University Press, 2009), 966–74.

33   **books, not sagas**: Whaley, "Useful Past," 169.

33   **oral tales**: Sigurðsson, *Medieval Icelandic Saga and Oral Tradition*, 329.

33   **not self-conscious authors**: M. I. Steblin-Kamenskij, *The Saga Mind* (Odense: Odense University Press, 1973), 51.

34   **Odd Snorrason**: Theodore Andersson, *The Growth of the Medieval Icelandic Sagas* (Ithaca, NY: Cornell University Press, 2006), 25, 40; and *Morkinskinna*, trans. Theodore Andersson and Kari Ellen Gade (Ithaca, NY: Cornell University Press, 2000), 3.

34   **Brother Gunnlaug**: Helgi Þorláksson, "Historical Background," in Rory McTurk, ed., *A Companion to Old Norse–Icelandic Literature and Culture* (Malden, MA: Blackwell, 2005), 147.

34   *Rotten Parchment*: Ciklamini, *Snorri Sturluson*, 41; Whaley, "Useful Past," 180; Andersson and Gade, *Morkinskinna*, 81; Theodore Andersson, "Snorri Sturluson and the Saga School at Munkaþverá," in Wolf, *Snorri Sturluson*, 21, 23; Theodore Andersson, "The Politics of Snorri Sturluson," *Journal of English and Germanic Philology* 93, no. 1 (January 1994): 55–78.

34   **dark and grubby**: Christine M. Schott, "Footnotes on Life: Marginalia in Three Medieval Manuscripts" (master's thesis, University of Iceland, 2010), 8–9.

34   *Skjoldunga Saga*: Faulkes, "Sources of *Skáldskaparmál*," 59; and Guðrún Nordal, *Tools of Literacy*, 310.

34   **Saxo Grammaticus**: Translated by Sigurðsson, *Medieval Icelandic Saga and Oral Tradition*, 4–5.

35   **"I have counted ten rulers"**: Guðrún Nordal, *Tools of Literacy*, 130; Torfi Tulinius, "*The Matter of the North*," in Clunies Ross, *Old Icelandic Literature*, 246; Magnus Magnusson, introduction to Snorri Sturluson, *King*

Harald's Saga, trans. Magnusson and Hermann Pálsson (1966; repr., New York: Dorset, 1986), 16; and Guðmundsson, *Snorri*, 47, 57.

35   **"game of puzzles"**: Jesse Byock, "Egil's Bones," *Scientific American*, January 1995, 85.

35   **He loved poetry**: Sigurður Nordal, *Snorri Sturluson* (1920; repr., Reykjavík: Helgafell, 1973), 76; Faulkes, "Sources of *Skáldskaparmál*," 59; Sigurðsson, *Medieval Icelandic Saga and Oral Tradition*, 5–6, 15; and Frog, "Snorri Sturluson and Oral Traditions," in Williams, Ney, and Ljungqvist, *Á Austrvega*, 270–72.

35   **"stepmothers' sagas"**: Quinn, "From Orality to Literacy," 39–40; and Andersson, "King of Iceland," 926.

35   **"what his mother taught"**: Guðrún Nordal, *Tools of Literacy*, 29.

36   **Ghost stories**: Andersson, *Growth of the Medieval Icelandic Sagas*, 16.

36   **kernels of sagas**: Sigurðsson, *Medieval Icelandic Saga and Oral Tradition*, 45, who credits the idea to Carol Clover.

36   **Saga of Hvamm-Sturla**: Peter G. Foote, "Sturlusaga and Its Background," *Saga-Book* 13 (1946–53): 235. See also Úlfar Bragason, "Sturla the Trickster," in Williams, Ney, and Ljungqvist, *Á Austrvega*, 958–65.

36   **On stylistic grounds**: Jónas Kristjánsson, "The Life and Works of Snorri Sturluson," online at www.snorrastofa.is/default.asp?sid_id=21065&tre_rod=002|009|001|&tId=1. See also Gwyn Jones, "Mabinogi and Edda," *Saga-Book* 13 (1946–53): 45; Bagge, *Society and Politics*, 33; Whaley, *Heimskringla*, 88, 96; and Sveinsson, *Age of the Sturlungs*, 97.

Chapter Two: The Uncrowned King of Iceland

37   **"the Golden Age"**: *Edda* (Faulkes), 16.

37   **Frigg**: *Edda* (Young), 48.

38   **Fridays**: John Lindow, *Norse Mythology* (Oxford: Oxford University Press, 2001), 36, 202. *Friday* could also come from *Frigg* or even *Freyr*.

38   **Lovesick Freyr**: *Edda* (Young), 61–62.

38   **Loki**: *Edda* (Faulkes), 26–29.

39   **"until God breathes"**: Einar Ól. Sveinsson, *Age of the Sturlungs* (Ithaca, NY: Cornell University Press, 1953), 24.

40   **Hvamm-Sturla**: *Saga of Hvamm-Sturla*, 60, 62, 72.

40   **Gudny**: *Saga of Hvamm-Sturla*, 87, 88, 95; and *Saga of the Icelanders*, 117–19, 125–26, 164. To distinguish Saga-Sturla's work from *The Book of the Icelanders*, I refer to it simply as part of *Sturlunga Saga*.

40 **skörungur**: Sigurður Nordal, *Snorri Sturluson* (1920; repr., Reykjavík: Helgafell, 1973), 11. The translators are George Dasent (1861, 1866); Eiríkr Magnusson and William Morris (1892–1901); W. C. Green (1893); Sir Edmund Head (1866); F. York Powell (1896); Muriel Press (1899); W. G. Collingwood and J. Stefánsson (1901); Reeves, Beamish, and Anderson (1901); G. H. Hight (1914); Magnus Magnusson and Hermann Pálsson (1960s); Denton Fox and Hermann Pálsson (1970s); Jenny Jochens (1995); Keneva Kunz (1990s); Anthony Faulkes (2001); Bo Almquist (2001); and Eric V. Youngquist (2002).

41 **Thord**: *Saga of the Icelanders*, 119–20. See also Guðbrandur Vigfússon, *Sturlunga Saga* (Oxford: Clarendon Press,1878), xcvi; and Diana Whaley, *Heimskringla* (London: Viking Society for Northern Research, 1991), 29.

41 **Sighvat**: *Saga of the Icelanders*, 123–25.

41 **inherited only a book**: *Saga of the Icelanders*, 126; and Monsen, introduction to *Heimskringla* (Monsen), xiv.

42 **Marriages in Iceland**: Jenny Jochens, *Women in Old Norse Society* (Ithaca, NY: Cornell University Press, 1995), 26, 31, 37.

43 **Aud the Deep-Minded**: *Laxdaela Saga*, trans. Magnus Magnusson and Hermann Pálsson (1969; repr., New York: Penguin, 1987), 55–57; and *The Book of Settlements*, trans. Hermann Pálsson and Paul Edwards (Manitoba: University of Manitoba, 1972), 50–55.

43 **wedding of Snorri**: Óskar Guðmundsson, *Snorri* (Reykjavík: JPV útgáfa, 2009), 77–78.

43 **Laxdaela Saga was written by**: Gísli Sigurðsson, *The Medieval Icelandic Saga and Oral Tradition* (Cambridge, MA: Harvard University Press, 2004), 97; and Vésteinn Ólason, "Er Snorri höfundur *Egils sögu?*" *Skírnir* 142 (1968): 53.

44 **their double shadow**: Gunnar Benediktsson, *Snorri skáld í Reykholti* (Reykjavík: Heimskringla, 1957), 64–67.

45 **"Sighvat liked it less"**: *Saga of the Icelanders*, 126–27.

45 **Egil's Saga**: On Snorri's authorship see Ólason, "Er Snorri höfundur *Egils sögu?*", 53–58, 63; Jónas Kristjánsson, *Eddas and Sagas* (Reykjavík: Hið íslenska bókmenntafélag, 2007), 268–69; Torfi Tulinius, *The Matter of the North* (Odense: Odense University Press, 2002), 234, 288; Torfi Tulinius, *Skáldið í skriftinni* (Reykjavík: Hid íslenska bókmenntafélag, 2004), 12, 168–71; and Bjarni Einarsson, "Skaldið í Reykjaholti," in Finn Hødnebø et al., eds., *Eyvindarbók* (Oslo: Institutt for nordistikk or litteraturvitenskap, 1992), 38–40.

47 **"expressing his own identity"**: Tulinius, *Matter of the North*, 288.

47 **Harald the Shaggy**: *Egil's Saga*, 21–61.

47   **revenge**: Ibid., 70–71.

48   **"symbol of unity"**: Axel Kristinsson, "Lords and Literature," *Scandinavian Journal of History* 28 (2003): 7–10, 14; and Jens Ulff-Möller, "The Gene-alogies of West-Icelandic Family Sagas and Their Relation to the Sturlung Family," in Henrik Williams, Agneta Ney, and Fredrik C. Ljungqvist, eds., *Á Austrvega: Saga and East Scandinavia* (Gävle: Gävle University Press, 2009), 970–71.

48   **Skalla-Grim**: *Egil's Saga*, 73–80; and Jesse Byock, "Egil's Bones," *Scientific American*, January 1995, 83.

49   **ball game**: *Egil's Saga*, 94–95.

49   **"I made a mockery"**: Ibid., 104.

49   **"Head Ransom"**: Ibid., 156–63.

50   **"Lament for My Sons"**: Ibid., 203–9.

50   **"My bald pate bobs"**: Ibid., 235.

51   **estate like Borg**: Árni Daníel Júlíusson, "Manorial Desmesnes in Medi-eval Iceland," *Viking and Medieval Scandinavia* 6 (2010): 10–18; and Mc-Grew and Thomas, *Saga of the Men of Svinafell*, 333.

51   **Stafholt**: Júlíusson, "Manorial Desmesnes," 10.

52   **cheerful host**: Viðar Pálsson, "Var engi höfðingi slíkr sem Snorri," *Saga* 41 (2003): 76–78.

53   **Dancing-Berg . . . Chess-Berg**: Whaley, *Heimskringla*, 32.

53   **lampoons**: *Saga of Thorgils and Haflidi*, 41.

53   **"The horn does not get to dry out"**: *Edda* (Faulkes), 183.

53   **drink "unmeasured"**: *Heimskringla* (Monsen), 231, 8, 87, 578.

53   **Stout**: Sigurður Nordal, *Snorri Sturluson*, 67, 68.

53   **hard drinker**: *Egil's Saga*, 79.

54   **"what with their folly and their fury"**: *Saga of the Icelanders*, 155–56.

54   **Art of War**: Danny Danziger and John Gillingham, *1215: The Year of Magna Carta* (London: Hodder and Stoughton, 2003), 117.

55   **Some kings**: *Heimskringla* (Monsen), 179, 218, 231, 237–38, 573.

55   **Sigurd Jerusalem-Farer**: *Heimskringla* (Laing), 298–300; and Helgi Þorláksson, "Hvernig var Snorri í sjón?" in *Snorri: átta alda minning* (Reykjavík: Sögufélag, 1979), 177–80.

57   **Egil had a dream**: *Saga of the Icelanders*, 131; verse translated by Kevin J. Wanner, *Snorri Sturluson and the "Edda"* (Toronto: University of Toronto Press, 2008), 19.

57   **frowning terribly**: *Egil's Saga*, 128.

58   **Reykholt**: Guðrún Sveinbjarnardóttir and Guðmundur H. Jónsson, *Reyk-holt í Borgarfirði 1999* (Reykjavík: National Museum of Iceland, 1999);

Guðrún Sveinbjarnardóttir, *Reykholt í Borgarfirði 2000* (Reykjavík: National Museum of Iceland, 2000); Guðrún Sveinbjarnardóttir, "Reykholt, A Centre of Power," in Else Mundal, ed., *Reykholt som makt og lærdomssenter* (Reykholt: Snorrastofa, 2006); Guðrún Sveinbjarnardóttir et al., "The Palaeoecology of a High Status Icelandic Farm," *Environmental Archaeology* 12 (2007): 187–206; Guðrún Sveinbjarnardóttir et al., "Land in Landscapes Circum *Landnám*," *Journal of the North Atlantic* 1 (2008): 1–15; Guðrún Harðardóttir, "The Physical Setting of Reykholt According to *Sturlunga Saga*," in Mundal, *Reykholt som makt og lærdomssenter*, 43–64; *Reykjaholtsmáldagi*, 7, 15, 32–34, 40; Sveinsson, *Age of the Sturlungs*, 85; and Guðmundsson, *Snorri*, 118.

59   **"hankering"**: *Saga of the Icelanders*, 130–31, 162.

61   **The buckler**: Ibid., 160–62; and Guðmundsson, *Snorri*, 243.

63   **eighty Norwegians**: Guðrún Nordal, "Snorri and Norway," in Mundal, *Reykholt som makt og lærdomssenter*, 78.

64   **divorce**: *Njal's Saga*, trans. Magnus Magnusson and Hermann Pálsson (1960; repr., New York: Penguin, 1976), 52; and Jochens, *Women in Old Norse Society*, 56–59.

65   **Gudmund the Good**: Eiríkr Magnússon, "The Last of the Icelandic Commonwealth," *Saga-Book* 5 (1906–1907): 324, 339; W. P. Ker, "The Life of Bishop Gudmund Arason," *Saga-Book* 5 (1906–1907): 91–92; and Sverrir Jakobsson, "The Peace of God in Iceland in the 12th and 13th Centuries," in Pavel Krafl, ed., *Sacri canones servandi sunt* (Prague: Historicky ustav AV CR, 2008), 205–13.

65   **Snorri wrote a love poem**: Guðmundsson, *Snorri*, 95–104.

65   **Bishop Thorlak**: *Saga of Gudmund Arason the Priest*, 110–11; and Guðmundsson, *Snorri*, 95–102.

67   **"delightful to converse with her"**: *Saga of the Icelanders*, 195.

67   **"man of many pleasures"**: Ibid., 131.

Chapter Three: On the Quay at Bergen

69   **"I cut the ice-cold wave"**: *Edda* (Faulkes), 184

69   **build the gods a wall**: Ibid., 35–36.

70   **Odin rode Sleipnir into Giantland**: Ibid., 77–78.

73   **"illustrations of heroic legends"**: *Egil's Saga*, 217.

73   **alum-fixed dyes**: Helgi Þorláksson, "Snorri Sturluson og Oddaverjar," in *Snorri: átta alda minning* (1979), 54, 58–59; and E. Lipson and F. Lipson,

The History of the Woollen and Worsted Industries (1921; repr., New York: Routledge, 1965), 8.

73 **dressed sumptuously**: *Heimskringla* (Monsen), 238, 603, 578, 520; and *Egil's Saga*, 177, 219.

74 **poem for King Sverrir**: Monsen in *Heimskringla* (Monsen), xvi; and Kevin J. Wanner, *Snorri Sturluson and the "Edda"* (Toronto: University of Toronto Press, 2008), 19–20, 69, 73.

74 **skald named Mani**: *Saga of the Icelanders*, 162; and Guðrún Nordal, *Tools of Literacy* (Toronto: University of Toronto Press, 2001), 178.

75 **They supported the tithe**: Gunnar Karlsson, *The History of Iceland* (Minneapolis: University of Minnesota Press, 2000), 39–41.

76 **Bishop Gudmund**: *Saga of the Icelanders*, 128; *Saga of Gudmund Arason the Priest*, 100, 106–8, 113–14, 121–23; Eiríkr Magnússon, "The Last of the Icelandic Commonwealth," *Saga-Book* 5 (1906–1907): 324, 339; W. P. Ker, "The Life of Bishop Gudmund Arason," *Saga-Book* 5 (1906–1907): 91–92; Lois Bragg, "Disfigurement, Disability, and Dis-Integration in *Sturlunga Saga*," *Alvíssmál* 4 (1994 [1995]): 23; Marlene Ciklamini, "Sainthood in the Making," *Alvíssmál* 11 (2004): 62, 66; and *The Life of Gudmund the Good, Bishop of Holar*, trans. G. Turville-Petre and E. S. Olszewska (Coventry, UK: Viking Society for Northern Research, 1942), 47–48.

77 **Bishop Thorlak**: Mary Charlotte J. Leith, *Stories of the Bishops of Iceland Translated from Biskupa sögur* (London: J. Masters, 1895), 111–13, 117; Kirsten Wolf, "Pride and Politics in Late-Twelfth-Century Iceland," in Thomas A. DuBois, ed., *Sanctity in the North* (Toronto: University of Toronto Press, 2008), 246, 255–63; and Turville-Petre and Olszewska, *Life of Gudmund the Good*, xxvi.

79 **"right to judge him"**: *Saga of the Icelanders*, 147; Magnusson and Pálsson, *Njal's Saga*, 159; Sverrir Jakobsson, "The Peace of God in Iceland in the 12th and 13th Centuries," in Pavel Krafl, ed., *Sacri canones servandi sunt* (Prague: Historicky ustav AV CR, 2008), 205–13; John Megaard, "Was *Njal's Saga* Written by Sturla Þórðarson?", paper presented at the Fourteenth International Saga Conference, Uppsala, August 9–15, 2009, 3, http://www.saga.nordiska.uu.se.

80 **chieftain Kolbein Tumason**: *Saga of Gudmund Arason the Priest*, 136; *Saga of the Icelanders*, 128, 134–41, 144–45; and Turville-Petre and Olszewska, *Life of Gudmund the Good*, xx, 50.

80 **Historians blame Gudmund**: Foote, *Age of the Sturlungs*, 237; Ker, "Life of Bishop Gudmund Arason," 91; Halldór Hermannsson, *Sæmund Sigfússon*

and the Oddaverjar (Ithaca, NY: Cornell University Press, 1932), 19; Diana Whaley, *Heimskringla* (London: Viking Society for Northern Research, 1991), 26; and Magnússon, "Last of the Icelandic Commonwealth," 339.

80   **martyrdom of Thomas Becket**: *Saga of Gudmund Arason the Priest*, 100; and Turville-Petre and Olszewska, *Life of Gudmund the Good*, xxv, 61.

81   **"there was grumbling"**: *Saga of the Icelanders*, 140–47.

82   **"scrutinized thoroughly the books"**: *Saga of Gudmund Arason the Priest*, 114.

83   **Snorri sailed to Norway**: *Saga of the Icelanders*, 164.

84   **medieval notebooks**: Nancy Marie Brown, *The Abacus and the Cross* (New York: Basic Books, 2010), 80.

84   **Bergen**: *Heimskringla* (Hollander), 664–65, 699, 721–24; and Asbjørn E. Herteig, "The Excavation of 'Bryggen,'" *Medieval Archaeology* 3 (1959): 177–86. See also Clifford D. Long, "Excavations in the Medieval City of Trondheim, Norway," *Medieval Archaeology* 19 (1975): 1–32; and Henry Goddard Leach, *Angevin Britain and Scandinavia* (Cambridge, MA: Harvard University Press, 1921), 53.

85   **Snorri again took ship**: On the following places, see *Heimskringla* (Hollander): Moster, 189; Hauga Sound, 94; Karmoy and Avaldsnes (or Ogvaldsnes), 203, 377–87, also *Ólafs saga hins helga*, ed. R. Keyser and C. R. Unger (Christiania: Feilberg and Landmarks Forlag, 1849), 35 and *Heimskringla* (Monsen), 5. On Jæren, see Peter G. Foote and David M. Wilson, *The Viking Achievement* (New York: Praeger, 1970), 39. On Larvik see David Keys, "Vikings' Home Reveals Extent of Their Wanderlust," *National Geographic News*, February 22, 2001, http://news.nationalgeographic.com/news/2001/02/0222_viking.html. On Geirstadir (Gokstad), see *Heimskringla* (Hollander), 48–49. On Tunsberg see *Heimskringla* (Hollander), 201, 89, 324; *King Hakon's Saga*, 42–49; and Óskar Gudmundsson, *Snorri* (Reykjavík: JPV útgáfa, 2009), 234.

89   **"The earl was very well disposed toward Snorri"**: *Saga of the Icelanders*, 164; and Wanner, *Snorri Sturluson and the "Edda,"* 21.

91   **Lady Kristin had remarried**: Guðmundsson, *Snorri*, 177. On Sarpsborg see *Heimskringla* (Hollander), 295. On Sighvat the Skald's poems, see *Heimskringla* (Hollander), 334–38; and Foote and Wilson, *Viking Achievement*, 368.

93   **"the lawspeaker makes answer"**: *Heimskringla* (Hollander), 316, 318, 320–21, 341, 343–46.

94   **laws of West Gautland were written down**: Guðmundsson, *Snorri*, 177.

95   **"Svegdir leaped into the stone":** *Heimskringla* (Monsen), 9.

95   **Snorri returned west:** On Konungahella, see *Heimskringla* (Hollander), 350, 714, 724–30. On Egil's insult pole, see *Egil's Saga*, 148. On Stad, see *Heimskringla* (Hollander), 68, 199. On Agdanes, see Richard Perkins, "The Gateway to Trondheim," *Saga-Book* 25 (1998–2001): 180; and *Heimskringla* (Hollander), 699.

96   **Long Serpent:** *Heimskringla* (Hollander), 220–21.

97   **winter of 1219 in Trondheim:** *Heimskringla* (Hollander), 276–78, 287–89, 275–76, 511, 699.

98   **called a knight:** Einar Ól. Sveinsson, *Age of the Sturlungs* (Ithaca, NY: Cornell University Press, 1953), 38.

98   **merchants of Bergen were in an uproar:** *Saga of the Icelanders*, 162–64.

99   **"each man did the best he could":** *Saga of Thorgils Skardi*, 440.

99   **what Snorri did is unclear:** *Saga of the Icelanders*, 171–73; *King Hakon's Saga*, 52; Theodore Andersson, *The Growth of the Medieval Icelandic Sagas* (Ithaca, NY: Cornell University Press, 2006), 108–10; Sverre Bagge, *Society and Politics in Snorri Sturluson's* Heimskringla (Berkeley: University of California Press, 1991), 133; Guðmundsson, *Snorri*, 189; and Gunnar Benediktsson, *Snorri skáld í Reykholti* (Reykjavík: Heimskringla, 1957), 100, 167.

101   **fifteen other magnificent gifts:** *Edda* (Faulkes), 218.

101   **"Hard-mouthed was Skuli":** *Saga of the Icelanders*, 173.

102   **"To us it seems ill to kiss an earl":** Translated by Wanner, *Snorri Sturluson and the "Edda,"* 88. See also Roberta Frank, *Old Norse Court Poetry* (Ithaca, NY: Cornell University Press, 1978), 125.

Chapter Four: Norse Gods and Giants

103   **"Most poets":** *Edda* (Faulkes), 106.

103   **the giant Utgard-Loki:** Anthony Faulkes, ed., *Edda* (London: Viking Society for Northern Research, 2007), 1:xxiv; and *Edda* (Faulkes), 37–46.

105   **sort of royal court:** Guðrún Nordal, *Tools of Literacy* (Toronto: University of Toronto Press, 2001), 136.

106   **a vast building project:** Óskar Guðmundsson, *Snorri* (Reykjavík: JPV útgáfa, 2009), 116, 233–37; Guðrún Sveinbjarnardóttir, "Reykholt, A Centre of Power," 28–31, 34–36, 39–40; Guðrún Harðardóttir, "The Physical Setting of Reykholt According to *Sturlunga Saga*," in Else Mundal, ed., *Reykholt som makt og lærdomssenter* (Reykholt: Snorrastofa, 2006), 45–60; Þorkell Grímsson and Guðmundur Ólafsson, "Fornar leiðslur í Reykholti í

Borgarfirði," *Árbók hins íslenzka fornleifafélags* 87 (1988): 120–21; Guðrún Sveinbjarnardóttir et al., "The Palaeoecology of a High Status Icelandic Farm," *Environmental Archaeology* 12 (2007): 188–94; and Viðar Pálsson, "Var engi höfðingi slíkr sem Snorri," *Saga* 41 (2003): 80.

107   **Snorri supported five clerics**: Benedikt Eyþórsson, "Í Þjónustu Snorra," *Sagnir* 23 (2003), 23–24; Helgi Þorláksson, "Reykholt som lærdoms-senter," 22–23; and "Snorri Sturluson, Reykholt, og augustinerordernen," in Mundal, *Reykholt som makt og lærdomssenter*, 75.

107   **Styrmir the Wise**: *Saga of the Icelanders*, 264; Eyþórsson, "Í Þjónustu Snorra," 24; Guðbrandur Vigfússon, *Sturlunga Saga* (Oxford: Clarendon Press, 1878), 1:lxxxi; *Edda* (Faulkes), xiii; and Diana Whaley, "A Useful Past," in Margaret Clunies Ross, ed., *Old Icelandic Literature and Society* (Cambridge, UK: Cambridge University Press, 2000), 180.

108   **"a good poet and farmer"**: Einar Ól. Sveinsson, *Age of the Sturlungs* (Ithaca, NY: Cornell University Press, 1953), 51. Also see Guðmundsson, *Snorri*, 256; and Torfi Tulinius, *The Matter of the North* (Odense: Odense University Press, 2002), 1.

108   **Poets, even moody types**: Alison Finlay, "Pouring Odinn's Mead," in Geraldine Barnes and Margaret Clunies Ross, eds., *Old Norse Myths, Literature, and Society* (Sydney: University of Sydney, 2000), 86, 98; Roberta Frank, *Old Norse Court Poetry* (Ithaca, NY: Cornell University Press, 1978), 27; Guðrún Nordal, *Tools of Literacy*, 165, 189, 174, 172; Eyþórsson, "Í Þjónustu Snorra," 24; *King Hakon's Saga*, 196; and *Saga of the Icelanders*, 364, 254.

110   **Snorri's rich literary life**: *Saga of the Icelanders*, 242; Guðrún Nordal, *Tools of Literacy*, 166, 190; and Anthony Faulkes, *What Was Viking Poetry For?* (Birmingham: University of Birmingham, 1993), 14.

110   **brothers Saga-Sturla and Olaf**: Vigfússon, *Sturlunga Saga*, 1:xcvi; Guðrún Nordal, *Tools of Literacy*, 191; Whaley, "Useful Past," 163; and John Megaard, "Was *Njal's Saga* Written by Sturla Þórðarson?", paper presented at the Fourteenth International Saga Conference, Uppsala, August 9–15, 2009, 3, http://www.saga.nordiska.uu.se.

110   **the *Third Grammatical Treatise***: Vigfússon, *Sturlunga Saga*, 1:cxi; Guðrún Nordal, *Tools of Literacy*, 181; Faulkes, *Edda*, 2:xliii; and Gísli Sigurðsson, *The Medieval Icelandic Saga and Oral Tradition* (Cambridge, MA: Harvard University Press, 2004), 93–98.

111   **Poetry had real power**: Margaret Clunies Ross, *A History of Old Norse Poetry and Poetics* (Cambridge, UK: D. S. Brewer, 2005), 13, 232, 72; *Saga of*

the Icelanders, 177; *Heimskringla* (Hollander), 3, 4; and Anthony Faulkes, "The Viking Mind," *Saga-Book* 31 (2007): 53.

112 **skaldic poetry**: Guðrún Nordal, *Tools of Literacy*, 178, 12, 214, 201, 36; Frank, *Old Norse Court Poetry*, 33–35, 28, 23, 21, and, on *scold*, 125; *About Sturla Thordarson*, 496; Kevin J. Wanner, *Snorri Sturluson and the "Edda"* (Toronto: University of Toronto Press, 2008), 107, 57, 73–75 (for the literal translation of the verse); Christopher Abram, *Myths of the Pagan North* (New York: Continuum, 2011), 14; Faulkes, *What Was Viking Poetry For?*, 10, 12, 14–15, 9; Peter Hallberg, *Old Icelandic Poetry* (Lincoln: University of Nebraska Press, 1975), 20; *Heimskringla* (Hollander), 277; Faulkes, "Viking Mind," 53; and Diana Whaley, "Skalds and Situational Verses in *Heimskringla*," in Alois Wolf, ed., *Snorri Sturluson* (Tübingen: Gunter Narr, 1993), 246–47.

115 **the best-educated king**: Wanner, *Snorri Sturluson and the "Edda*," 81; Henry Goddard Leach, *Angevin Britain and Scandinavia* (Cambridge, MA: Harvard University Press, 1921), 54–55; Sveinsson, *Age of the Sturlungs*, 35, 37, 41; and *Heimskringla* (Monsen), 218.

116 **Iceland's cultural capital**: Tulinius, *Matter of the North*, 10; Wanner, *Snorri Sturluson and the "Edda*," 15; and Jón Jóhannesson, *Íslendinga saga* (Reykjavík: Almenna bókafélagið, 1956), 1:373–74.

116 **"Hattatal"**: Clunies Ross, *History of Old Norse Poetry*, 164–66, 173; Wanner, *Snorri Sturluson and the "Edda*," 114, 117, 112; Faulkes, *Edda*, 4:ix; *Edda* (Faulkes), 170; and Frank, *Old Norse Court Poetry*, 32.

117 **A one-eyed chieftain**: Guðrún Nordal, *Tools of Literacy*, 127; and Óskar Halldórsson, "Sagnaritun Snorra Sturlusonar," in *Snorri: átta alda minning* (Reykjavík: Sögufélag, 1979), 117.

118 **"the lesser meters"**: *Edda* (Faulkes), 218–20.

118 **"Skaldskaparmal"**: Wanner, *Snorri Sturluson and the "Edda*," 128–30, 6, 8; Faulkes, *Edda*, 4:xxxv; and *Edda* (Faulkes), 64, xviii.

119 **Loki the Trickster**: *Edda* (Faulkes), 60–61, 96–97.

120 **sequence of information**: Martin Arnold, *Thor* (New York: Continuum, 2011), 14.

121 **Odin's lost eye**: *Edda* (Young), 43; see also *Edda* (Faulkes), 17–19, 56; and John Lindow, *Norse Mythology* (Oxford: Oxford University Press, 2001), 143.

122 **elves**: *Edda* (Faulkes), 19–20, 56; and T. A. Shippey, "Light-elves, Dark-elves, and Others," *Tolkien Studies* 1 (2004): 1–15. See also Lindow, *Norse Mythology*, 99–101, 109–10.

122   **Valkyries:** *Heimskringla* (Hollander): 125; Magnusson and Pálsson, *Njal's Saga*, 349–51; and H. R. Ellis Davidson, *Gods and Myths of Northern Europe* (Middlesex, England: Penguin, 1964), 61, 64–65.

123   **Thor's fishing trip:** *Edda* (Faulkes), 46–47, 142; Sigurðsson, *Medieval Icelandic Saga and Oral Tradition*, 10; Abram, *Myths of the Pagan North*, 40, 10, 33, 36–37; Ellis Davidson, *Gods and Myths of Northern Europe*, 89; Preben Meulengracht Sørensen, "Þórr's Fishing Expedition," in Paul Acker and Carolyne Larrington, eds., *The Poetic Edda* (London: Routledge, 2002), 123.

124   ***Poetic Edda:*** Sigurður Nordal, "The Author of Völuspá," *Saga-Book* 20 (1978–81): 115–19; Ursula Dronke, *Myth and Fiction in Early Norse Lands* (Brookfield: Ashgate, 1996), 12, 19; Stefanie Würth, "The Role of Völuspá in the Perception of Ragnarök in Old Norse–Icelandic Literature," in Margaret Clunies Ross, *Old Norse Myths, Literature, and Society* (Odense: University Press of Southern Denmark, 2003), 223; Sigurður Nordal, introduction to *Edda* (Young), 13; Meulengracht Sørensen, "Þórr's Fishing Expedition," 121; Clunies Ross, *History of Old Norse Poetry*, 8; Hallberg, *Old Icelandic Poetry*, 27; and Tim William Machan, ed., *Vafþrúðnismál* (Toronto: Pontifical Institute of Mediaeval Studies, 2008), 5–6.

125   **"Hymir's Lay":** Sigurðsson, *Medieval Icelandic Saga and Oral Tradition*, 12; and Paul B. Taylor and W. H. Auden, *The Elder Edda* (New York: Vintage, 1970), 89–94.

126   **making things up:** Margaret Clunies Ross, *Old Icelandic Literature and Society* (Cambridge, UK: Cambridge University Press, 2000), 131–32; Faulkes, *Edda* 1:xxvi, 99n; Joseph Harris, "The Masterbuilder Tale in Snorri's Edda and Two Sagas," *Archiv för nordisk filologi* 91 (1976): 66–101; Guðrún Nordal, *Tools of Literacy*, 273–74, 279, 281; Heather O'Donoghue, *From Asgard to Valhalla* (London: I. B. Tauris, 2007), 16; Marlene Ciklamini, *Snorri Sturluson* (Boston: Twayne, 1978), 54; Arnold, *Thor*, 12, 10, 15; John Lindow, "Bloodfeud and Scandinavian Mythology," *Alvíssmál* 4 (1994): 58; Ellis Davidson, *Gods and Myths*, 149; Svava Jakobsdóttir, "Gunnlöð and the Precious Mead," in Acker and Larrington, *Poetic Edda*, 34, 52; Lindow, *Norse Mythology*, 14, 303; John Lindow, "Þórr's Visit to Útgarðaloki," *Oral Tradition* 15 (2000): 170–71, 180, 182; and Gwyn Jones, "Mabinogi and Edda," *Saga-Book* 13 (1946–1953): 43.

128   **death of Baldur:** *Edda* (Faulkes), 48–51; the verse "Thokk will weep," *Edda* (Young), 84; Jones, "Mabinogi and Edda," 44–46; Abram, *Myths of the Pagan North*, 186, 215, 219, 217; Anatoly Liberman, "Some Controversial Aspects

of the Myth of Baldr," *Alvíssmál* 11 (2004): 17–54; Lewis Hyde, *Trickster Makes This World* (New York: Farrar, Straus and Giroux, 1998), 103–5; Ellis Davidson, *Gods and Myths*, 187, 176; Würth, "Role of Völuspá," 222–23; Anthony Faulkes, "Pagan Sympathy," in R. J. Glendinning and H. Bessason, eds., *Edda* (Manitoba: University of Manitoba Press, 1983), 31; Christopher Abram, "Representations of the Pagan Afterlife in Medieval Scandinavian Literature" (PhD diss., University of Cambridge, 2003), 20, 141–48, 174; Christopher Abram, "Snorri's Invention of Hermóðr's Helreið," paper presented at the Thirteenth International Saga Conference, Durham and York, August 6–12, 2006, 1–7; and Vésteinn Ólason, "The Un/Grateful Dead—From Baldr to Bægifótr," in Clunies Ross, *Old Norse Myths*, 156.

129   **Baldur's death causes Ragnarok**: Liberman, "Some Controversial Aspects," 42–43; Würth, "Role of Völuspá," 217; and Ciklamini, *Snorri Sturluson*, 57.

131   **a subtle Christian coloring**: *Edda* (Faulkes), 9, 56–57, 7–8; Abram, "Snorri's Invention of Hermóðr's Helreið," 8; Faulkes, "Pagan Sympathy," 31, 26; Clunies Ross, *History of Old Norse Poetry*, 180, 174, 182.

132   **Odd the Monk was Snorri's source**: *Heimskringla* (Hollander), 203–4; and Oddr Snorrason, *The Saga of Olaf Tryggvason*, trans. J. Sephton (London: David Nutt, 1895), 303–4.

133   **frame narrative**: Rory McTurk, "Fooling Gylfi," *Alvíssmál* 3 (1994): 3–18.

134   **wrote a boring prologue**: *Edda* (Faulkes), 1–5, xviii; Paul Acker, introduction to Acker and Larrington, *Poetic Edda*, xiii; Faulkes, *Edda*, 1:xxii–iii; Clunies Ross, *History of Old Norse Poetry*, 175–76; Abram, *Myths of the Pagan North*, 200; and Lindow, *Norse Mythology*, 22.

135   **to ransom his head**: Faulkes, *What Was Viking Poetry For?*, 23.

Chapter Five: Independent People

137   **"Age of axes"**: *Edda* (Faulkes), 53–57.

138   **no greater men in Iceland**: *Saga of the Icelanders*, 172, 177, 199, 183, 179; (verse adapted); 194–99, 190, 181, 201; Gunnar Benediktsson, *Snorri skáld í Reykholti* (Reykjavík: Heimskringla, 1957), 64, 12; Jón Jóhannesson, *Íslendinga saga* (Reykjavík: Almenna bókafélagið, 1956), 1:286–88; Óskar Guðmundsson, *Snorri* (Reykjavík: JPV útgáfa, 2009), 220–21; Torfi Tulinius, *The Matter of the North* (Odense: Odense University Press, 2002), 7; and *Reykjaholtsmáldagi*, 16.

146   **"talk was about chieftains"**: *Saga of the Icelanders*, 217; verse translated by Kevin J. Wanner, *Snorri Sturluson and the "Edda"* (Toronto: University

of Toronto Press, 2008), 47. On Hrolf Kraki, see *Edda* (Faulkes), 110–12; and Pálsson, "Var engi höfdingi slíkr sem Snorri," *Saga* 41 (2003): 64.

148 **Snorri's fiercest rival**: *Saga of the Icelanders*, 200, 125, 153–54, 180–81, 188, 217, 220–21; Benediktsson, *Snorri skáld í Reykholti*, 15; and *Egil's Saga*, 78–80.

153 **homestead of Saudafell**: *Saga of the Icelanders*, 223–38; Jonathan Grove, "Skaldic Verse-making in Thirteenth-century Iceland," *Viking and Medieval Scandinavia* 4 (2008): 85–131; and Einar Ól. Sveinsson, *Age of the Sturlungs* (Ithaca, NY: Cornell University Press, 1953), 91–92.

156 **skin disease erysipelas**: *Saga of the Icelanders*, 232–34; Guðmundsson, 296; and Diana Whaley, *Heimskringla* (London: Viking Society for Northern Research, 1991).

156 **Snorri's critical flaw: greed**: Benediktsson, *Snorri skáld í Reykholti*, 50.

156 **Snorri's daughter Hallbera**: *Saga of the Icelanders*, 234, 245.

157 **"The great hostility"**: *Saga of the Icelanders*, 240–42.

157 **"Men were more grim"**: Bogi Th. Melsted, quoted by George Thomas in the introduction to *Sturlunga Saga*, 1:23–24.

157 **too late for Jon Trout**: *Saga of the Icelanders*, 242.

158 **blames Ingibjorg**: Ibid., 246.

159 **a volcanic eruption**: Ibid., 212.

161 **"Sturla will keep the truce"**: Ibid., 248, 258–59; truce formula from *Grettir's Saga*, trans. Denton Fox and Hermann Pálsson (Toronto: University of Toronto Press, 1974), 150; and Ármann Jakobsson, "Snorri and His Death," *Scandinavian Studies* 75 (2003): 330–31.

161 **Oraekja**: *Saga of the Icelanders*, 263, 275, 282, 289, 291.

163 **return of Sturla**: Ibid., 266; *King Hakon's Saga,* trans. Theodore Andersson, "The King of Iceland," *Speculum* 74 (October 1999): 928; and Theodore Andersson, *The Growth of the Medieval Icelandic Sagas* (Ithaca, NY: Cornell University Press, 2006), 108–10.

164 **conflicting feelings about kingship**: Theodore Andersson, "The Politics of Snorri Sturluson," *Journal of English and Germanic Philology* 93 (January 1994): 55–78; Richard Gaskins, "Visions of Sovereignty in Snorri Sturluson's *Heimskringla*," *Scandinavian Journal of History* 23 (September 1998): 177–83; Andersson, "King of Iceland," 930; Nils Hallan, "Snorri fólgsnarjarl," *Skirnir* 146 (1972): 174; Benediktsson, *Snorri skáld í Reykholti*, 128; and Sveinsson, *Age of the Sturlungs*, 11.

164 **"If you wish to have my opinion"**: *Heimskringla* (Hollander), 395.

165 **"We may be in trouble"**: *Egil's Saga*, 23–26.

166 **lost his nerve:** *Saga of the Icelanders,* 293–95, 297, 298–300, 308, 311; Jónas Kristjánsson, and Jónas Kristjánsson, "The Life and Works of Snorri Sturluson," Snorrastofa, http://www.snorrastofa.is/default.asp?sid_id=21065 &tId=1&Tre_Rod=002|009|001|&qsr; and Wanner, *Snorri Sturluson and the "Edda,"* 3–4.

Chapter Six: The Ring

171 **"In this book":** *Heimskringla* (Monsen), xxxv.

172 **"Otter's ransom":** *Edda* (Faulkes), 99–105; Humphrey Carpenter, *Tolkien* (Boston: Houghton Mifflin, 1977), 22; and J. R. R. Tolkien, *The Legend of Sigurd & Gudrún,* ed. Christopher Tolkien (New York: HarperCollins, 2009), 3.

174 **Sturla Battle-Strong had overstepped:** *Saga of the Icelanders,* 313–45; and Axel Kristinsson, "Lords and Literature," *Scandinavian Journal of History* 28 (2003): 10–11.

175 **a power vacuum—an opportunity:** *Saga of the Icelanders,* 349–50; *King Hakon's Saga,* 234; Nils Hallan, "Snorri fólgsnarjarl," *Skirnir* 146 (1972): 162–70; Jón Jóhannesson, *Íslendinga saga* (Reykjavík: Almenna bókafélagið, 1956), 1:299; and Stefán Karlsson, "Hákon gamli og Skúli hertogi í Flateyjarbók," *Árbók hins íslenzka fornleifafélags* (1979): 149–54.

176 **Snorri gave the scriptorium:** *Reykjaholtsmáldagi,* 15.

176 **new web of power:** *Saga of the Icelanders,* 353, 356.

177 **Snorri could not recover:** Ibid., 357–60.

179 **avenge Snorri's death:** Ibid., 400–1.

180 **greeted Saga-Sturla coldly:** *About Sturla Thordarson,* 493–99; and Guðbrandur Vigfússon, *Sturlunga Saga* (Oxford: Clarendon Press, 1878), 1:cvi.

180 **three of Snorri's *Edda*:** Heimir Pálsson, "A Short Report from the Project on *Codex Upsaliensis* of *Snorra Edda,*" in Henrik Williams, Agneta Ney, and Fredrik C. Ljungqvist, eds., *Á Austrvega: Saga and East Scandinavia* (Gävle: Gävle University Press, 2009), 369; Eiríkr Magnússon, "Edda," *Saga-Book* 1 (1896): 332; and Judy Quinn, "*Eddu list:* The Emergence of Skaldic Pedagogy in Medieval Iceland," *Alvíssmál* 4 (1994): 87, 88; the English poet quoted is William Morris in Alan Boucher, *The Iceland Traveller* (Reykjavík: Iceland Review, 1989), 114; and Guðbrandur Vigfússon and F. York Powell, *Corpus Poeticum Borealis* (Oxford: Clarendon Press, 1883), 1:xxxvi–vii.

181   **Outside Iceland**: Saxo Grammaticus translated by Gísli Sigurðsson, *The Medieval Icelandic Saga and Oral Tradition* (Cambridge, MA: Harvard University Press, 2004), 4–5; and the fifteenth-century English poet and Thomas Nashe are quoted by Andrew Wawn, ed., *The Iceland Journal of Henry Holland* (London: Hakluyt Society, 1987), 5.

182   **Arngrim Jonsson**: *Brevis commentarius de Islandia* (1593), in Richard Hakluyt, *The Principal Navigations, Voyages, Traffiques, and Discoveries of the English Nation* (London: 1598–1600), 1:303, 307, 313, 296, 316; Arngrímur Jónsson, *Crymogaea* (1609), in Samuel Purchas, *Hakluytus Posthumus or Purchas His Pilgrimes* (1625; repr. Glasgow: James Maclehose and Sons, 1906), 13:420; Mats Malm, "The Nordic Demand for Medieval Icelandic Manuscripts," in Gísli Sigurðsson and Vésteinn Ólason, eds., *The Manuscripts of Iceland* (Reykjavík: Árni Magnússon Institute in Iceland, 2004), 102; Gunnar Karlsson, *The History of Iceland* (Minneapolis: University of Minnesota Press, 2000), 158; Heather O'Donoghue, *From Asgard to Valhalla* (London: I. B. Tauris, 2007), 107; Vigfússon and Powell, *Corpus Poeticum Borealis*, 1:xxi–ii, xlv; Martin Arnold, *Thor* (New York: Continuum, 2011), 79; Anthony Faulkes, "The Sources of *Skáldskaparmál*," in Alois Wolf, ed., *Snorri Sturluson* (Tübingen: Gunter Narr, 1993), 59; and Guðrún Nordal, *Tools of Literacy* (Toronto: University of Toronto Press, 2001), 310.

183   **Ole Worm**: Malm, "Nordic Demand," 102; Frederick Metcalfe, *The Englishman and the Scandinavian* (London: Trübner, 1880), 265, 262, 234; and Vigfússon and Powell, *Corpus Poeticum Borealis*, 1:xliv.

184   *Codex Regius*: Vigfússon and Powell, *Corpus Poeticum Borealis*, 1:xlivi; Margaret Clunies Ross, *A History of Old Norse Poetry and Poetics* (Cambridge, UK: D. S. Brewer, 2005), 7–8; and John Lindow, *Norse Mythology* (Oxford: Oxford University Press, 2001), 12.

184   **ethics of the North**: Árni Björnsson, *Wagner and the Völsungs* (London: Viking Society for Northern Research, 2003), 81; Malm, "Nordic Demand," 103; and Arnold, *Thor*, 83.

184   *Heimskringla* **too had been printed**: Björnsson, *Wagner and the Völsungs*, 81; and Óskar Halldórsson, "Sagnaritun Snorra Sturlusonar," in *Snorri: átta alda minning* (Reykjavík: Sögufélag, 1979), 120.

184   **Icelander named Arni Magnusson**: Árni Magnússon Institute for Icelandic Studies, "Árni Magnússon (1663–1730)—life and work," www.arnastofnun.is/page/a_arni_magnusson_en; Arnold, *Thor*, 86; and Karlsson, *History of Iceland*, 159.

185   **gothic literature**: Anthony Faulkes, "The Viking Mind," *Saga-Book* 31
        (2007): 57; O'Donoghue, *From Asgard to Valhalla*, 118; and Thomas Percy,
        preface to *Five Pieces of Runic Poetry* (London: R. and J. Dodsley, 1763).

187   *Northern Antiquities:* Björnsson, *Wagner and the Völsungs*, 81–90; Arnold,
        Thor, 88; and Thomas Percy, *Northern Antiquities* (1770; rev. ed., London:
        Henry G. Bohn, 1847), 75–76, 79, 236–39.

188   **"simple and martial as themselves"**: Thomas Percy, quoted by O'Donog-
        hue, *From Asgard to Valhalla*, 125.

188   **"that liberty which we now enjoy"**: Joseph Sterling, quoted by Wawn,
        Iceland Journal of Henry Holland, 10.

188   **Herder, father of nationalism**: Lars Lönnroth, "Andrew Ramsay's and
        Olof Dalin's Influence on the Romantic Interpretation of Old Norse My-
        thology," in Geraldine Barnes and Margaret Clunies Ross, eds., *Old Norse
        Myths, Literature, and Society* (Sydney: University of Sydney, 2000), 237;
        Ulrich Gaier, "Myth, Mythology, New Mythology," 165–88; Karl Menges,
        "Particular Universals," in Hans Adler and Wulf Köpke, eds., *A Companion
        to the Works of Johann Gottfried Herder* (Rochester, NY: Boydell & Brewer,
        2009), 189–214; and Óskar Bjarnason, "The 'Germanic' heritage in Icelan-
        dic books," in Sigurðsson and Ólason, *Manuscripts of Iceland*, 121.

188   **In Norway**: T. A. Shippey, "Light-elves, Dark-elves, and Others," *Tol-
        kien Studies* 1 (2004): 5; Diana Whaley, *Heimskringla* (London: Viking
        Society for Northern Research, 1991), 114, 10; Jónas Kristjánsson, *Ed-
        das and Sagas* (Reykjavík: Hið íslenska bókmenntafélag, 2007), 75; and
        Einar Ól. Sveinsson, "The Value of the Icelandic Sagas," *Saga-Book* 15
        (1957–1961): 3.

188   **Patriotic Icelanders**: Sveinsson, "Value of the Icelandic Sagas," 1–2; Jón
        Karl Helgason, "Continuity? The Icelandic Sagas in Post-Medieval Times,"
        in Rory McTurk, ed., *A Companion to Old Norse–Icelandic Literature and
        Culture* (Malden, MA: Blackwell, 2005), 73; Karlsson, *History of Iceland*,
        200–6 (including the verse translation), 267, 283; *Heimskringla* (Monsen),
        139–40; Gísli Sigurðsson, "Bring the Manuscripts Home!", in Sigurðsson
        and Ólason, *Manuscripts of Iceland*, 172, iii–iv; Jón Karl Helgason, "Par-
        liament, Sagas, and the Twentieth Century," in Sigurðsson and Ólason,
        Manuscripts of Iceland, 153.

191   **the Brothers Grimm**: Vigfússon and Powell, *Corpus Poeticum Borealis*,
        1:xciii; Arnold, *Thor*, 118–19; Jacob Grimm, *Teutonic Mythology*, trans.
        James Steven Stallybrass (London: W. Swan Sonnenschein & Allen, 1880),
        92, 99.

192   **philology**: T. A. Shippey, *The Road to Middle-Earth* (Boston: Houghton Mifflin, 1983): 7–10; Lindow, *Norse Mythology*, 30; and Vigfússon and Powell, *Corpus Poeticum Borealis*, 1:xcvii.

192   **"Scandinavian paganism"**: Lindow, *Norse Mythology*, 3; and James Stallybrass, preface to Grimm, *Teutonic Mythology*, v, viii.

193   **Richard Wagner**: Björnsson, *Wagner and the Völsungs*, 111, 7, 25–26, 79, 277; Bjarnason, "'Germanic' Heritage in Icelandic Books," 122; and Arnold, *Thor*, 129.

194   **Hitler's favorite composer**: Robert L. Jacobs, "Wagner's Influence on Hitler," *Music & Letters* 22 (1941): 81–83; Andreas Dorpalen, "Hitler—Twelve Years After," *Review of Politics* 19 (1957): 486–506; Paul Lawrence Rose, *Wagner: Race and Revolution* (New Haven, CT: Yale University Press, 1996), 78, 68; O'Donoghue, *From Asgard to Valhalla*, 145, 177, 196–97; Bjarnason, "'Germanic' Heritage in Icelandic Books," 123, 129; and Philip Andrew Shaw, "Uses of Wodan" (PhD diss., Leeds University, 2002), 10.

195   **"burning private grudge"**: *The Letters of J. R. R. Tolkien*, ed. Humphrey Carpenter (Boston: Houghton Mifflin, 2000), 55–56.

195   **"good sense and liberty"**: Thomas Percy, quoted in O'Donoghue, *From Asgard to Valhalla*, 125.

195   **Expeditions to Iceland**: On Joseph Banks, Lord Dufferin, and William Morris, see Boucher, *Iceland Traveller*, 81, 3, 215–16, 7, 10, 12, 16, 139, 151, 153, 166, 236; and Metcalfe, *Englishman and the Scandinavian*, 294. On Sir Walter Scott, see Andrew Wawn, "Victorian Vínland," in Andrew Wawn and Þórunn Sigurðardóttir, eds., *Approaches to Vínland* (Reykjavík: Sigurður Nordal Institute, 2001), 195. On George Dasent, see Andrew Wawn, "The Idea of the Old North in Britain and the United States," in Sigurðsson and Ólason, *Manuscripts of Iceland*, 137. On Samuel Laing, see Whaley, *Heimskringla*, 112; and *Heimskringla* (Laing), 1.

197   **Benjamin Thorpe**: *Northern Mythology* (London: Edward Lumley, 1851), ix–x; and Richard M. Dorson, *The British Folklorists* (Chicago: University of Chicago Press, 1968), 379.

197   **William Morris**: David Ashurst, "William Morris and the Volsungs," in David Clark and Carl Phelpstead, eds., *Old Norse Made New* (London: Viking Society for Northern Research, 2007), 43, 45, 53, 56, 59–60; Peter Faulkner, *Against the Age* (London: Allen & Unwin, 1980), 28, 62, 56; William Morris, *Journals of Travel in Iceland, 1871–73* (1911; repr., Elibron Classics, 2005), 225; Whaley, *Heimskringla*, 11; *Heimskringla* (Monsen), xix; Wawn, "Victorian Vínland," 195; Lin Carter, introduction to William

Morris, *The Well at the World's End* (New York: Ballantine, 1970), 1:ix, xi; and Carpenter, *Tolkien*, 69.

198   **J. R. R. Tolkien**: Carpenter, *Tolkien*, 22, 35; Shippey, *Road to Middle-Earth*, 7; Carpenter, *Letters of J. R. R. Tolkien*, 13, 143, 185, 104, 145; Carpenter, *Inklings*, 28, 5, 7; 56, 43; Andrew Lazo, "Gathered Round Northern Fires," in Jane Chance, ed., *Tolkien and the Invention of Myth* (Lexington: University of Kentucky Press, 2004), 198.

200   **The wizard Gandalf**: Carpenter, *Letters of J. R. R. Tolkien*, 119; Marjorie Burns, *Perilous Realms* (Toronto: University of Toronto Press, 2005), 95, 104; and T. A. Shippey, "Tolkien and the Appeal of the Pagan," in Chance, *Tolkien and the Invention of Myth*, 159.

200   **elves, and dwarfs**: *Edda* (Young), 16, 19; *Heimskringla* (Monsen), 8–9; Shippey, "Light-elves, Dark-elves, and Others," 11; Terry Gunnell, "How Elvish Were the Alfar?", in Andrew Wawn, ed., *Constructing Nations, Reconstructing Myth* (Turnhout: Brepols, 2007), 127; Lindow, *Norse Mythology*, 109–10; Shippey, *Road to Middle-Earth*, 48; and John D. Rateliff, *The History of the Hobbit* (New York: HarperCollins, 2007), 1:424.

201   **dragons**: T. A. Shippey, *Tolkien, Author of the Century* (Boston: Houghton Mifflin, 2001), 36; and Rateliff, *History of the Hobbit*, 1:373.

201   **Beorn**: *Heimskringla* (Monsen), 5; *Egil's Saga*, 21; Aðalheiður Guðmundsdóttir, "The Werewolf in Medieval Icelandic Literature," *Journal of English and Germanic Philology* (July 2007): 277–303; and Rateliff, *History of the Hobbit*, 1:261.

201   **giant eagles**: *Edda* (Young), 60.

202   **trolls**: *Heimskringla* (Monsen), 379.

202   **Bilbo Baggins's ride**: Burns, *Perilous Realms*, 81–87; and Morris, *Journals of Travel in Iceland*, 88–89.

203   **"theory of courage"**: Shippey, *Road to Middle-Earth*, 62, 61, 117; Burns, *Perilous Realms*, 41; and J. R. R. Tolkien, "Beowulf: The Monsters and the Critics," *Proceedings of the British Academy* 22 (1936): 245–95.

203   **By *fantasy* Tolkien meant**: Shippey, *Tolkien, Author of the Century*, 262; and Burns, *Perilous Realms*, 91.

203   **The Hobbit**: Carpenter, *Inklings*, 65; and Anne T. Eaton, "New Books for Young Readers," *New York Times*, March 13, 1938.

203   **Lord of the Rings**: Carpenter, *Tolkien*, 26; Philip Norman, "The Prevalence of Hobbits," *New York Times Magazine*, January 15, 1967; and Shippey, *Tolkien, Author of the Century*, xx.

205   **Michael Chabon**: Preface to *D'Aulaire's Book of Norse Myths* (New York: New York Review of Books, 1995), ix–x.

205   **A. S. Byatt**: *Ragnarok: The End of the Gods* (Edinburgh: Canongate, 2011), 160, 169.

205   **Neil Gaiman**: Interview by Paul Kane and Marie O'Regan, November 2005, www.shadow-writer.co.uk/neilinterview.htm; and Neil Gaiman, *American Gods* (New York: HarperTorch, 2002), 132.

206   **"Make what use of it you can"**: *Edda* (Faulkes), 64; and *Edda* (Young), 92.

Further Reading

Snorri's Works in Translation

Snorri's *Edda, Heimskringla,* and *Egil's Saga* are available in many English translations. Here are the versions I prefer, even though some are rather old-fashioned.

Sturluson, Snorri. *Edda.* Translated and edited by Anthony Faulkes. 1987. Reprint, Vermont: Charles E. Tuttle, 1995.
———. *Egil's Saga.* Translated by Hermann Pálsson and Paul Edwards. New York: Penguin, 1978.
———. *Heimskringla: History of the Kings of Norway.* Translated by Lee M. Hollander. 1964. Reprint, Austin: University of Texas Press, American-Scandinavian Foundation, 2009.
———. *The Prose Edda: Tales from Norse Mythology.* Translated by Jean I. Young. 1954. Reprint, Los Angeles: University of California Press, 1964.

Snorri's Life and Times—

For those who can read Icelandic, Óskar Guðmundsson's 2009 biography, *Snorri: Ævisaga Snorra Sturlusonar 1179–1241* (Reykjavík: JPV útgáfa), cannot be matched. I also recommend Sigurður Nordal's *Snorri Sturluson* (1920; repr., Reykjavík: Helgafell, 1973); Gunnar Benediktsson's *Snorri skáld í Reykholti* (Reykjavík: Heimskringla, 1957); the beautiful eight-hundredth-birthday collection of essays by Halldór Laxness and others, *Snorri: átta alda minning* (Reykjavík: Sögufélag, 1979); and Torfi H. Tulinius's *Snorri skáld í Reykholti: Snorri Sturluson og Egils saga* (Reykjavík: Hið íslenska bókmenntafélag, 2004).

I found the following books in English to be particularly useful:

Andersson, Theodore. *The Growth of the Medieval Icelandic Sagas, 1180–1280*. Ithaca, NY: Cornell University Press, 2006.

Bagge, Sverre. *Society and Politics in Snorri Sturluson's* Heimskringla. Berkeley: University of California Press, 1991.

Ciklamini, Marlene. *Snorri Sturluson*. Boston: Twayne, 1978.

Clunies Ross, Margaret. *A History of Old Norse Poetry and Poetics*. Cambridge, UK: D. S. Brewer, 2005.

Hermannsson, Halldór. *Sæmund Sigfússon and the Oddaverjar*. Ithaca, NY: Cornell University Press, 1932.

Jochens, Jenny. *Women in Old Norse Society*. Ithaca, NY: Cornell University Press, 1995.

Karlsson, Gunnar. *The History of Iceland*. Minneapolis: University of Minnesota Press, 2000.

Kristjánsson, Jónas. *Eddas and Sagas: Iceland's Medieval Literature*. Reykjavík: Hið íslenska bókmenntafélag, 2007.

McGrew, Julia, and George Thomas, trans. *Sturlunga Saga,* vols. 1 and 2. New York: Twayne, 1970, 1974.

Nordal, Guðrún. *Tools of Literacy: The Role of Skáldic Verse in Icelandic Textual Culture of the Twelfth and Thirteenth Centuries*. Toronto: University of Toronto Press, 2001.

Ólason, Vésteinn. *Dialogues with the Viking Age: Narration and Representation in the Sagas of the Icelanders*. Reykjavík: Heimskringla, 1998.

Sigurðsson, Gísli. *The Medieval Icelandic Saga and Oral Tradition*. Cambridge, MA: Harvard University Press, 2004.

Sigurðsson, Gísli, and Vésteinn Ólason, eds. *The Manuscripts of Iceland*. Reykjavík: Árni Magnússon Institute in Iceland, 2004.

Sveinsson, Einar Ól. *Age of the Sturlungs*. Ithaca, NY: Cornell University Press, 1953.

Tulinius, Torfi. *The Matter of the North: The Rise of Literary Fiction in Thirteenth-Century Iceland*. Odense: Odense University Press, 2002.

Wanner, Kevin J. *Snorri Sturluson and the "Edda": The Conversion of Cultural Capital in Medieval Scandinavia*. Toronto: University of Toronto Press, 2008.

Whaley, Diana. *Heimskringla: An Introduction*. London: Viking Society for Northern Research, 1991.

Snorri's Influence

All books about Norse mythology derive from Snorri. Here are a few recent ones I've found enjoyable:

Abram, Christopher. *Myths of the Pagan North: The Gods of the Norsemen.* New York: Continuum, 2011.

Arnold, Martin. *Thor: Myth to Marvel.* New York: Continuum, 2011.

Burns, Marjorie. *Perilous Realms: Celtic and Norse in Tolkien's Middle-earth.* Toronto: University of Toronto Press, 2005.

Lindow, John. *Norse Mythology: A Guide to the Gods, Heroes, Rituals, and Beliefs.* Oxford: Oxford University Press, 2001.

O'Donoghue, Heather. *From Asgard to Valhalla: The Remarkable History of the Norse Myths.* London: I. B. Tauris, 2007.

Index